"Big data have come to dominate how we rethink about economies and the applications of big data offer new areas of research and new insights into urban science. Geographers and economists point to the increasing heterogeneity of mobility, wellbeing and development within and between cities, and their importance of local and regional prosperity. This book provides useful evidence that has correspondingly directed attention to the interactions of places and people as the foci of urban management and planning policies."

Professor Tao Sun, Dean of Zhou Enlai School
of Government, Nan Kai University, China

"New forms of data can enrich our understanding of cities. This book offers valuable insights into understanding the significant transformations taking place in Chinese cities through analytics of novel data sources. This is a helpful approach as traditional data sources in this context are relatively limited at the fine temporal and spatial scales needed to derive such understanding. The lessons learned with big data provides crucial understanding of what drives the dynamics of urban development, activity patterns, human mobility and wellbeing."

Piyushimita (Vonu) Thakuriah, Distinguished Professor
and Dean, Edward J. Bloustein School of Planning
and Public Policy, Rutgers University, USA

The Geography of Mobility, Wellbeing and Development in China

Big data is increasingly regarded as a new approach for understanding urban informatics and complex systems. Today, there is unprecedented data availability, with detailed remote-sensed data on the built environment and rich mineable web-based sources in the form of social media, web mapping, information services and other sources of unstructured "big data".

This book brings together a group of international contributors to consider the geographical implications of mobility, wellbeing and development within and across Chinese cities through location-based big data perspectives. The degree of urban sprawl, productive density and vibrancy can be reflected from location-based social media big data. The challenge is to identify, map and model these relationships to develop cities at different places in the urban hierarchical system that are more sustainable. This edited book aims to tackle these issues through two inter-related geographical scales: inter-city level and intra-city level.

The text is designed for graduate courses in planning, geography, public policy and administration, and for international researchers who are involved in urban and regional economics and economic geography.

Dr. Wenjie Wu is a Professor at the College of Economics, Jinan University, Guangzhou, China, and a research affiliate at the China Institute for Urban Governance, Shanghai Jiaotong University. He formerly worked as a tenured assistant professor (lecturer) and associate professor in UK universities such as the University of Glasgow where he remains as a Co-Investigator of the ESRC Urban Big Data Centre. His research focuses on the economic and geographical implications of urban environment and development, using empirical methods and data to inform public policy. His latest book is the *Economics of Planning Policies in China: Infrastructure, Location, and Cities* (Routledge, 2017). He has been named the World Social Science Fellow (Big Data in an Urban Context) by the International Social Science Council. He has served on the Global Board of Directors of the International Association for China Planning.

Dr. Yiming Wang is a Senior Lecturer in Cities and Public Policy and Director of the MSc Public Policy Programme within the School for Policy Studies, University of Bristol. Yiming's research specialises in the application of geographic information technologies to study government interventions in the urban transport infrastructure and real estate markets. He also has a longstanding interest in studying China's urban economic development policies, mainly from empirical and comparative perspectives. Yiming's peer-refereed publications can be found in major urban planning and public policy journals.

Routledge Advances in Regional Economics, Science and Policy

The Geography of Mobility, Wellbeing and Development in China

Understanding Transformations Through Big Data

Edited by Wenjie Wu and Yiming Wang

Routledge
Taylor & Francis Group

LONDON AND NEW YORK

First published 2020 by Routledge

2 Park Square, Milton Park, Abingdon, Oxon OX14 4RN

605 Third Avenue, New York, NY 10017

Routledge is an imprint of the Taylor & Francis Group, an informa business

First issued in paperback 2021

Publisher's Note

The publisher has gone to great lengths to ensure the quality of this reprint but points out that some imperfections in the original copies may be apparent.

British Library Cataloguing-in-Publication Data
A catalogue record for this book is available from the British Library

Library of Congress Cataloging-in-Publication Data
Names: Wu, Wenjie, 1985– editor. | Wang, Yiming, 1959– editor.
Title: The geography of mobility, wellbeing and development in China : understanding transformations through big data/edited by Wenjie Wu, Yiming Wang.
Description: Abingdon, Oxon ; New York, NY : Routledge, 2020. | Series: Routledge advances in regional economics, science and policy | Includes bibliographical references and index. |
Identifiers: LCCN 2019040843 (print) | LCCN 2019040844 (ebook)
Subjects: LCSH: Regional planning—China—Statistical methods. | Economic development—China. | Urbanization—China. | Migration, Internal—China. | Big data—China.
Classification: LCC HT395.C55 G465 2020 (print) | LCC HT395.C55 (ebook) | DDC 307.1/20951—dc23
LC record available at https://lccn.loc.gov/2019040843
LC ebook record available at https://lccn.loc.gov/2019040844

ISBN: 978-1-138-08132-1 (hbk)
ISBN: 978-1-03-217497-6 (pbk)
DOI: 10.4324/9781315112954

Typeset in Times New Roman
by Apex CoVantage, LLC

Contents

Figures

Tables

Contributors

Jianquan Cheng Department of Natural Sciences and MMU Crime and Well-being Big Data Centre, Manchester Metropolitan University (MMU), UK

Tianshi Dai College of Economics, Jinan University, Guangzhou, China

Anrong Dang School of Architecture, Tsinghua University, China

Guanpeng Dong Department of Geography and Planning, University of Liverpool, UK

Zhaoya Gong School of Geography, Environmental and Earth Sciences, University of Birmingham and School of Architecture, Tsinghua University, China

ChengHe Guan Department of Urban Planning and Design, Graduate School of Design, Harvard University, USA

Cheng Jin School of Geographical Sciences, Nanjing Normal University, China

Changcheng Kan Baidu Online Network Technology (Beijing) Co., Ltd.

Weifeng Li Department of Urban Planning and Design, Faculty of Architecture, The University of Hong Kong, Hong Kong, and Shenzhen Institute of Research and Innovation, The University of Hong Kong, Shenzhen, China

Xiaoming Li Shenzhen University, Research Institute for Smart Cities, Shenzhen, China

Jianzheng Liu School of Public Affairs, Xiamen University, China

Zhaoliang Luan Shenzhen University, Key Laboratory of Spatial Information Smart Sensing and Services, School of Architecture and Urban Planning, Shenzhen, China

Qiwe Ma School of Architecture, Tsinghua University, China

Terry Pulford Sigma Information Technology Pty Ltd

Peter G. Rowe Department of Urban Planning and Design, Graduate School of Design, Harvard University, USA

Yao Shen University College London, Centre for Advanced Spatial Analysis, London, UK

Wei Tu Shenzhen University, Key Laboratory of Spatial Information Smart Sensing and Services, School of Architecture and Urban Planning, Research Institute for Smart Cities, Shenzhen, China

Jianghao Wang State Key Laboratory of Resources and Environmental Information System, Institute of Geographic Sciences and Natural Resources Research, Chinese Academy of Sciences, Beijing, China

Yifei Wang The Center for Modern Chinese City Studies and The Future City Lab and School of Urban and Regional Science, East China Normal University, Shanghai, China

Yiming Wang Centre for Urban and Public Policy Research, School for Policy Studies, University of Bristol, UK

Wenjie Wu College of Economics, Jinan University, Guangzhou, China

Wenqiang Wu Centre for Urban and Public Policy Research, School for Policy Studies, University of Bristol, UK and Centre for Chinese Public Administration, School of Government, Sun Yat-sen University, China

Tian Xu Department of Urban Planning and Design, Faculty of Architecture, The University of Hong Kong, Hong Kong, China

Le Yuan Department of Chemistry, University of Cambridge, Cambridge, UK

Weiyang Zhang The Center for Modern Chinese City Studies and The Future City Lab and School of Urban and Regional Science, East China Normal University, Shanghai, China

Chen Zhong Strand Campus King's College London, Department of Geography, London, UK

Weijiang Zhu Bartlett School of Construction and Project Management, Bartlett Faculty of the Built Environment, University College, London, UK

Foreword I

Michael Batty

New insights into urban development through big data

The fastest growth in urban populations over the last 30 years has been in the development of cities in China. China has quickly moved from a relatively closed agrarian society in the mid-20th century – what used to be called a developing country – to a highly urbanised, modern society, which is increasingly dominated by professional, financial and scientific activities. This process of development began in the south of the country and in the coastal cities, particularly in the big cities of Guangzhou, Shanghai and of course Beijing, diffusing westwards, with commercial and industrial activities rapidly modernising as the nation has sought to integrate the less developed areas with the developed. The latest policy imperative to attempt this integration is the Belt and Road Initiative (BRI), the policy of developing westward, reinvigorating the countries of middle Asia, the Middle East, and onwards into Europe with spurs through Africa, and ultimately to Latin America.

At the same time as this rapid urban transformation, western societies and now the entire world have been immersed in the development of new information technologies, building on the technologies of the first industrial revolution that gave rise to electro-mechanical devices of all kinds that changed the way we work and live in cities. Cities have sprawled from their original cores, largely due to falling transportation costs and the widespread use of the automobile, while information technologies now underpin global forces that have generated a new type of connected world economy. As computers have become ever smaller, as their costs have decreased exponentially and as communications that enable them to be stitched together get denser and faster, these technologies have become embedded in the built environment. We are now getting data from our use of such computers as sensors in real time, and combined with the use of our personal sensors – smartphones – there is a veritable cornucopia of data that is gushing out of the city, giving us the possibility of developing a new understanding, a new science of the city, that will enable us to get a much more complete picture of how the city functions. This data is big in volume, certainly, and in the velocity at which it comes. It is often said to be the 'new oil'.

Big data flowing in real-time from sensors that are either embedded in the built environment or generated from our own devices either when we are stationary or on the move, tends to be highly unstructured. This is in comparison to traditional data sources such as censuses of population. The data is so large that it requires massive new storage to conserve and archive it, and very new software to explore and understand what it is telling us about the city and the functions that the sensors are used to control and manage. Anything that moves routinely in real time is subject to such automation. Mobile phone usage, for example, is the raw data in terms of the strength, duration, frequency and location of calls, while purpose-built sensors for transport – for payment systems, for managing and controlling the supply of vehicles, for energy usage and so on – are typical flows of data that grow linearly with time. This data is big in that it is often recorded second by second and only ever ends when the sensors in question are switched off. The frequency of such data is very variable at the finest level and can be aggregated to produce smoother trajectories, but the spatial scales over which it is generated also vary substantially. For example, airline traffic, automobiles at the city scale, transport either timetabled such as public buses or on demand such as Uber, all kinds of activities that require some record of appointment or attendance, usage of energy in terms of heat and light, water delivery, waste removal and disposal, pollution and weather events all combine to generate a massive number of flow patterns that signify how the city is working in terms of its space-time economy. And this is before we define all the electronic data from email to multiple web applications to social media that dominate our working and, to an extent, our social lives.

Flows are thus of the essence in thinking about the contemporary city, as I have argued in my book *The New Science of Cities* (MIT Press, 2013). As China continues its dramatic trajectory towards development, increasingly we are seeing the generation and use of big data used for the process of understanding the transformations that are occurring as well as for managing and controlling the structure of the city with respect to its employment, financial services and trade and tourism. For China and for all of us elsewhere in the world, this is a unique time. Here we see a society adjusting very rapidly to the modern world – indeed, one might say it has already adjusted and is now in the vanguard of future change – and a society that at the same time is advancing so rapidly in terms of new technologies that our theories no longer stand up with respect to what we know about how cities are changing. We are running everywhere just to stand still, and this is as critical in China as it is anywhere else. We simply have no idea of how cities are adjusting to the flows of global capital, the new rootlessness and the massive changes in migration that are taking the attention away from growth itself to redistribution within the world economy.

This book is about all these developments, building on typical snapshots of the new data – the big data – that is being generated and captured in many Chinese cities and regions. Unlike parts of the West where we do have some historical appreciation of urban change in terms of physical flows of people and traffic, we do not have this heritage in China, and thus what we see in terms of contributions to this book are snapshots of flows and interdependencies that we have not seen before in Chinese cities. Indeed, the lesson is wider than this because it is very probable that what we can now see in China is the outline of this new mobility which can detect in other places too; and in this sense, the chapters in this book represent a snapshot of the future. Moreover, the tenor of this book is not only to display this kind of big data using various network and flow systems but to illustrate how cities are developing with respect to their form and function where such networks increasingly underpin the loosening of this form from function and vice versa.

In the first main part of the book, the first chapter deals with flow data pertaining to location-based social media such as that generated by systems such as Weibo (a little like but not the same as Twitter). This data is used to examine the connectivity and strength of flows between the largest 326 Chinese cities. The flow data is measured in terms of millions of tweets, while in the second chapter, some 179 airline hubs are examined with respect to millions of airline flights. In this case, the focus is more on the network than the flows – but as in this science, flows are but one side of the coin, networks the other, and there is considerable correlation between them. The distribution of flows at hubs is explored and familiar power law relations are exposed. The next chapter switches to automobile networks, where geographically weighted regression (GWR) variants of the spatial interaction model are fitted to data in Jiangsu province. Transit data captured from smart cards is then used to provide an overall picture of mobility in Shenzhen, where there is excellent data about many features pertaining to mobility, and this chapter thus provides a very comprehensive view of mobility in one of the fastest growing cities in China. The last chapter in this first main part deals with modelling land development, in particular house prices in Beijing, again using a variant of GWR. This provides a nice closure to these chapters, which present a useful and informative approach to thinking about flows and locations in Chinese cities and regions.

In the second main part of the book, the focus changes to the form of cities. First the residential housing market is explored in Shanghai with respect to the structure of rents. An econometric model, log-linear in its parameters, is calibrated to the data, and some interesting analysis of the communities that are identified by this analysis is made. The next chapter focuses more generally on the polycentric nature of urban form, using indicators of centrality and density to explain different clusters in the Beijing and Shanghai, where these clusters are explained using regression analysis. A chapter follows which looks at retail development in 20 small towns in China, taking the analysis down to the site-specific level and identifying different risks associated with locating retail facilities in different areas of the towns in question. The last chapter deals with pollution levels across China and explores how data on particulate matter can be used to look at concentrations over space and time.

Big data is the focus of all the analyses in this book, which provides a clear and impressive picture of the state of the art in developing models that grasp the challenge of explaining big data in the rapidly developing cities of mainland China. There is much that the reader can learn from these experiences, and besides providing a very balanced snapshot of research in mobility and urban form in fast-growing cities, the chapters point directly to an impressive amount of work in China dealing with similar questions at different scales and over different time periods. In fact, more work on mining big data for understanding patterns of mobility is now evident in China than anywhere else, and the work that is reported in what follows suggests that the researchers involved are grappling with some of the big problems facing the field. Readers will gain much from absorbing the methods, models and applications which are presented below. Read on, learn, and enjoy!

Michael Batty

Centre for Advanced Spatial Analysis,
University College London
Friday, 5 April 2019

Foreword II

China's ongoing transformation is remarkable in many ways, as it seemingly defies the laws of gravity while rising steadily as a rapidly emerging global power. Two facets of China's rise that are of especial interest here are seen in the unprecedented pace of *urbanization*, on the one hand, and China's growing prowess as a front-runner in the proliferation of social media platforms and other *data-driven technologies*. These two facets are closely intertwined, and a unique contribution of this book is to examine the important relationship between the two. It does so through a systematic exploration of how big data methods and applications can inform a more detailed understanding of urbanization trends, and thus support more finely tuned and effective planning practices in China.

Just 40 years ago, only 20% of China's population resided in urban areas.[1] Today, it is 60%, with a resulting average increase of 16 million urban residents per year.[2] To put that into perspective, China has been adding an urban population exceeding the current size of metropolitan London every year for four decades! The growth of social media and other big data generators in China is even more astonishing. According to China Internet Watch, the number of internet users in China rose from about 300 million 10 years ago to 830 million today, with the corresponding internet penetration rising from 22.6% to 59.6% over the same interval. Almost three-quarters of these internet users reside in China's urban areas, and almost all of them access the internet via mobile devices.[3] These dual trends in urbanization and social media connectivity are combining to create an unprecedented volume of urban data. The contributors to this book volume have undertaken a collective effort to deploy such data to generate new insights into urbanization trends in China.

Importantly, this rapidly emerging cyberspace layer of urbanization is helping to knit together the physical and human layers as well, because spatially tagged data of this type link individual users to specific geographic locations. We are no longer confined to viewing urban phenomena from a relatively static macro scale; instead, we can recast these macro-level observations in terms of dynamic observable behaviors at the "molecular" scale. This approach is in evidence in this book across a range of sectors or application areas:

- Using social media user data to reveal the nature and scope of social inequalities induced through urban migration flows;

- Combining social media and air traffic data to shed light on imbalances in aviation networks;
- Drawing upon traffic flows data at both the regional and local level to explore the heterogeneous socio-economic determinants of travel behavior;
- Employing finely granulated data to generate insights into the local provision of affordable housing in China's largest cities;
- Likewise, to investigate retail location behavior, air pollution dispersion patterns, and other aspects the underlying social, economic and spatial behaviors that shape urban form and other macrolevel phenomena at the urban scale.

These and other applications are not only valuable for the insights they provide into China's fascinating urban transformation, they are also important as harbingers of a fundamentally new approach to research into urban phenomena in an age of big data. One can anticipate that this new approach will bring with it a whole new set of formidable and exciting challenges. Some of these challenges will pertain to the practical and theoretical aspects of urban modelling, while others will be framed more in terms of new urban policies that may be informed by such developments.

In certain respects, the challenges ahead recall the perennial debates in economics over the micro foundations of observed macro-level phenomena. Will the increasing availability of big data increase or obviate the need for stronger theoretical foundations? An analogy to language translation may be instructive. Early research into machine translation sought to replicate a rules-based approach that encoded principles of grammar, syntax and other linguistic properties directly into the application. With the advent of big data, combined with increasingly sophisticated artificial intelligence (AI) methods, however, it became increasingly feasible to develop translation software that does not rely on explicit linguistic structures. Fed enough data, machines can learn that *this* phrase in English translates into *that* corresponding phrase in the target language. Massive volumes of parallel texts in source and target languages from official United Nations reports or transcripts, for example, can help machine learning vehicles to find their way.

Similarly, for the first time ever, a machine learning chess engine, Lc0, recently won the Computer Chess Championship title.[4] Using AI methods, it taught itself how to play chess without needing to have the formal rules of chess encoded into its software. With sufficiently large volumes of data from prior games fed into the training materials, Lc0 can recognize, for any particular situation, what the correct move is. Can we expect a similar process to evolve in urban planning? Fed sufficient volumes of data, will machine-learning *urban planning engines* learn to make the "right moves" in any given situation? If so, perhaps it might not then be necessary to encode principles or procedures of good urban planning into the process explicitly, but it will likely still require human intervention to indicate through training examples which *outcomes* are preferred under particular circumstances. This could be the ultimate movement away from structural models of human behavior in urban settings, replaced instead by these special kinds of reduced form models. We may not understand why or even how they work, but as long as they perform well, perhaps that will be sufficient. Or perhaps not. Such urban planning engines might also learn to delineate between solutions that work in China versus those that make sense elsewhere. Again, we may not understand why, other than to recognize that "*this* is China" while "*that* is not China".

A related challenge that urban scholars may encounter in this context is not just how big data can help us gain insights into the evolution of urban places – the question may increasingly become one of how big data, together with allied tools and technologies, actually shapes the urban evolutionary process itself. An obvious example is the emergence of high-tech zones in Shenzhen, Beijing and elsewhere in China, which in turn follow the emergence of Silicon Valley and similar urban phenomena elsewhere abroad. We see it also in the way that ride-share companies or short-term accommodation platforms rely upon (and generate) big data as a core part of their business model while they in turn reshape the urban places that are the venues for such activities. Big data may not only help us understand urban change, it may become a key underlying impetus for that change.

Finally, and perhaps most importantly, how will big data affect our ability to formulate effective urban planning and other policies to guide change? One possibility is that policies themselves may become more finely tuned to individual behaviors and circumstances rather than to average propensities. For example, the tolls for use of exclusive lanes of traffic may vary by the characteristics of the vehicles or the occupants. Likewise, enforcement of policies may be facilitated by big data, but this raises the specter of Big Brother as well. Big Brother may be watching us, but who is watching Big Brother? The European Union's recent General Data Protection Regulation (GDPR)[5] may be one of the more progressive examples of how data rights can be shifted in favor of individual persons, thereby limiting the potential intrusiveness of big business or big government. We are on the cusp of a new era and perhaps a correspondingly new social contract, and it will be in cities – both in China and beyond – that these future-shaping developments will unfold.

Eric J. Heikkila

Professor and Director of Office of Global Engagement
USC Price School of Public Policy
University of Southern California

Notes

1 https://ourworldindata.org/urbanization
2 www.populationpyramid.net/china/2020/
3 www.chinainternetwatch.com/29010/china-internet-users-snapshot/
4 www.chess.com/news/view/lc0-wins-computer-chess-championship-makes-history
5 https://ec.europa.eu/commission/priorities/justice-and-fundamental-rights/data-protection/2018-reform-eu-data-protection-rules_en

Part I

1 Introduction

Transformation is taking place in cities across the globe. This is particularly the case in the developing world, where the majority of people now live in urban areas and are attracted to cities for opportunities of development, wellbeing and mobility. Data play a fundamental role in modeling, mapping and visualizing much of the transformations which impact in complex ways on the geography of development, wellbeing and mobility. The emergence of (big) data in urban contexts offers new and alternative strategies for social science research (Batty, 2016). This is particularly important for developing countries where traditional census data are poor.

Modern cities can be viewed as spaces with multiple dimensional layers. The first dimensional layer refers to the physical and built environment space made up of concrete elements such as roads and buildings, lakes and trees. The second-dimensional layer includes the human society space functioned by social behavior and economic interactions of people and places. The third-dimensional layer is based purely on the big data space through which one can understand how cities function as a type of organism at temporal and spatial scales. Specifically, big data offers a valuable real-time information collection base for exploring new research challenges and gaining new insights into geography and social science (Graham and Shelton, 2013; Elwood et al., 2012). It includes a huge amount of dynamic and unstructured data information generated from various social media platforms, public facilities, institutions and individuals. Recent studies have summarized the key features of big data (e.g., volume, velocity, variety, veracity, hierarchy, integrity among others). See recent reviews by Batty (2013), Goodchild (2013) and Kitchin (2013). In many cases, big data information can be administered and extracted by public sectors, private sectors and individuals using new methods and technologies. When such big data information could be shared, mined and integrated in real time, policy makers and scholars could make use of big data to gain a more complete understanding of dynamic situations of urban settings and issues. This new data structural setting of cities calls for new areas of research, new methods, new philosophies and practices for analyzing the spatial-temporal variation of development, wellbeing and mobility patterns and problems in a more innovative and systematic way.

China is in the midst of a data revolution. Billions of daily internet searches are made through Baidu, and hundreds of millions communicate via Weibo, WeChat and active smart mobile devices. Now with hundreds of millions of users, the big data is fundamentally capturing the fabric of development and daily life in cities. Understanding China's transformations through data such as survey data, traffic flows data, air pollution data, land parcel data, human activity and smart card data is the source of offering potential solutions for socioeconomic and environmental challenges for development, wellbeing and mobility. This edited volume presents theoretical and empirical works around the discussions and applications of using big data for understanding patterns and dynamics of development, wellbeing and mobility within cities and/or across cities. The edited book aims to offer useful food for thoughts for policy makers, researchers, and students who have interests in this relatively new and cross-disciplinary area and considers many of the methodological, policy and practical challenges that we urban researchers should do more rather than less.

Understanding China's transformations makes tracking the patterns and characteristics of traditional surveys and newly emerged big data sources important. As shown in the following chapters, this is a daunting but meaningful task. Take human mobility as an example: An intercity human mobility footprint will be generated based on the "geo-tagged" linkage of an individual's social media posts such as Weibo. Indeed, Weibo provides a location-tracked application tool (commonly known as a "geo-tagged" service) for identifying users' geographical locations. A geo-tagged record, therefore, includes spatial information for studying users' mobility patterns across cities. By mining and aggregating millions of users' geo-tagged records, it is possible to construct the origin-to-destination city matrix based on the topology network method. However, a full cost-benefit analysis of differences in the motivations of human mobility behavior would be beyond the capacity of social media big data. It is likely that some people may visit other cities for business purposes, whereas others may travel to distant places for family and leisure purposes. One critical assumption is that cities with high in-flow human mobility patterns are likely to be correlated with better market potentials and economic development. This basic viewpoint – that the geography of mobility is important for productive development – colors most of urban science research and has influenced most thinking on the evaluations of what public policies work better for people's wellbeing.

China's rapid and uneven spatial expansion in human mobility provides incentives for land use configurations and public investment in social infrastructure and will transform and shape the location and liveliness of activities in cities for decades to come. The aim of this book is to generate new insights into the geographical implications of mobility, wellbeing and development through a combination of traditional data sources and location-based big data perspectives. It sheds light on many of the priorities identified in the planning and geography literature, with a specific focus on two levels: At the national/regional level, the need for understanding the role of data evidence to play in offering the insights on the patterns and dynamics of human mobility and development and the rationales of public policies such as air pollution controls that shape environmentally friendly development pathways. At the city level, this book focuses on the data-informed evidence based on analyzing both new and conventional urban data. Our intention is to shed new light on geographic uncertainties of mobility and development through interactions across physical spaces, human society spaces and cyber spaces. The book is organized in two parts that spawn new areas of research methods and data in transport these discussions, with the final part providing some concluding remarks. Figure 1.1 provides an overview of book chapters.

Part I: Introduction and overview (Chapter 1)
- An overview for understanding the book episodes and key building blocks of understanding China's transformations through data, with a specific focus on development, mobility and wellbeing.

Part II: From periphery to core: Patterns and dynamics of mobility and traffic flows
A multi-level set of data-informed evidence to model, map and mine the patterns and dynamics of urban mobility and traffic flows under spatial-temporal varying contexts.
- Chapter 2: Mining China's Urban Social Interaction Footprint Patterns (national level)
- Chapter 3: Long distance mobility and airline networks (national level)
- Chapter 4: Spatial weighted interaction model of traffic flows on motorway networks (regional level)
- Chapter 5: Profiling Rapid Urban Transformations through Urban Mobility Data (city level)

Part III: Development and policy: Locational contexts and analyses
Modern-day empirical evidence on clarifying the importance of considering locational contexts into understanding the heterogeneity in development and air pollution patterns, and generating policy implications.
- Chapter 6: Modeling Land Development: Heterogeneity in Space, Time and Context (city level)
- Chapter 7: Modeling distributional patterns of residential rental housing markets (city level)
- Chapter 8: Evaluating Polycentric Spatial Strategy of Megacities (inter-city level)
- Chapter 9: Multi-criteria locational analysis for retail development in small towns (inter-city level)
- Chapter 10: Profiling PM2.5 Pollution Patterns and Policy Development (national level)

Part IV: Concluding remarks (Chapter 11)
- A critical summary of a big data evidence-base for evaluating the geographical division of social-spatial mobilities, and related forms of urban development in China.
- A discussion of shaping the rise, decline and dynamics of mobility, wellbeing and development through an insightful understanding of China's socioeconomic transformations in urban contexts.

Figure 1.1 An overview of book chapters

In the following part, patterns and dynamics of mobility and traffic flows are identified in Chapters 2 through 5 through location-based big data from social media platforms, smart card records and traffic networks at different spatial scales. Chapters tackle myriad uncertain patterns and dynamics through mining geographically tagged information, which highlights how big data can enrich our understanding of urban mobility in a variety of dimensions and the considerations that are needed for making it guide many of policy instruments and interventions (Kwan, 2012; Kwan, 2013). Chapter 2 examines the national-level human mobility footprints across cities using social media user data with the aim to understand the social interactions between periphery cities and core cities at different times of the year. Using an airline network as a lens, Chapter 3 provides clear evidence on the inter-city linkages between air transport networks and long-distance mobility networks in China using social media big data and air traffic data. An ideal public policy for guiding long-distance and short-distance mobility patterns across periphery and core regions needs to consider economic agglomeration drivers and market potentials in addition to the optimized planning of transport infrastructure systems towards enhancing accessibility for cities and regions.

Chapter 4 explores the mobility patterns and dynamics at the regional level by using traffic flow data. By looking at the county-level changing patterns at a highly developed province in China, this chapter provides clear evidence on the spatially heterogeneous socio-economic determinants of traffic flows. It is expected that the spatial non-stationarity in traffic flow driving forces may reflect the spatial imbalance in the regional development patterns between core and periphery areas. If this is the case, China's unbalanced regional development pathways are likely to continue in a systematic way. In turn, this makes the spatial inequality of wellbeing across places more pronounced in a large developing-country context. Chapter 5 follows this line of research but looking at the characteristics of urban mobility patterns in more detail at a case-study city – Shenzhen. Functional and structural urban mobility patterns can be identified by mining smart card data. Areas with higher cumulative population, dense intra-inter travel, and better proximity to the city center are likely to be more attractive for productive work, modern life and leisure. Taken together, one fundamental viewpoint from here is that data-informed methods could generate good values for urban planning and policy, though an integrated framework is needed for piecing together multi-source new and traditional data sources in the empirical assessments.

China's development is spatially uneven. Before economic reforms in the 1980s, land parcels were allocated to work units as a social welfare good provided by the state. The dominance of public housing was prevalent in urban China (Huang and Li, 2014). This socialist welfare land and housing allocation system largely met with the traditions of people's wellbeing expectations in which it is not common to generate inequalities of wellbeing among people and places. This was paralleled with the centrally planned development pathways of urban growth in the pre-reform Chinese cities. In the post-reform era, market-oriented mechanisms could lead to the rise of differences in development patterns. First, expansion of rural–urban migration has been rapid. This rapid urbanization has come alongside the development of retail sectors and land markets in cities that place great opportunities and pressures on people's wellbeing. Second, the emergence of private-sector businesses that once allowed to sacrifice the environment to generate production outputs in cities has gradually been restricted to limit air pollutant emissions. This may impose wellbeing effects for residents in the longer term. Third, urban development in the post-reform era is characterized by the rise of sub-centres and polycentric spatial development strategy. In turn, this makes designing policy toolkits important for identifying the centrality of places and evaluating the performance of subcenters as an empirical evaluation of the polycentric spatial strategy.

The third part of the book explores these building blocks in detail. As Chapters 6 through 10 acknowledge, the set of data-informed evidence is intended to familiarize international scholars and policy makers with how big data can be applied to help us understand China's development through analyzing real estate markets, retail sectors, urban spatial structures and environmental dimensions. Chapter 6 looks at the development patterns of residential land markets in Beijing. Based on the availability of location-specific data resources, this chapter clarifies the importance of considering the heterogeneity in space, time and contextual characteristics. Following this viewpoint, Chapter 7 provides the evidence on the distributional patterns of residential rental housing markets and submarkets in Shanghai using real estate big data, covering more than 2,000 residential complex communities. Careful assessments are needed to show if public investments in social infrastructure can affect the dynamic patterns of housing and land development.

Taking Beijing and Shanghai as comparable examples, big data approaches are used to explore urban spatial structures in Chapter 8. Specifically, this chapter makes use of the centrality of places as a lens for showing the evidence of urban polycentric spatial development outcomes as reflected from the decentralization trends of mobile phone positioning data. Chapter 9 examines retail locational development at small towns in Zhejiang province. Exposure to accessibility and site location characteristics are measured to conduct the risk analysis for the relative size of retail development. This chapter, albeit from a stylized retail location choice model, highlights the nature of local comparative location advantages that reinforce master plans decision-making processes about retail developments in the era of digital data.

Chapter 10 reviews the air pollution distributional patterns based on the daily PM2.5 concentration data records throughout the country. This chapter also compares China's air pollution conditions with the US and Asian countries to imply the development pathways for pollution mitigation policies across time and space. One implication is that public policies of environmental regulations have been powerful tools to foster spatial configurations of development, mobility and wellbeing patterns.

Together, chapters highlight different urban challenges that need to be addressed to ensure big data can answer critical policy-relevant questions. The potential of big data has been emerging. Big data offers the scientific evidence base for exploring the refinement of spatial, temporal and individual trajectory data due to its nature of massive volume and real-time information collection. The geo-computation of such data has attracted growing interest from various disciplines such as economics, geography and planning policy (Batty, 2017a). These data could be decomposed into different dimensions, enabling researchers to look at temporal-spatial dynamic elasticity, fragmentation and mutual overlapping with traditional survey and census data sources.

Understanding urban transformations involved with the complexities and institutional forces is not easy (Cheshire et al., 2014). The scope of this book would not be able to cover all topics and needs for adopting emerging data sources into the evaluation of successful and diverse cities (Batty, 2017b). As a baseline, we hope the collection of chapters in this book demonstrates an important starting point.

We would like to acknowledge the support of the National Natural Science Foundation of China. We would like to thank International Association for China Planning for event opportunities that offer new generations of ideas and discussions for understanding China's transformations. A special thank you to Professor Michael Batty, Chairman of the Centre for Advanced Spatial Analysis (CASA), University College London (UCL), inspiring our thoughts with care. We thank Yanwen Yuan and numerous research assistants who have helped us with excellent editorial assistance. We are also indebted to chapter contributors and the anonymous reviewers who took their time to read chapter selections and provide feedback. Future researchers are encouraged to formulate the integrated framework for piecing together multi-source new and traditional data and providing the micro foundation on the spatial and social assignments of public policies.

References

Batty, M. 2013. Big data, smart cities and city planning. *Dialogues in Human Geography*, 3 (3), 274–279.

Batty, M. 2016. Big data and the city. *Built Environment*, 42 (3), 321–337.

Batty, M. 2017a. Geocomputation. *Environment and Planning B: Urban Analytics and City Science*, 44 (4), 595–597.

Batty, M. 2017b. Urban studies: Diverse cities, successful cities. *Nature Human Behaviour*, 1 (1). doi:10.1038/s41562-016-0022

Cheshire, P., M. Nathan, and H. G. Overman. 2014. *Urban Economics and Urban Policy: Challenging Conventional Policy Wisdom*. London: Edward Elgar.

Elwood, S., M. F. Goodchild, and D. Z. Sui. 2012. Researching volunteered geographic information: Spatial data, geographic research, and new social practice. *Annals of the Association of American Geographers*, 102 (3), 571–590.

Goodchild, M. F. 2013. The quality of big (geo)data. *Dialogues in Human Geography*, 3 (3), 280–284.

Graham, M., and T. Shelton. 2013. Geography and the future of big data, big data and the future of geography. *Dialogues in Human Geography*, 3 (3), 255–261.

Huang, Y., and S. M. Li. 2014. *Housing Inequality in Chinese Cities*. Abingdon: Routledge.

Kitchin, R. 2013. Big data and human geography: Opportunities, challenges and risks. *Dialogues in Human Geography*, 3 (3), 262–267.

Kwan, M.-P. 2012. The uncertain geographic context problem. *Annals of the Association of American Geographers*, 102 (5), 958–968.

Kwan, M.-P. 2013. Beyond space (as we knew it): Toward temporally integrated geographies of segregation, health, and accessibility. *Annals of the Association of American Geographers*, 103 (5), 1078–1086.

Part II

Part II

2 Mining China's urban social interaction footprint patterns using big data

Wenjie Wu, Jianghao Wang, and Tianshi Dai

This chapter explores the geography of China's social interaction footprint patterns based on a unique location-based social media database. At its heart, a geo-tagged computational framework is designed to extract and aggregate millions of social media users' space-time footprints for network analysis about human mobility flows at different spatiotemporal scales. Our visual exploration results present evidence in support of the existence of heterogeneous social interaction patterns between peripheral and metropolitan regions. Additional results suggest that footprints are not distributed evenly over time, with substantial travel flows out of and into metropolitan regions during traditional Chinese holiday months. Finally, we quantify new evidence about important roles of tangible market potentials and intangible cultural ties to play in influencing human mobility flows at a detailed spatial degree.

1 Introduction

The emergence of location-based social media (LBSM) data is, increasingly, an important cyberspace of mapping social networks in and between cities across the globe (Sui and Goodchild, 2011; Manyika et al., 2011; Jiang and Miao, 2014). Typical examples include Twitter, Facebook and Foursquare. In large developing and emerging economies with massive numbers of social media users via computers and mobile phones, real-time 'geo-tagged' human mobility information from social media data sources are clearly large. However, despite widespread policy interests, there is virtually no direct evidence on exploring the configuration of urban social footprint networks and its interactions with a city's market potentials and cultural ties between city pairs in a large developing country context.

This chapter provides the first robust evidence on these questions by using a unique location-based social media database from China. China provides an ideal laboratory for our experiment. Expansions of the cyberspace infrastructure and social media markets have been rapid. Since 2010, China embarked on an ambitious programme of cyberspace infrastructure investment, investing over 1500 billion RMB (1 USD = approximately 6.5 RMB). Today, China is one of the world's largest social media markets, carrying more than approximately 556 million tweets (Weibo) per month in 2013. This rapid expansion means that people can easily access to the internet for posting social networking activities on which we can base big data mining.

This research contributes to several strands of literature. First, it adds to the work on spatial applications of big data resources. The existing studies have allowed for the simulation and modeling of dynamics of traffic flows (Steiger et al., 2014), mobile users (Malleson and Andersen, 2014), urban population (Aubercht et al., 2011), social networks (Ahern et al., 2007; Backstrom et al., 2010; Sun et al., 2013) and food health (Widener and Li, 2014) as well as predictions of natural disaster progresses (e.g. earthquake, forest fire). These studies are of interest in their own right and are important for the development of optimal public policy.

There is a substantial literature that investigates various aspects of human mobility behaviors. Much of it is concerned with variation in local amenities (e.g. crimes) and population distribution within cities, an issue not directly related to our work. A growing body of literature looks at social and spatial interactions of individuals across cities using GIS techniques (Wang, 2010; Wright and Wang, 2011) and social media data sources (Crandall et al., 2009; Gao et al., 2012; Stephens, 2013; Rosler and Liebig, 2013; Stefanidis et al., 2013; Liu et al., 2014; Lovelace et al., 2014; Hollenstein and Purves, 2014). A typical application is the human mobility analysis of Twitter-based social networks to inform how cities grow and connect to each other. Our aim is to test if these findings hold in China and, if yes, do any distinctive social footprint patterns emerge in relation to China's urban systems? This is novel in developing countries.

In what is probably the most closely related paper to our own, Cao et al. (2015) uses a 1% sampling tweet database to examine intercity mobility flows of Twitter users within a weekly time window among major US cities. But more careful consideration reveals three important differences between our research context and that in Cao et al. (2015). First, the existing literature focuses almost exclusively on the U.S. in the early 21st century. We are among the first to investigate urban social interaction footprint patterns in a developing country where social media markets are booming and where cities are much denser than in developed countries. Second, the application programming interface (API) system of social media data in the U.S. and in China is radically different. In contrast to the publicly API access of tweets data in the U.S., China's limited API access of LBSM data hindered potential big data mining applications. Conventional data computational methods cannot directly track individuals' space-time trajectories and read the unstructured text data (e.g. words, pictures, videos) in China. We implement a novel web crawler program for transforming the unstructured LBSM data with limited API access into a structured framework for exploring China's social interaction footprint patterns. Third, unlike most studies on network analysis by computational scientists, studies by geographers (including our study) have interests beyond testing the statistical properties of social networks. Distinctive roles of network nodes and edges with actual travel flows at different spatial scales are the primary interests of our geographic inquiry.

Finally, our work is related to the economic geography literature dealing with the spillovers of agglomeration effects (Andersson et al., 2004; Rosenthal and

Strange, 2008; Arzaghi and Henderson, 2008). By showing that human mobility flows from periphery cities tend to cluster into large metropolitan cities, recent studies suggest that external economies of agglomeration are substantial but sharply attenuated by geographical distance across cities. The extant literature focuses on distance-based geographical thinking but provides little insight into the implications of cultural ties on social interaction footprints. In addition to the importance of distance-based market agglomeration forces, we document the critical roles of intangible cultural diversity to play in shaping the spatial distribution of human mobility flows.

The remainder of this chapter is organized as follows. Section 2 introduces the spatially integrated data mining framework for extracting and aggregating location-based social media data information. In Section 3 we describe the data for our empirical implementation. Section 4 implements the methodology into mapping spatiotemporal patterns of travel flows of social media users. Section 5 examines economic geography implications of social interaction footprints. Section 6 presents the concluding remarks.

2 A spatially integrated data computational framework

2.1 Defining activity trajectories of social media users

The starting point for our analysis is to extract and build the space-time trajectories of social media users for identifying individuals' footprints in a geographic space. Assume that there is a country space which contains M cities available for individuals' mobility. A set of N individuals would post their daily social activities (e.g. traveling) through a location-based social media platform. The measurement of "space-time trajectory" for capturing human mobility is followed by Hägerstraand's (1970) implicit function which has been widely used in the geographical analysis (Zheng and Zhou, 2011; Gao and Liu, 2013; Cao et al., 2015).

We define that a social media user, $u_i (i \in [1,N])$, has a space-time trajectory W_i within a country. This real-life trajectory W_i is approximately identified by WT_i; Where WT_i represents a set of geographically tagged footprints of location (s_i), timestamp (t_i) and message content (c_i) posted in social media.

For each user u_i, the space-time trajectory can be written as:

$$WT_i = \{(s_i^j, t_i^j, c_i^j), (s_i^{j+1}, t_i^{j+1}, c_i^{j+1}), \dots (s_i^{j+k}, t_i^{j+k}, c_i^{j+k}) \dots\} \tag{1}$$

Where $j \geq 0$; $k \geq 0$; $t_i^{j+k} \geq t_i^{j+k-1} \dots \geq t_i^j$. One fundamental issue to build human trajectory is to identify the user's *origin* city. Existing studies have often used the most frequently visited city as the origin city and used a spatial radius to track individuals' footprints (Gonzalez et al., 2008; Cao et al., 2015). However, this kind of identification method may contain error because of disparities in individuals' initial motivations. For a more rigorous assessment, we apply the text mining methods (Rao et al., 2010; Burger et al., 2011; Wang et al., 2013) to analyse the historical tweets to derive and validate social media users' current residence information. To be specific, we define social media user's current residence as his or her origin city and other cities in space-time trajectories as visited destination cities.

2.2 Dimensional mobility algorithm

Adopted from Leonardi et al. (2014), a graphical framework for data warehousing and data cuboid is employed in this study to represent the dimensional mobility algorithm of social media users across cities. In the social media data cuboid, we stratify three dimensions: first, user dimension. To avoid data privacy concerns, we restrict our focus to extracting users' origin city information and geo-tagged footprint information from its registration location, historical social media sending place and text-based contents. Second, spatial dimension. It identifies the number of users in each city as the basic spatial cuboid scenario. We define the cuboid (C)-based geometric measures as follows:

> $C(u_i)$: the number of social media users in the origin location O;
> $OutC(u_i)$: the number of mobility visits made by the user i from the origin location O to other destinations.
> $InC(u_i)$: the number of mobility visits made by the user i from other locations into the origin location O.

The third dimension is related to the temporal information. We break down the temporal measurement intervals into days as our baseline temporal cuboid. Evidently, by interacting the temporal dimension with spatial-user dimensions, we can quantify human mobility flow patterns between city pairs over time and space.

2.3 Aggregation function

Incorporating individuals' space-time trajectories into the dimensional mobility geometrics measures requires appropriate aggregation functions for efficient data query operations (Gray et al., 1997).

Assume that U is an aggregated spatiotemporal hierarchy corresponding to a set of human mobility patterns of social media users u_i between a pair of cities: p_1 and p_2. Specifically, p_1 and p_2 represent the higher levels of the hierarchy cuboids (e.g. month&city-based cuboid), aggregated by a series of basic individual measures: $p_1 = \sum_{i=1}^{k} P_{1,i}$, where ($p_{1,i}, ^i = 1,2, \ldots k$); and $p_2 = \sum_{j=1}^{k} P_{2,j}$, where ($p_{2,j}, j = 1,2, \ldots k$). Thus we can write the aggregation function for measuring mobility flows between p_1 and p_2 as follows:

$$F\left(p_1, p_2\right) = \sum_{i=1}^{k}\sum_{j=1}^{k}\left(p_{1,i}, p_{2,j}\right) \tag{2}$$

In addition to the mobility flows between city pairs, it would also be interesting to know the total out-flow volume and in-flow volume of social media users for each city. Recall that we assume that there are M cities (p_m) available for individuals' mobility in China. By deducting the space-time trajectories that occurred within the city boundaries of p_m, we can finalize the aggregation function for measuring total out-flow volume $(OutC(p_m))$ and in-flow volume $(InC(p_m))$ of social media users of p_m as:

$$OutC\left(p_m\right) = \sum_{i=1}^k OutC\left(p_{m,i}\right) - \sum_{i=1}^k F\left(p_{m,i}\right)$$ (3)

$$InC\left(p_m\right) = \sum_{i=1}^k InC\left(p_{m,i}\right) - \sum_{i=1}^k F\left(p_{m,i}\right)$$ (4)

2.4 Mapping network topology

Hypothetical urban social interaction footprints are defined as individuals' inter-city mobility behaviors based on aggregated social media data. The logic behind this is that, an intercity connection 'geo-tagged' linkage will be created if an individual's Twitter account is registered in city A (corresponding to individuals' current residence city) but sends a tweet from city B (corresponding to individuals' geo-tagged cities). This assumption is critical because it has allowed for the transformation of social media users' geo-tagged records into the topology of intercity social networks, as detailed below.

We adopt the directed star network topology approach to construct the matrix between a social media user's origin city and destination cities. In line with the common practice, we calculate the origin–destination matrix using a two-step procedure.

In the first step, we use the web crawler methods to retrieve all users' geo-tagged records throughout China. This involves massive computing exercises due to the large amount of LBSM data. A typical example for illustrating a user's trajectories from geo-tagged record is {< origin city = City O>, <City-D_1, t_1>, <City-D_2, t_2>, <City-D_3, t_3>, <City-D_2, t_4>, <City-D_4, t_5> . . .}. This simple example illustrates the trajectory of a user from the origin city (City-O) to four geo-tagged destination cities (City-D_1, City-D_1, City-D_1, City-D_1) in five times from t_1 to t_5.

The second step reads and calculates the intensity of linkages between city pairs within the directed star topology network. First, the origin cities are defined as the core nodes in the network, whereas other geo-tagged destination cities are defined as leaf nodes that include connections to the origin city. Second, we characterize the direction of city-pair linkages from the core code to leaf codes. This means that directed intercity travel flows are drawn from assigning an outward direction from the core code to each leaf code in the topology network. Third, we use the frequencies of geo-tagged destination cities to weight the linkages of intercity connections in the topology network. We also calculate the accumulative travel flows out of this city and towards this city. By doing so, we can adjust the origin–destination human mobility flows along the network to reflect the intensity of intercity linkages.

3 Implementation

We focus on the most commonly used location-based social media data available in China – Weibo (www.weibo.com). Weibo (literally means 'microblog' in

English), which is often seen as the Chinese version of Twitter, is essentially a web-based or mobile-based social media platform. Similar to Twitter, Weibo users can post a short text message (with a 140-character limit) for showing subjective impressions and daily activities (Java et al., 2007). With more than 50 million daily active users since 2013, Weibo has provided us a new way to explore real-time travel flows between city pairs in China.

Seeing urban social networks in a large developing country through social media users' travel flows is new to the existing literature (Guo et al., 2006; Wang, 2010; Verbeek et al., 2011). We improve on the applications of LBSM data in two ways: First, we design a sophisticated web crawler program to search, fetch and extract billions of Weibo records from Weibo's limited access application programming interface (API) system. Second, Weibo provides a location-tracked application tool (commonly known as a 'geo-tagged' service) for identifying users' geographical locations. A geo-tagged record, therefore, includes spatial information for studying users' mobility behaviors across cities. By mining and aggregating millions of users' geo-tagged records, we can construct the origin-to-destination city matrix based on the directed star topology network method.

A full cost–benefit analysis of differences in the motivations of human mobility behaviors would be beyond the scope of this chapter. Indeed, it is highly possible that some people may visit other cities for business purposes, whereas others may travel to distant places for family and leisure purposes. In this study, we focus on the first-order effect that only considers an intercity social connection as a human mobility linkage along the origin-to-destination routes between city pairs.

By applying the spatially integrated data computational framework, we gathered the geo-tagged records submitted over the period from January 2014 to November 2014. Our overall sample contains 220 million geo-tagged records and covers 328 cities throughout China, where each record provides a Weibo user's basic information (such as user ID, origin city, gender, the number of connected Weibo friends and so on), messages sent by days and by locations (geographic coordinates).

4   Geo-tagged footprint flows as proxy for exploring urban social networks

4.1   Spatiotemporal decomposition of mapping single-source flow disparities

This sub-section uses the visualized flow mapping techniques to explore spatiotemporal patterns of travel flows (including in-flows and out-flows) made by hundreds of millions of social media users by single-source regions.

Panel A of Table 2.1 lists basic statistics of out-flow travel flows by regions, whereas Panel B of Table 2.1 shows basic statistics of in-flow travel flows by

Table 2.1 Statistical characteristics of monthly geo-tagged travel flows by regions

		Mean	STD
Nationwide	*Average (1 million person)*	*6.38*	*1.48*
	Growth rate (%)	*10.24*	*22.93*
Panel A. Out-flow by regions			
From Eastern region	Average (1 million persons)	3.16	0.81
	Growth rate (%)	12.12	28.32
From Central region	Average (1 million persons)	1.38	0.24
	Growth rate (%)	7.01	15.29
From Western region	Average (1 million persons)	1.35	0.32
	Growth rate (%)	10.08	22.99
From Northeastern region	Average (1 million persons)	0.43	0.11
	Growth rate (%)	10.48	21.21
Panel B. In-flow by regions			
To Eastern region	Average (1 million persons)	3.30	0.73
	Growth rate (%)	9.56	23.26
To Central region	Average (1 million persons)	1.33	0.32
	Growth rate (%)	10.58	23.41
To Western region	Average (1 million persons)	1.24	0.30
	Growth rate (%)	11.08	22.79
To Northeastern region	Average (1 million persons)	0.42	0.11
	Growth rate (%)	11.86	23.81

regions. Following the convention, we divide the whole sample into four regions: Eastern region, Central region, Western region, and Northeastern region. The monthly average out-flow footprint records of the Eastern region is 3.16 million, much higher than the Central region (1.38 million), Western region (1.35 million) and Northeastern region (0.43 million). In terms of regional in-flow patterns, we also find substantial in-flow mobility footprint records in the Eastern region (3.03 million) as compared to other regions.

Figure 2.1 (a–b) visualizes the spatial distributions of total in-flows and out-flows for sampled Chinese cities. It should be noted that we adopt the head/tail break scheme (instead of traditional Jenks natural breaks) for classification with respect to Figures 2.2 and other figures in this study. The key presumption is that the head/tail break scheme is a more reliable visualization classification method than the traditional Jenks natural break scheme for scaling of right-skewed/heavy-tailed rank distributions in geographic space (Jiang, 2013).

Figure 2.2 (a–b) plots the city rank distribution of travel flows, along with its log-log plot of the complementary cumulative distribution function (CCDF). To simplify the interpretation, we restrict our focus on cities with travel flows larger than 500 footprint records. As can be seen, the rank distribution of

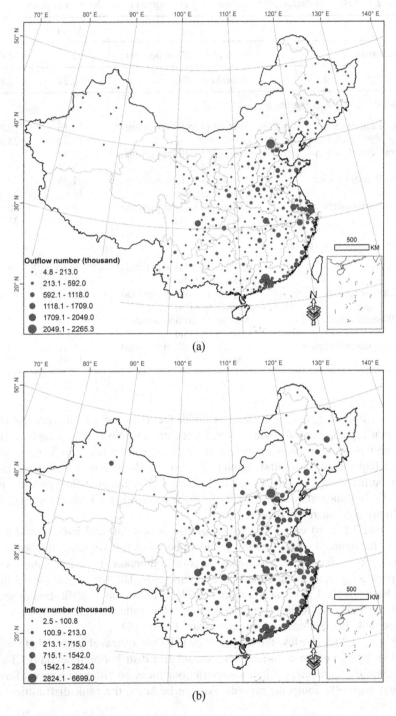

Figure 2.1 Spatial distribution of geo-tagged travel flows across 328 cities

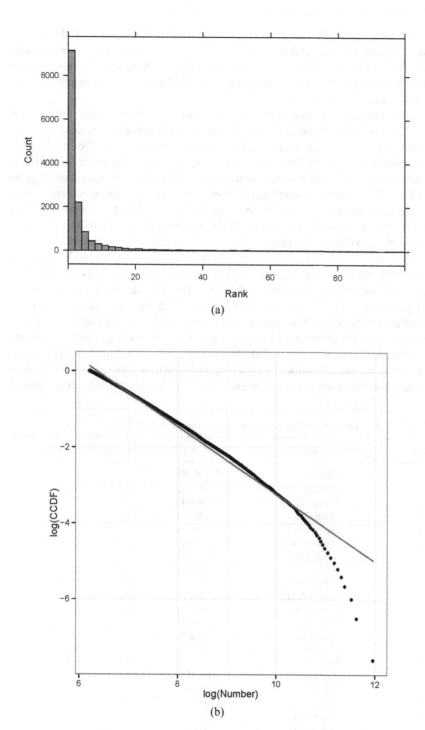

Figure 2.2 City rank distribution of total travel flows based on geo-tagged footprint

travel flows generally conforms to a power-law function. That said, the number of travel flows increases dramatically with the city's ranking: a high percentage of cities in the tail and a low percentage of cities in the head. This right-skewed distribution is consistent with recent findings about urban social networks in other countries (Jiang, 2015).

By listing the rank distribution of top 20 cities with the largest in-flow and out-flow volumes, Table 2.2 provides additional supportive evidence on this claim. Top 20 cities have occupied almost 40% of total travel flows of China. Over half of the top 20 cities are in the Eastern region, about one-fourth in the Central region and less than one-fourth in the Western and Northeastern regions (Table 2.2). In terms of total travel flows, the most dynamic cities are mainly clustered around the Greater Beijing area, the Yangtze River Delta and the Pearl River Delta regions. Provincial capital cities such as Xi'an, Chengdu, Shenyang, Zhengzhou, Wuhan and Changsha also have high travel flow volumes.

In the results not reported, we find that travel flows of social media users are correlated with monthly average temperature and air pollution levels. This suggests that social media users are likely to travel during warmer months with lower air pollution levels, though we cannot pin down precise mechanisms at work. Further investigations about potential economic geography channels at work are discussed in the following section. Perhaps more surprisingly, higher-mobility months are mostly concentrated at March, May, July and October across regions. This peak temporal variation is plausibly in line with Chinese traditional public holiday months, such as post–Chinese New Year Holiday (March), International

Table 2.2 Top 20 cities with most dynamic social media travel flows

Rank	City name	City travel flows/nationwide travel flows (%)
1	Beijing	6.468262
2	Guangzhou	3.449366
3	Shanghai	3.096601
4	Chengdu	2.706658
5	Shenzhen	2.429031
6	Wuhan	2.104649
7	Hangzhou	1.913715
8	Xi'an	1.797241
9	Nanjing	1.792341
10	Zhengzhou	1.720537
11	Chongqing	1.468156
12	Suzhou	1.326507
13	Changsha	1.323233
14	Tianjin	1.24535
15	Fuzhou	1.167929
16	Xiamen	1.085996
17	Jinan	1.071414
18	Hefei	1.039932
19	Shenyang	1.003613
20	Dongguan	0.997718

Labor Holiday (May), Summer vacations for kids (July) and China's National Day (October). This pattern is consistent with recent findings from social media data studies about peak-flow periods during the Christmas and New Year's Eve holidays in developed countries.

Looking specifically at regional disparities, intra-region travel flows are much denser than inter-region travel flows, even in the context of falling trade costs and shortened commuting distances between regions. Despite heterogeneous travel modes and motivations, residents are more likely to make local travels by visiting neighboring cities within the same region.

In terms of inter-region variations, there is a general travel flow tendency from West to East regions over space. This West-to-East mobility flow pattern may partly reflect the correlations with uneven population and economy distributions in China, where western and central regions are less developed than the eastern region. Furthermore, travel flows between specific region pairs are not distributed evenly over time. It is evident that the Eastern region is the second-largest destination region for travel flows sourced from other regions, and such patterns are not distributed evenly over time. In particular, there is a sharp rise of travel flows during March, May, July, and October. For example, we find higher mobility flows, moving from the Western region, Central region and Northeastern region to the Eastern region during March (after the Chinese New Year period). This typical polarization pattern could be related to a unique large-scale human mobility process (*Chun yun*, http://en.wikipedia.org/wiki/Chunyun) – a highly sensitive issue in China. Together, these findings provide new evidence about regional disparities of monthly human mobility flows in a large developing country.

4.2 *Spatiotemporal decomposition of mapping pair-wise flow disparities*

The single-region flow graphs provide valuable insights into how social media users move in and out of a particular region over time. In this section, we make a step further by mapping spatiotemporal patterns of pair-wise flows between cities and regions.

Figure 2.3 shows the spatial distribution of urban social interaction networks (USIN) across 328 Chinese cities. We reach three novel patterns: First, it is apparent that USIN is globally connected as a hub-and-spoke circling pattern, and is anchored by three national hub cities such as Beijing, Shanghai, Guangzhou. In terms of total travel flows, these hub cities have a combined market share of over 12% relative to the nationwide level (see Table 2.2 for details). Like the UK government's initiative to expand the Great London Area, China's State Council adopted a new urban planning system to advance potential market catchment areas for megacities by promoting periphery cities to link with megacities via high-speed rails and other high-speed transportation modes. Consequently, hub cities dominate the entire urban social network and connect with all other cities throughout China.

The second pattern is the regional trunk pattern. This pattern captures travel flow variations between province capital cities and non-province capital cities.

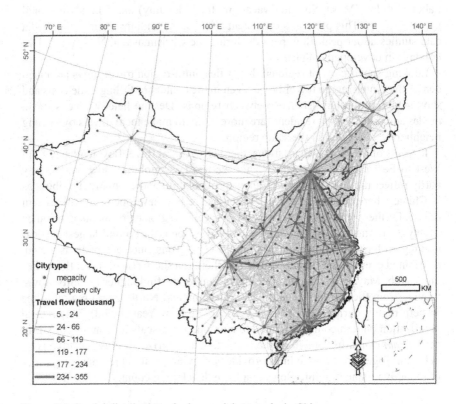

Figure 2.3 Spatial distribution of urban social networks in China

As shown in Figure 2.3 multiple regional hub cities (province capital cities) began to emerge by either anchoring routes with secondary-and third-tier cities in its province or strengthening new linkages with cities in neighboring provinces. For example, provincial capitals such as Xi'an, Chengdu, Zhengzhou, Wuhan and Changsha have experienced substantial social interaction flows with neighboring cities. This pattern expands the geographic coverage and the hinterlands of regional trunk cities and is useful for forming localized loops and improving the core–periphery structure of China's urban systems. This pattern is in line with findings from recent studies that the formation of social mobility nodes and edges has close relations with the economic and geopolitical forces at stake (Liu et al., 2015).

Third, we find the formation of community patterns surrounding Kunming and Urumqi. For example, Kunming (the capital city of the Yunnan province) connected many edge cities with only one major flow route, such as Zhaotong, Lincang, Simao, Baoshan etc. Urumqi (the capital city of the Xinjiang province) is another typical example for illustrating this pattern, where most cities such as Kashi and Aksu mainly connect to Urumqi instead of other places in China. A natural question is to ask what is the underlying mechanism of the local community

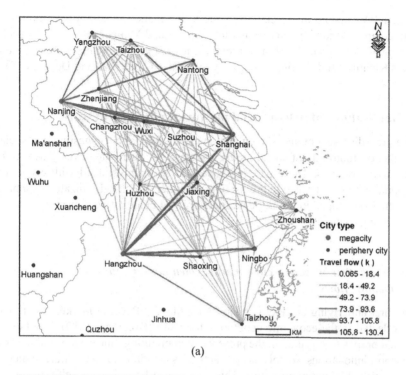

(a)

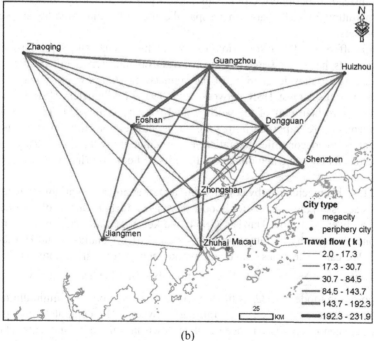

(b)

Figure 2.4 Social interaction networks in the Yangtze River Delta and Pearl River Delta metropolitan regions

pattern? A possible interpretation is due to the market integration, cultural ties and complex landscape constraints in Xinjiang and Yunnan provinces. In truth, this picture is similar to findings from the transport geography literature about the roles Kunming and Urumqi play as key brokers in China (Wu and Dong, 2015).

5 Implications of urban social networks: channels at work

The preceding section has shown new evidence for China suggesting that social interaction footprints of social media users are not distributed evenly over time and across regions. These patterns appear to be mainly linked with economic geography forces at stake. In this section, we generalize the visualization mapping evidence developed in the big data literature and quantitatively examine several underlying channels at work.

5.1 Association between a city's market potentials and human mobility flows

The first underlying channel is related to spillover effects of market integration as reflected in the economic geography literature (Krugman, 1980). The fundamental proposition is that, in the presence of commuting time savings induced by transport innovations, socioeconomic activities are likely to concentrate in megacities instead of periphery cities. This pattern can be driven by self-reinforcing agglomeration forces that arise in the spatial context of human mobility and social interactions.

China offers a textbook scenario for studying this mechanism. Since 2007, State governments have spent massive investments on high-speed rail (HSR) infrastructure as a policy lever to boost the connectivity across cities. Today, China has the world's largest HSR network, with 19369.8-kilometers HSR lines and carrying more than half of the world's total passengers in 2014. Transportation improvements are important in that they have allowed for falling trade costs and stimulating socioeconomic integration. In particular, individuals can easily access megacities for enjoying agglomeration benefits without suffering from megacities' high social costs.

We test this mechanism by constructing a market potential variable to measure a city's access to the markets for goods, services and labor. Our guiding principle here has been to follow Harris's (1954) market potential function used in the economic geography literature (Gibbons et al., 2012; Donaldson and Hornbeck, 2013). We can write cities' calculated market access (or market potential index) as follows: $A_i = \sum_j P_j \Omega_{ij}^{-\alpha}$. Where A_{it} is an index of market access in city i, by rail transportation mode, and Ω_{ij} is the transportation cost along the minimum travel time route from city i to city j by railroad networks. The computation of travel times between city pairs has been broken down into three components: (1) the least-length road routes from an origin city i to the nearest rail station m that can offer the shortest railway time to the destination city j; (2) the shortest railway distance from the departure rail station *m* to the arrival rail station *n* that is located near the destination city *j*; (3) the least-length road routes from a destination city *j* to the rail station *n*. P_j is the pre-existing population in city *j*. The parameter of α is the cost–distance decay function from the origin *i* to destination *j*. Potential weighting schemes of the parameter of α are well discussed in the existing literature. Following the convention, we use the inverse cost weighting scheme ($\alpha = 1$), in which the transportation cost is the 'optimal' travel time between locations *j* and *k*.

In addition, high-speed rail networks could spur the development of second- and third-tier cities in metropolitan regions. We see strong evidence about this claim: shortened commuting distances between *ex ante* asymmetric markets could be a positive force for the diffusion of social interactions to peripheral cities in the decentralized metropolitan regions. Typical examples include the Yangtze River Delta and Pearl River Delta metropolitan regions (Figure 2.5). Dynamic social interaction networks are concentrated not just between megacities (Shanghai, Nanjing, Hangzhou, Guangzhou and Shenzhen) but also across peripheral cities like Suzhou, Wuxi, Changzhou, Taizhou, Zhenjiang, Foshan, Dongguan etc. In the presence of comparative market access advantages, intense social interaction flows may increase the implicit social values and productivity of second- and third-tier cities, whereas sparse social interaction flows could reflect frictions in the reallocation of factors such as labor and capital fundamentals across cities.

It is important to note that what we may learn about geo-tagged social interaction patterns is well beyond the realm of conventional economic theory-based assessments. Many explanations of market potentials rely on the microfoundation of spillover effects that lead to theories of trade and market competition, industrial clustering, and economic integration. In this chapter, however, we step back from casual concerns and focus on new stylized relationships to be explained. A direction for future research is to look into how the opening of an HSR line can exactly shape changes in market potentials and how changes in market potential affect changes in travel flows at affected areas versus unaffected areas. For a rigorous causal identification, one nice aspect of this story is that we know how geo-tagged footprints are changed between any pair of cities over a relatively short time. Excellent recent examples focusing on explaining pervasive causal effect investigations using transport network data at least include Banerjee et al. (2012) and Baum-Snow et al. (2013).

5.2 Association between a city pair's cultural diversity and human mobility flows

The second underlying channel is related to cultural diversity across cities. While most of existing studies are still much constrained by distance-/market-based geographical thinking, there is a growing literature that investigates cultural-based psychological costs of human mobility patterns. Culture is a sophisticated concept and is hard to quantitatively measure. Empirical progresses in anthropology and sociology literature have shown that the cultural identity evolution proceeds in parallel with linguistic characteristics, and thus dialect can be used as a reliable proxy for cultural identity (see e.g. Cavalli-Sforza, 2000; Brewer, 1991). This is consistent with Charles Darwin's classical evolution theory.

We present the empirical analysis to quantitatively examine the association between pair-wise human mobility flows and cultural diversity. Our focus is novel because we study linguistics, i.e. city-level linguistic variation of the same language within a large developing country. Our analysis uses the linguistic data from the atlas of the Chinese linguistic census. This census has documented all direct and indirect characteristics of dialects used at the local areal level since the 19th century and therefore mitigates the endogenous concerns of cultural diversity and contemporary human mobility flows between city pairs.

We follow Greenberg's (1956) classic function used in the linguistic literature to measure the 'dialect distance' between city pairs. Building on Fearon's (2003) formula, we set a dialect distance decay parameter $\delta_{i,j}$ for two cities i and j that works as follows: δ_{ij} is zero when two cities' languages come from completely different dialect groups and share no common dialect characteristics. δ_{ij} is 1 when the two groups' linguistic share exactly the same set of dialect characteristics. δ_{ij} will be set between 0 and 1 when there are some shared classifications between i's and j's dialects.

In the spirit of Sjaastad (1962), we examine the relationship between cultural diversity and human mobility flows between city pairs.

Human mobility flows decline with dialect distance between city pairs, and such a pattern has a nonlinearity nature at spatial scales. The tendency for non-pecuniary costs to fall steeply with mobility flows in the lower part of the dialect distance distribution (x-axis) could indicate that the general mobility pattern is significantly affected by dialect differences, and individuals tend to flow into culturally familiar areas. The implication is that if two cities share many dialect non-similarities, the cultural diversity here may influence intercity social interaction patterns even if these two cities belong to the same province. But if two cities share many dialect similarities, cultural ties here could stimulate human mobility flows even if these cities belong to different provinces. Indeed, there is strong evidence of local cultural identity variations in China, as reflected in the dialect regions of Cantonese and Fukienese. For example, high Cantonese dialect similarities between Wuzhou (Guangxi province) and cities in the Guangdong province tend to be associated with intense social interactions between these regions.

Before concluding, it is important to note that are there any other factors that may influence human mobility flows across space? Of course the answer is yes. A full cause-sense factor analysis, which would need data on controlling for observed and unobserved labor markets, environmental and socioeconomic characteristics, is beyond the scope of this chapter. But as a baseline, our study is intriguing because it offers new insights for the configuration of urban social networks and other countries' planning to enlarge social media markets and infrastructure investments. First, high mobility flows of social media users, a sufficient number of megacities and secondary cities in reasonable proximity to transport networks are key factors that can be used to predict travel demands and the cost-effectiveness of transport infrastructure investments. These factors are also linked to a city's economic gains in market potentials and social interactions as reflected from intangible cultural ties. These conditions may hold not just in China but also other fast-developing countries in the Latin American and African regions. Second, China's unique political structure allows us to explore the association between cultural diversity and social interactions efficiently. China is not a federal country in the constitutional sense. This implies that the institutional barriers are reasonably assumed to be homogenous across space. But these conditions are less likely to hold in federal countries where cultural borders might be coincided with federal administration borders like in Russia, India, Canada (Quebec) and some European federal countries.

6 Conclusion

This chapter uses a unique pair-wise location-based social media users' mobility-footprint database and innovative methods to examine the configuration of urban social interaction networks in a large developing country, China. Our results suggest that heterogeneous social interaction footprint patterns largely meet with polycentric core–periphery urban systems in China: Human mobility flows tend to concentrate between megacities relative to periphery regions, leading to significant regional disparity patterns. Additional results suggest that social interaction footprint patterns are not distributed evenly over time, with larger travel flows out of and into metropolitan regions during traditional Chinese festival months.

Our study has direct and important policy implications. In a modern economy, emerging social media data sources are new proxies for understanding city social interaction networks and the spatiotemporal layout of human mobility patterns. Evolution of intercity social interactions could affect Zipf's urban systems (Zipf, 1949), generating implicit social values of cities through their effects on urban productivity, social externalities and the density of migration flows. While political leaders in developing countries ultimately want to determine the optimal scale and spatial layout of social interactions for digital cities, a necessary precursor to describing the optimal level is a mapping of how a city's social interaction flows could be correlated with economic geography channels at work. In addition to the importance of market potentials, we document that human mobility flows are associated with linguistic similarities between city pairs. These findings plausibly suggest that both tangible market potentials and intangible cultural ties within a country affect social interaction footprints and may influence the long-term dynamics of a country's economic integration process.

With the emergence of social media data and innovations of geographic information science, we have presented the first study about inter-city social interaction patterns, as well as their correlations with linguistic barriers and market potentials at fine spatial scales. There are several limitations of our study, primarily due to the lack of data and space. First, our analysis is based on a monthly sliced flow data throughout a whole-year period. It is certainly the case that weekly sliced, daily sliced or even hourly sliced flow data can offer more precise information about human mobility patterns. But visual explorations of such micro-data with precise geographical information on individual-level space-time trajectories would be beyond the scope of this chapter due to the space limits. Second, our results may not reflect the long-term dynamics of social interaction trends across cities and regions. Given the rapid urbanization and economic growth in China, we expect that the evolution of urban social interaction networks at a longer temporal dimension would be even more striking. Third, we focus on the development of computational models in mining and mapping visualized travel flows over space. Future research would concentrate on applications of statistics and mathematics and on simulating more general-equilibrium economic geography impacts in a cause sense.

Acknowledgements

This research was supported by National Nature Science Foundation projects (Grant No. 41971194, 41230632 and 71473105) and National Science & Technology Support Program during the 12th Five-Year Plan Period (Grant No. 2012BAI32B06 and 2012BAI32B07).

References

Ahern, S., Naaman, M., Nair, R., and Yang, J. H.-I. (2007). World explorer: Visualizing aggregate data from unstructured text in geo-referenced collections. In *Proceedings of the 7th ACM/IEEE-CS joint conference on digital libraries* (pp. 1–10). ACM.

Andersson, R., Quigley, J. M., and Wilhelmson, M. (2004). University decentralization as regional policy: The Swedish experiment. *Journal of Economic Geography*, 4(4), 371–388.

Arzaghi, M., and Henderson, J. V. (2008). Networking off Madison Avenue. *Review of Economic Studies*, 75(4), 1011–1038.

Aubercht, C., Ungar, J., and Freire, S. (2011). Exploring the potential of volunteered geographic information for modeling spatio-temporal characteristics of urban population. *Proceedings of 7VCT*, 11, 13.

Backstrom, L., Sun, E., and Marlow, C. (2010). Find me if you can: improving geographical prediction with social and spatial proximity. In *Proceedings of the 19th international conference on world wide web* (pp. 61–70). ACM.

Banerjee, A., Duflo, E., and Qian, N. (2012). *On the road: Access to transportation infrastructure and economic*, National Bureau of Economic Research, NBER Working Paper No. 17897.

Baum-Snow, N., Brandt, L., Henderson, V., Turner, M., and Zhang, Q. (2013). *Roads, railroads and decentralization of Chinese cities*. Brown University Working Paper.

Brewer, M. B. (1991). The social self: On being the same and different at the same time. *Personal and Social Psychology Bulletin*, 17(5), 475–482.

Burger, J. D., Henderson, J., Kim, G., and Zarrella, G. (2011). Discriminating gender on Twitter. In *Proceedings of the conference on empirical methods in natural language processing* (pp. 1301–1309). Association for Computational Linguistics.

Cao, G., Wang, S., Hwang, M., Padmanabhan, A., Zhang, Z., and Soltani, K. (2015). A scalable framework for spatiotemporal analysis of location-based social media data. *Computers, Environment and Urban Systems*, 51, 70–82.

Cavalli-Sforza, L. L. (2000). *Genes, peoples, and languages*. London: Penguin.

Crandall, D. J., Backstrom, L., Huttenlocher, D., and Kleinberg, J. (2009). Mapping the world's photos. In *Proceedings of the 18th international conference on world wide web* (pp. 761–770). ACM.

Donaldson, D., and Hornbeck, R. (2013). *Railroads and American economic growth: A market access approach*, NBER Working Paper, No. 19213.

Fearon, J. D. (2003). Ethnic and cultural diversity by country. *Journal of Economic Growth*, 8(2), 195–222.

Gao, H., and Liu, H. (2013). Data analysis on location-based social networks. In A. Chin and D. Zhang (Eds.), *Mobile social networking: Computational social sciences* (pp. 165–194). New York: Springer.

Gao, H., Tang, J., and Liu, H. (2012). Exploring social-historical ties on location-based social networks. In *Sixth International AAAI Conference on Weblogs and Social Media*.

Gibbons, S., Lyytikäinen, T., Overman, H. G., and Sanchis-Guarner, R. (2012). *New road infrastructure: The effects on firms*, SERC Discussion Papers, SERCDP0017. Spatial Economics Research Centre (SERC), London School of Economics and Political Sciences, London, UK.

Gonzalez, M. C., Hidalgo, C. A., and Barabasi, A.-L. (2008). Understanding individual human mobility patterns. *Nature*, 453, 779–782.

Gray, J., Chaudhuri, S., Bosworth, A., Layman, A., Reichart, D., Venkatrao, M., et al. (1997). Data cube: A relational aggregation operator generalizing group-by, cross-tab, and sub-totals. *Data Mining and Knowledge Discovery*, 1, 29–53.

Greenberg, J. (1956). The measurement of linguistic diversity. *Language*, 32, 109–105.

Guo, D., Chen, J., MacEachren, A. M., and Liao, K. (2006). A visualization system for space-time and multivariate patterns (vis-stamp). *IEEE Transactions on Visualization and Computer Graphics*, 12, 1461–1474.

Hägerstraand, T. (1970). What about people in regional science? *Papers in Regional Science*, 24, 7–24.

Harris, C. (1954). Market as a factor in the localization of industry in the United States. *Annals of the Association of American Geographers*, 44(4), 315–348.

Hollenstein, L., and Purves, R. (2014). Exploring place through user-generated content: Using Flickr tags to describe city cores. *Journal of Spatial Information Science*, 21–48.

Java, A., Song, X., Finin, T., and Tseng, B. (2007). Why we twitter: Understanding microblogging usage and communities. In *Proceedings of the 9th WebKDD and 1st SNA-KDD 2007 workshop on Web mining and social network analysis* (pp. 56–65). ACM.

Jiang, B. (2013). Head/tail breaks: A new classification scheme for data with a heavy-tailed distribution. *The Professional Geographer*, 65(3), 482–494.

Jiang, B. (2015). Head/tail breaks for visualization of city structure and dynamics. *Cities*, 43, 69–77.

Jiang, B., and Miao, Y. (2014). The evolution of natural cities from the perspective of location-based social media. *The Professional Geographer*, 67(2), 295–306.

Krugman, P. (1980). Scale economies, product differentiation, and the pattern of trade. *The American Economic Review*, 70(5), 950–959.

Leonardi, L., Orlando, S., Raffaetà, A., Roncato, A., Silvestri, C., Andrienko, G., et al. (2014). A general framework for trajectory data warehousing and visual OLAP. *GeoInformatica*, 18, 273–312.

Liu, X., Song, Y., Wu, K., Wang, J., Li, D., and Long, Y. (2015). Understanding urban China with open data. *Cities*. Retrieved 2015, March 29 from http://dx.doi.org/10.1016/j.cities.2015.03.006

Liu, Y., Sui, Z., Kang, C., and Gao, Y. (2014). Uncovering patterns of inter-urban trip and spatial interaction from social media check-in data. *PLoS ONE*, 9, e86026.

Lovelace, R., Malleson, N., Harland, K., and Birkin, M. (2014). Geotagged tweets to inform a spatial interaction model: A case study of museums. *arXiv preprint arXiv:1403.5118*.

Malleson, N., and Andersen, M. A. (2014). The impact of using social media data in crime rate calculations: Shifting hot spots and changing spatial patterns. *Cartography and Geographic Information Science*, 1–10.

Manyika, J., Chui, M., Brown, B., Bughin, J., Dobbs, R., Roxburgh, C., and Byers, A. H. (2011). *Big data: The next frontier for innovation, competition, and productivity*. McKinsey Global Institute, pp. 1–137. http://www. mckinsey.com/Insights/MGI/Research/ Technology_and_Innovation/Big_data_The_next_frontier_for_innovation.

Rao, D., Yarowsky, D., Shreevats, A., and Gupta, M. (2010). Classifying latent user attributes in Twitter. In *Proceedings of the 2nd international workshop on search and mining user-generated contents* (pp. 37–44). ACM.

Rosenthal, S. S., and Strange, W. C. (2008). The attenuation of human capital spillovers. *Journal of Urban Economics*, 64(2), 373–389.

Rosler, R., and Liebig, T. (2013). Using data from location based social networks for urban activity clustering. In *Geographic information science at the heart of Europe*. Switzerland: Springer.

Sjaastad, L. A. (1962). The costs and returns of human migration. *Journal of Political Economy*, 70(5), 80–93.

Stefanidis, A., Cotnoir, A., Croitoru, A., Crooks, A., Rice, M., and Radzikowski, J. (2013). Demarcating new boundaries: mapping virtual polycentric communities through social media content. *Cartography and Geographic Information Science*, 40, 116–129.

Steiger, E., Ellersiek, T., and Zipf, A. (2014). Explorative public transport flow analysis from uncertain social media data. In *Proceedings of the 3rd ACM SIGSPATIAL international workshop on crowdsourced and volunteered geographic information* (pp. 1–7). ACM.

Stephens, M. (2013). Featured graphic. Mapping the geoweb: A geography of Twitter. *Environment and Planning A*, 44, 100–102.

Sui, D., and Goodchild, M. (2011). The convergence of GIS and social media: Challenges for GIScience. *International Journal of Geographical Information Science*, 25, 1737–1748.

Sun, Y., Fan, H., Helbich, M., and Zipf, A. (2013). Analyzing human activities through volunteered geographic information: Using Flickr to analyze spatial and temporal pattern of tourist accommodation. In J. M. Krisp (Ed.), *Progress in location-based services*. Berlin and Heidelberg: Springer.

Verbeek, K., Buchin, K., and Speckmann, B. (2011). Flow map layout via spiral trees. *IEEE Transactions on Visualization and Computer Graphics*, 17, 2536–2544.

Wang, S. (2010). A CyberGIS framework for the synthesis of cyberinfrastructure, GIS, and spatial analysis. *Annals of the Association of American Geographers*, 100, 535–557.

Wang, S., Cao, G., Zhang, Z., and Zhao, Y. (2013). A CyberGIS environment for analysis of location-based social media data. *Advanced Location-based Technologies and Services*, 187.

Widener, M. J., and Li, W. (2014). Using geolocated Twitter data to monitor the prevalence of healthy and unhealthy food references across the US. *Applied Geography*, 54, 189–197.

Wright, D., and Wang, S. (2011). The emergence of spatial cyberinfrastructure. *Proceedings of the National Academy of Sciences*, 108, 5488–5491.

Wu, W. J., and Dong, Z. B. (2015). *Exploring the geography of China's airport networks during 1980s–2000s*, SERC Discussion Papers, SERCDP00173. Spatial Economics Research Centre (SERC), London School of Economics and Political Sciences, London, UK.

Zheng, Y., and Zhou, X. (2011). *Computing with spatial trajectories*. New York: Springer Science & Business Media.

Zipf, G. K. (1949). *Human behavior and the principles of least effort*. Cambridge, MA: Addison Wesley.

3 Is China's airline network similar to its long-distance mobility network?

A comparative analysis

Weiyang Zhang, Yifei Wang, and Jianghao Wang

1 Introduction

Air transportation has long been one of the primary means of transporting goods and people over long distances. As a consequence, a tendency has emerged to use airline networks as a proxy for long-distance trips, as well as to simulate the spatial spread of infectious diseases and exotic species in urban studies literature (Balcan et al., 2009; Tatem, 2009). However, the key issue here concerns the gap between airline networks and long-distance mobility. On the one hand, long-distance movement is enabled by the coexistence of multiple forms of transport, including intercity buses, trains, and aircraft; these different forms of transport have various spatial structures and span different geographical scales (Liu et al., 2016). On the other hand, there are also multi-layered definitions as to what an airline network actually is. According to Neal's (2012) conceptualisation of transportation networks, an infrastructure network (air route) enables intercity trips via aircraft, a capacity network (volume of flights) reflects information on how many trips are possible, while a network of air passenger flows captures the more tangible interactions between cities. Naturally, these different definitions of transport networks lead to projections of different urban networks: for instance, the distinctions between airline capacity networks and actual passenger flows have been widely discussed (Derudder and Witlox, 2005; Neal, 2010), with emphasis on the special hub-and-spoke mode of organisation in air transportation. As a result, the distinction between airline networks and long-distance movements is obviously existing but unclear. Accordingly, to fill this gap, this chapter offers a systematic investigation of this distinction by comparing the airline network and the intercity long-distance mobility network in China.

Before beginning this comparison, two fundamental concerns arise: how so-called long-distance trips might be defined and how two comparable networks might be generated. With regard to the first concern, we will here employ a threshold to define long-distance trips, in which air transport is the main means of transportation. The second concern relates to the fact that airline networks only connect cities with airports but also service other hinterland cities, while movement networks connect whole cities. In other words, it would be irrational to directly compare the two original networks, as airline networks may transport people to unconnected cities. Accordingly, a hinterland analysis for all airport cities has been carried out to counter this concern: we project the original mobility network into a transformed mobility network, in which trips of hinterland cities have been aggregated into their airport (and also gateway) cities. After the two-step pre-processing is complete, a number of statistical measures (such as degree distribution and clustering coefficient) are adopted to test the networks' basic properties, including the small-world and scale-free structures. This is followed by cluster analysis to detect the subgroup structures of the two networks and a quadratic assignment procedure (QAP) test to discover their structural correlations in general. Furthermore, three different centrality measures are employed to facilitate understanding of the fine distinctions between the roles played by cities in both networks. Residual analyses are then performed to identify and classify those city dyads that are well or less connected in the airline network when compared to the actual long-distance intercity movements.

The remainder of this chapter is organised as follows. We first describe the datasets, present the analytical framework used to generate the two comparable networks, and introduce the relevant methods used to compare the two networks. Next, we discuss the results of the empirical comparison, which are developed in three parts: we generally compare their structural similarities and differences, investigate the different roles played by cities, and discuss the results of residual analyses for city dyads. This chapter is concluded with a summary of our main findings.

2 Methodology

2.1 Data description

The airline data was gathered through the Official Airline Guide (OAG; www.oag.com). This database offers detailed digital information on all airlines and airports in the world. We extracted the data on all flights that operated within mainland China in 2014. A total of 3.63 million flight records were gathered, all of which provide corresponding origin–destination (O–D) airports and temporal information. Moreover, as the research object is cities rather than airports, we transform airport-to-airport connections into city-to-city connections by aggregating flights from multiple airports when more than one airport exists in a single city (e.g. Beijing and Shanghai). Furthermore, to facilitate analysis, we further transform the city-to-city network into a symmetrical network by averaging the dyad values between two cities.[1] As 179 cities at the prefecture level and above are interconnected through airline networks, the end product is a 179 cities × 179 cities matrix. The strongest connection in this network is Shanghai–Beijing (17150 flights), followed by Shanghai–Shenzhen (16427 flights). Figure 3.1a presents a map of the airline network.

The data on intercity movements are derived from Weibo, a popular social media platform in China, which can be roughly described as China's version of Twitter. Weibo's users can share their locational information via a geo-tagged mobile application. By employing an application programming interface (API) provided by Weibo, we were able to crawl millions of geo-tagged records containing rich information about the location of Weibo users. Data collection was carried out in 2015, and 210 million geo-tagged records submitted by 27.6 million Weibo users within

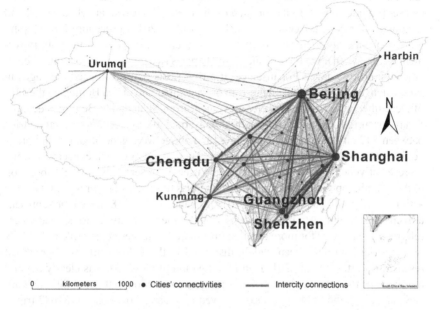

a: the airline network

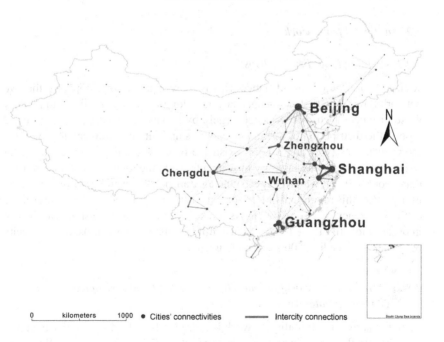

b: the mobility network

Figure 3.1 The airline network and the overall mobility network
Source: Derived from Weibo users' digital footprints in China.

mainland China from January 2014 to November 2014 were gathered. The original dataset provides post activity for each of the users, along with attached spatial and temporal information. According to Zhang et al.'s (2018) procedure for mapping individual intercity footprints from Weibo geo-tagged records, an intercity movement occurs when a Weibo user successively posts two geo-tagged posts in different cities within two days.[2] For instance, if a user posts two geo-tagged messages in succession, one in Shanghai on the 10th of December and one in Beijing on the 11th of December, an effective intercity movement from Shanghai to Beijing is deemed to have occurred. Following this methodology, 6.25 million records of intercity trips between 347 cities at the prefecture level and above were generated; the end product is thus a 347 cities × 347 cities matrix. There is, of course, a concern as to the representativeness of Weibo records: Weibo users represent only a small subsection of the overall population, with an underlying bias towards young groups and leisure activities (Li et al., 2013; Liu et al., 2014). Zhang et al. (2018) tested the representativeness of Weibo data by comparing it with other mobility datasets; readers are referred to that paper for more detailed information. Furthermore, while the pitfalls of using big data have been widely discussed in the field of urban-geographical research (Poorthuis et al., 2014), an investigation of these issues is clearly beyond the scope of the present chapter. The strongest connection in the mobility network is Shanghai–Suzhou (34757 trips), followed by Guangzhou–Foshan (31687 trips). Figure 3.1b presents a map of the network of intercity movements.

2.2 Analytical framework

2.2.1 Defining long-distance trips

A clear definition of long-distance trips is a prerequisite for comparing the two network types. The first step in an analysis of long-distance mobility is to identify those instances of trips that occur largely by means of air transport. Figure 3.2 reports the distribution of airline connections and intercity movements over different distances. We can note the existence of the same decaying tendency for airline connections and intercity movements when the total trip distance is more than about 500 km, which suggests that air transport tends to be the major means of trips after this rough 'cut-off' point. This is also supported by the change curve of the frequency of airline travel. As a result, we impose a threshold of 500 km in order to identify these long-distance movements; in other words, only intercity movements exceeding 500 km are included in our analyses.

2.2.2 Transferring the original mobility network into an assembled network of gateway cities

As noted above, the mobility network is more likely to be a fully connected network, while the airline network only connects main airport cities. In this case, airport cities are home to higher volumes of movement that exceed local demands (Derudder et al., 2007). More precisely, nodes in the movement network are single cities, while nodes in the airline network are metropolitan areas (Neal, 2014).

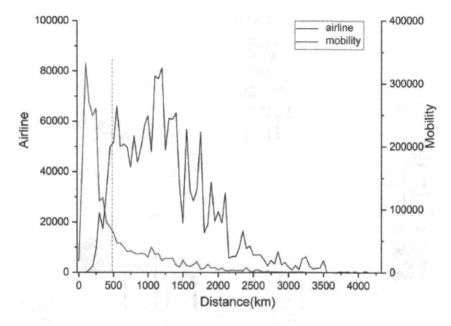

Figure 3.2 Distribution of airline and mobility across different distances

To facilitate comparison, we therefore transform the mobility network into an assembled network in which nodal cities are aggregated into metropolitan areas in which airports are located. In practice, we delimit the hinterlands for each of the airport cities according to the principle of shortest distance: cities without airports are classified into the hinterland of their nearest airport-cities. Figure 3.3 illustrates how the hinterlands are divided: for instance, city-D and city-E are grouped into the metropolitan area of city-C, in which the nearest airport-y is located. Following this logic, we then transform the 347 cities × 347 cities mobility matrix into a 179 gateway cities × 179 gateway cities mobility matrix by summing all cities' movements in each of the airport-containing metropolitan areas.

2.3 Methods

After generating the two comparable networks, several indices and measures are used to compare the two networks in terms of general network structures, nodal connectivities, and city dyad connectivities.

2.3.1 Network structures

SMALL-WORLD FEATURE

As has been observed in a large number of complex networks, many networks exhibit a highly clustered feature of regular lattices but short geodesic distance,

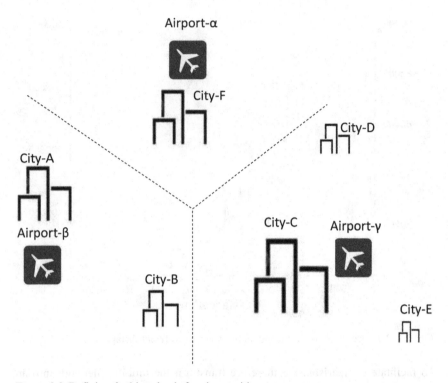

Figure 3.3 Defining the hinterlands for airport cities

like a random network; this has been termed a 'small-world' structure (Watts and Strogatz, 1998). The small-world phenomenon has been identified in many mobility networks and traffic networks and can also help to explain the spread of diseases and the circulation of economic resources throughout networks (Neal, 2014). The statistical testing of the small-world feature includes benchmarking a network's average path length (L) and clustering coefficient (C) by using a simulated random network. The measure of average path length (L) can be calculated as follows:

$$L = \frac{2}{n(n-1)} \sum_{i>j} d\left(v_i, v_j\right)$$

where $d(v_i, v_j)$ is the length of the shortest path for node-pairs (v_i, v_j), while n is the total number of nodes in the network.

The measure of clustering coefficient (C) can be defined according to the following formula:

$$C = \frac{1}{n} \sum_{i=1}^{n} \frac{2E_i}{k_i\left(k_i - 1\right)}$$

where $2/k_i(k_i-1)$ indicates the maximal possible edges between the node i and its $k_i(k_i-1)$ neighbors, and E_i is the actual number of edges between them.

SCALE-FREE FEATURE

A network can be described as having a scale-free feature when it has a power-law degree distribution. This can be described as $P(k) \approx k(-\alpha)$, where the exponent α is greater than 1. A scale-free network is characterised by the inclusion of a small number of nodes with high connectivities and a large number of nodes with low connectivities. The aim of testing for the scale-free structure is to compare the vulnerability of the networks when targeted or random nodes are attacked. To be more specific, having a fitter scale-free feature means that random attacks (such as airport closures, in this study) cannot affect network structure, while targeted attacks may destroy the general network very quickly. In practice, the scale-free feature can be tested for by fitting the degree distribution of nodes according to a power law statistical distribution.

COMMUNITY STRUCTURES

One of the important components of network structures is community formation: that is, sets of nodes having more close connections to each other than to other nodes can be grouped into clusters. Community-finding technologies can help us to observe the general structure of networks (Gurtner et al., 2014). In this chapter, we employ the fast greedy method (Clauset et al., 2004), a well-known community detection approach that functions by optimising Newman-Girvan modularity (Girvan and Newman, 2002) to divide the two networks into various groups. The modularity can indicate the presence of community strictures, with a modularity value of 0.3 to 0.7 signifying the existence of a community feature.

QAP CORRELATION

As mentioned before, air traffic is one of the most common modes of transport over long distances. We can therefore conceptually assume that both networks have similar features. To quantify the potential correlation between the two networks, we carry out a QAP correlation test, in which a standardised coefficient and p-value can be interpreted according to their meanings in traditional statistical approaches.

2.3.2 Nodal connectivities

Nodal connectivities reflecting the hierarchical positions of cities in a network can be defined in different forms. For instance, the sum of a city's connections represents its ability to connect other nodes, while the average connection distance between a city and others represents a city's proximity to or distance from a network 'centre'. In this chapter, we employ three kinds of centrality measures in social network analysis to carefully differentiate between the roles played by different cities in the two networks.

Degree centrality measures a node's connectivity in the network by counting the number of links each node has to others and can be defined as:

$$C_D(i) = \sum_{j=1}^{n} a_{ij}$$

where a_{ij} is the number of connections between city-i and another city-j. By quantifying the sum of cities' connections, this measure describes a city's general influence in a network, highlighting prestige and dominance.

Closeness centrality measures the proximity of a node to other nodes in the network and can be computed as follows:

$$C_C(i) = \frac{n-1}{\sum_{v_j \in V, i \neq j} d_{ij}}$$

where d_{ij} is the connection distance between vertices i and j. By measuring the extent to which one city can connect all other cities, the measure of closeness centrality reports on a city's ability to serve as a network centre.

Betweenness centrality is a measure of centrality based on shortest paths. The betweenness centrality of node v_i is defined as the ratio of the number of shortest paths between node v_k and v_j that pass through v_i (i.e., $\sigma_{kj}(i)$) to the sum of all shortest paths between node v_k and v_j (i.e. σ_{kj}). As indicated by the formula, betweenness centrality indicates cities' 'bridging' or 'brokering' function and is thus useful for identifying gateway cities in urban systems (Burghardt, 1971).

$$C_B(i) = \sum_{k \neq i \neq j \in N} \sigma_{kj}(i) / \sigma_{kj}$$

2.3.3 City dyad connectivities

A city dyad's connectivity is one of the important aspects involved in comparing the specific structure of urban networks. We employ residual analysis to compare city dyad connectivities in the two networks. To be more specific, after carrying out a regression analysis between corresponding city dyad connectivities in the two networks, the departures from the regression line (i.e. the residual values of city dyads) can be used to identify those city dyads that have distinctive connectivities in a specific network. In the regression analysis, where the X-axis represents the mobility network and the Y-axis represents the airline network, positive residuals indicate strong intercity links in the airline network relative to their connectivities in the mobility network, while negative residuals indicate strong intercity links in the intercity mobility network relative to their connectivities in the airline network.

3 Results

Figure 3.4 presents a map of the two networks, in which the original mobility network has been transformed into a comparable network consisting of gateway cities. The strength of intercity connections is shown by both the colour and thickness of the edges, while node sizes indicate cities' connectivities. Moreover, the various categories of the nodes represent the specific groups that each city belongs to in the community analysis. Rather than directly describing the two networks, we will blend the basic geographies of the two networks into the comparative analyses in terms of network structures, nodes, and linkages.

3.1 Network structures

Table 3.1 reports the average path length and clustering coefficient of the two networks, which are used to identify the small-world feature. The first observation is that both networks have relatively short path lengths, which are similar to the average path length of a random network of the same size. This implies that any two cities can reach each other easily (with less than two changes). In fact, almost all airports can be connected by one or two steps. The average path lengths of the mobility network, however, are shorter than those of the airline network. This finding is unsurprising: the mobility network approximates actual intercity flows, representing the combination of all means of transportation. In light of the clustering coefficient, this difference becomes even more pronounced. With a clustering coefficient of 0.746, which is much larger than that for a random network of the same size, the airline network exhibits a typical small-world feature. This suggests that the airline network has a greater tendency to cluster together to produce various groups with relatively high density, which also reflects the hub-and-spoke organisation model of the airline system (Wang et al., 2011). However, unlike the airline network, the long-distance-movement network does not display high levels of clustering. This observation is inconsistent with other types of migration networks reported on before (Fagiolo and Mastrorillo, 2013). This observation can be tentatively ascribed to the nature of daily mobility: the selected 48-hour interval makes it more likely that the movements will be skewed towards leisure and business activities and will thus be unlike long-period migration, which is characterised by obvious clustering (Davis et al., 2013).

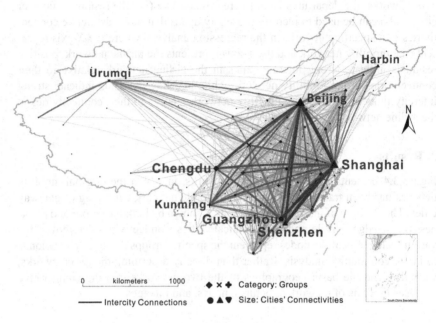

a: the airline network

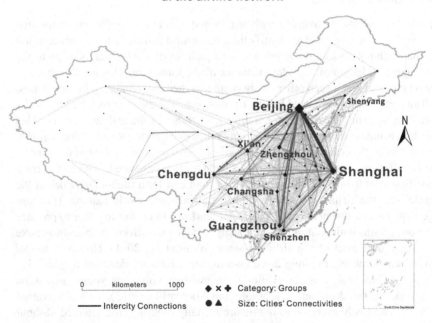

b: the mobility network

Figure 3.4 The airline network and the mobility network

Table 3.1 Average path lengths and clustering coefficients of the airline and mobility network

Network	Average Path Length (L)	Clustering Coefficient (C)
Airline	1.955	0.746
Random network with same size	1.931	0.124
Migration	1.197	0.820
Random network	1.197	0.803

As a scale-free structure can bring an optimal efficiency to the operation of airline networks, the existence of scale-free topology in airline networks has been widely reported in the existing literature (Guida and Maria, 2007). Unsurprisingly, and in line with previous studies, the degree distribution in this airline network appears to follow a power law (Figure 3.5a). The long-distance mobility network, however, exhibits an obvious exponential distribution (Figure 3.5b). This indicates that the two networks are different in essence, despite their nodal degree distributions being ostensibly similar. Airline networks tend to be resilient to random failure (such as bad weather or air traffic control) but can easily incur damage from the paralysis of key airports; by contrast, the general patterns of actual movement are less vulnerable to random and targeted attacks. Again, this underscores that airline networks offer only one of the means of transport that enable long-distance intercity commuting, and the infrastructure topology of airlines thus cannot cover the topology of substantive flows as such.

The community analysis revealed the module patterns of organisation of the two networks, which can be used to understand whether some cities have closer relations in one network than the other. Figure 3.4 maps the results of community detection produced by the fast greedy method, in which six and five communities were detected in the airline network and the mobility network, respectively (with modularity values of about 0.6, indicating the evident presence of community structures in both networks). The obvious distinctiveness of their community structures can be summarised with reference to two main points. First of all, in terms of nodal connectivities, the main cities (such as Beijing, Shanghai, Guangzhou, Chengdu, Chongqing, and Zhengzhou), which have dense intercity connections, are divided into one group and thus form the backbone of the mobility network. This confirms that it is a city's population size rather than economic performance that matters most where long-distance movements are concerned. For instance, Zhengzhou, Chongqing, and Changsha, which are home to large populations but do not have outstanding economic performance, stand out as being densely connected with other main cities. Conversely, only three main cities (i.e. Beijing, Shanghai, and Shenzhen), along with other small cities, are bonded within the same group. This provides a point of difference from the 'diamond backbone' of the airline network. These results can be explained by noting the fact that airline routes are operated by various airline companies, which leads to other main cities (such as Guangzhou and Chengdu) having their own linkage hinterlands. As

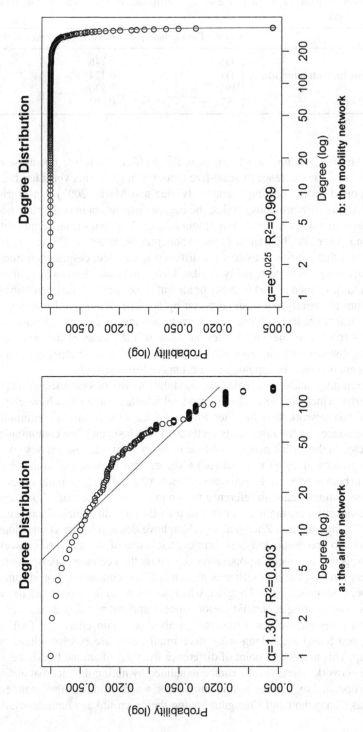

Figure 3.5 Cities' degree distribution in the airline and mobility network

a result, the members of the first community do not coincide with the members of the backbone of the airline network. Second, the community structures of the mobility network exhibit the typical characteristics of spatial variation. Two notable examples are the two spatially contiguous communities in the northwest and northeast of China. This suggests that spatial factors, along with related physical barriers and cultural affinities, play crucial roles in shaping intercity movements (Wu et al., 2016; Zhang et al., 2019). As a network of infrastructure connections, the airline typology does not display such apparent geographical configurations.

Although the structural distinctions have been discussed with reference to small-world and scale-free features, as well as clustering results, it is also necessary to note the existence of some degree of structural similarity between the two networks, such as the diamond-like typologies and the key positions of main cities. We next employ a QAP test to examine the correlation between the two networks. The Pearson correlation coefficient of 0.757 ($p < 0.001$) confirms that there is significant correlation between intercity connectivities in the two networks. Accordingly, it can be concluded that the structural similarities and differences between the two networks co-exist.

3.2 Nodal connectivities

To facilitate discussion, Table 3.2 presents the top 10 cities in the two networks in terms of degree, closeness and betweenness centralities. As noted above, different measures of centrality represent different roles played by cities in shaping networks. First, with regard to degree centrality, it is indeed remarkable that Beijing, Shanghai, and Guangzhou feature in the top three, which reveals their dominance in China's urban system in terms of not only infrastructure linkage but also tangible flows. The different rankings of other cities show that large cities by population, such as Zhengzhou and Wuhan, play key positions in the mobility network, while major aviation hubs such as Chengdu and tourism cities such as

Table 3.2 Top 10 cities in terms of their degree, closeness and betweenness centralities in the airline network and the mobility network

Rank	Degree centrality		Closeness centrality		Betweenness	
	Airline	Mobility	Airline	Mobility	Airline	Mobility
1	Beijing	Beijing	Beijing	Urumqi	Beijing	Shenzhen
2	Shanghai	Shanghai	Shanghai	Lhasa/Lasa	Shanghai	Beijing
3	Guangzhou	Guangzhou	Guangzhou	Xining	Guangzhou	Zhengzhou
4	Shenzhen	Zhengzhou	Shenzhen	Jieyang	Chongqing	Shijiazhuang
5	Chengdu	Xi'an	Chengdu	Harbin	Xi'an	Handan
6	Xi'an	Chengdu	Xi'an	Sanya	Chengdu	Xi'an
7	Kunming	Wuhan	Chongqing	Haikou	Shenzhen	Chengdu
8	Chongqing	Chongqing	Kunming	Changchun	Haikou	Mianyang
9	Hangzhou	Shenzhen	Haikou	Xiamen	Tianjin	Xining
10	Xiamen	Hangzhou	Hangzhou	Lanzhou	Hangzhou	Shanghai

Kunming, Hangzhou, and Xiamen tend to have relatively stronger connectivities in the airline network. This first observation can be traced back to the spatial mismatch between population and airport service in China. One example of this is Shenzhen, which is listed as the fifth-busiest airport in mainland China, although its population ranks in 10th place. In addition, major tourism cities tend to be well connected through airline routes. Second, the measure of closeness centrality of the airline network is generally consistent with its measure of degree centrality. However, with regard to the mobility network, some frontier cities in particular stand out. For instance, Urumqi, Lhasa, and Xining exhibit the strongest closeness centrality, which reflects their proximity to other cities along the shortest path. This is unsurprising, given that the mobility data used in the current research has a bias towards leisure trips. These frontier cities, with their stunning scenery, attract many Weibo users traveling from other cities and thus have more direct connections with other cities. For instance, Urumqi has direct connections with 164 cities out of all 176 cities, while Shanghai directly connects with only 155 cities. As a result, more direct connections produce higher closeness centralities. Furthermore, a comparison of closeness centrality and degree centrality reveals Haikou's unusual position in the airline network. As an offshore city, Haikou has more air routes with inland cities, as long-distance movements mainly rely on taking flights. Hence, Haikou is less dominant but still well connected in China's airline network. Third, an examination of cities' rankings in terms of betweenness in the airline network reveals results that are generally consistent with their rankings by degree and closeness centrality. By contrast, patterns of betweenness centrality for cities in the mobility network are notably different when compared with their rankings by degree and closeness centrality. We can observe that several cities, such as Shenzhen, Zhengzhou, and Shijiazhuang, stand out as having conspicuous betweenness centrality. This identifies their gateway function in the network of intercity mobility: for instance, Zhengzhou and Shijiazhuang are home to important junctions in the railway networks of China, while Shenzhen serves as an important port between the mainland and Hong Kong.

3.3 City dyad connectivities

The residual analysis helps us to differentiate between the two networks in terms of city dyad connectivities. Put simply, in our residual analysis, a positive residual indicates that a city dyad has more airline supply than intercity movement, while a negative residual shows that a city dyad has more intercity movement than airline supply. An analysis of this kind is consequently relevant in the practice of airline planning in order to optimise airline networks and the layout of other transport means.

Figure 3.6 presents the results of regression analysis, which reveal that some city dyads are indeed 'over-linked' in the airline or mobility network. To facilitate discussion, we list only the top 10 'over-linked' city dyads (i.e. those with the largest positive or negative residuals) for each of the networks (Table 3.3).

Looking at the top 10 'over-linked' city pairs in the airline network, we can observe that they are almost all separated by large distances. Shanghai–Lincang,

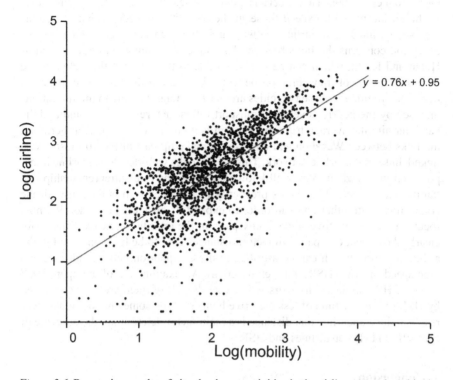

Figure 3.6 Regression results of city-dyad connectivities in the airline network and in the mobility network

Table 3.3 Top 10 'over-linked' city dyads in the airline and mobility network

	Well-connected in the airline network		Well-connected in the mobility network	
Rank	*City-pairs*	*Residuals*	*City-pairs*	*Residuals*
1	Shanghai-Lincang	1.10	Shenyang-Harbin	−3.49
2	Wenzhou-Guiyang	1.06	Nanjing-Jinan	−3.48
3	Urumqi-Hotan	0.91	Zhengzhou-Changsha	−3.40
4	Nanning-Dalian	0.88	Zhengzhou-Wuxi	−3.36
5	Jiayuguan-Guangzhou	0.88	Xuzhou-Hangzhou	−3.29
6	Urumqi-Kashi	0.86	Wuxi-Jinan	−3.28
7	Ordos-Nanning	0.82	Tianjin-Nanjing	−3.27
8	Wenzhou-Kunming	0.82	Dalian-Changchun	−3.27
9	Daxing'anling-Beijing	0.82	Jinan-Hefei	−3.27
10	Haikou-Enshi	0.81	Wuhan-Handan	−3.26

Nanning–Dalian, Guangzhou–Jiayuguan, Nanning–Ordos, and Beijing–Daxinganling in particular exhibit this feature. Clearly, this indicates that the supply of airlines for long-distance movements is sufficient, which further implies that air transportation rather than railway is the dominant means of transportation if two cities are far away from each other. This is because, in this case only, the intercity connections in the airline network exceed those in the mobility network, which represents the average linkages of airline, railway, and other transport means. One notable exception concerns the links between Urumqi and its hinterland cities, such as Hotan and Kashi, which can be explained due to the fact that the airline is the dominant means of transportation between them. Even the Euclidean distances between Urumqi and these two cities are not far enough; owing to the limitations imposed by the poorly developed transport infrastructure on the ground and the harsh terrain, the average trip time by train is more than 20 hours. Furthermore, the links between Wenzhou and other cities make up part of the 10 most 'over-linked' links in the airline network. This points to the well-developed airline transportation in Wenzhou. As a well-known cradle for private entrepreneurship and family-run business, Wenzhou's prosperity has enabled it to build dense airline connections with other cities in order to expand its business networks. We now focus on the top 10 'over-linked' city pairs in the mobility network. This result clearly shows that city pairs with short distances tend to be less connected in the airline network, which can be ascribed to the competition between airlines and high speed railway (HSR; Yang et al., 2018). An examination of the operational status of HSR in these city pairs will reveal that all of them are well connected by HSR (a journey time of less than five hours). While somewhat obvious, these results indeed underline that distance is a main factor determining the outcome of competition between airlines and HSR.

4 Conclusions

Airline networks have often been used as proxies for mapping intercity long-distance mobility. However, there are obvious differences between the two networks, as airlines are only one means of transportation over long distances, while airline supply and the tangible flows of passengers are two distinct layers of urban networks. In this chapter, we have examined the similarities and differences between the two networks using airline schedule data and approximated information on intercity movements (derived from Weibo).

Although these networks have certain similarities, the following differences are also evident. First, the structure of the airline network is characterised by apparent small-world and scale-free patterns, while the mobility network does not exhibit such features. Second, there are varied clustering structures in which the backbone of intercity connections and geographic proximity do not manifest in the clustering results of the airline network, as airline routes are operated by various airline companies. Third, considering different definitions of the importance of cities in networks reveals that large cities (by population), frontier cities, port cities, and junction cities for ground transportation are well connected in the mobility network, while tourism cities and major aviation hubs are well connected in the airline network. This relates to the spoke-and-hub model of airline network organisation on the one hand and the determinants that produce intercity movements on the other hand. However, it is also important to note that some findings are more or less related to the datasets we utilised. Fourthly, city pairs separated by long distances tend to be well-connected in the airline network, while city pairs in relatively close physical proximity tend to be well-connected in the mobility network. This confirms that the results of competition between airlines and HSR is highly dependent on intercity distance. Furthermore, harsh terrain, poorly developed transport infrastructure on the ground, and a prosperous business economy also stimulate the development of airline network.

In addition to achieving the stated objective of differentiating between the two kinds of intercity linkages, this chapter also is useful to policy makers and urban planners. More specifically, the present analysis offers useful background information regarding how airline networks can be optimised. Air transport always endeavours to optimise its airline networks in order to transport more people and give equal consideration to efficiency and equality. By identifying where and in which cities and city pairs airline connectivity is well developed or less developed, in conjunction with benchmarking against actual long-distance mobility, we can determine which airline routes should be added and which should be cut. Moreover, these results can also help to support the formulation of cities' development strategies. To be specific, cities with well-developed airline connectivity should fully utilise this advantage and focus on attracting more intercity travel, while cities with less-developed airline connectivity should move towards improving airline accessibility and access to border regions.

Acknowledgement

This work was supported by the Shanghai Philosophy and Social Sciences Fund (2018ECK009); Fundamental Research Funds for the Central Universities (2018ECNU-HLYT016); Major Projects of Humanities and Social Sciences Key Research Base of Ministry of Education (17JJD790007).

Notes

1 The original network in fact approximates a symmetrical network, as most of the flights are round-trip.
2 The reason behind the adoption of the two-day duration constraint is that people can travel across the city dyad spanning the greatest distance in mainland China within approximately 48 hours.

References

Balcan D, Colizza V, Gonçalves B, et al. (2009) Multiscale mobility networks and the spatial spreading of infectious diseases. *Proceedings of the National Academy of Sciences* 106(51): 21484–21489.

Burghardt AF. (1971) A hypothesis about gateway cities. *Annals of the Association of American Geographers* 61(2): 269–285.

Clauset A, Newman ME and Moore C. (2004) Finding community structure in very large networks. *Physical review E* 70(6): 066111.

Davis KF, D'Odorico P, Laio F, et al. (2013) Global spatio-temporal patterns in human migration: A complex network perspective. *PLoS ONE* 8(1): e53723.

Derudder B, Devriendt L and Witlox F. (2007) Flying where you don't want to go: An empirical analysis of hubs in the global airline network. *Tijdschrift Voor Economische En Sociale Geografie* 98(3): 307–324.

Derudder B and Witlox F. (2005) An appraisal of the use of airline data in assessing the world city network: A research note on data. *Urban Studies* 42(13): 2371–2388.

Fagiolo G and Mastrorillo M. (2013) International migration network: Topology and modeling. *Physical Review E* 88(1): 012812.

Girvan M and Newman ME. (2002) Community structure in social and biological networks. *Proceedings of the National Academy of Sciences* 99(12): 7821–7826.

Guida M and Maria F. (2007) Topology of the Italian airport network: A scale-free small-world network with a fractal structure? *Chaos, Solitons & Fractals* 31(3): 527–536.

Gurtner G, Vitali S, Cipolla M, et al. (2014) Multi-scale analysis of the European airspace using network community detection. *PLoS ONE* 9(5): e94414.

Li L, Goodchild MF and Xu B. (2013) Spatial, temporal, and socioeconomic patterns in the use of Twitter and Flickr. *Cartography and Geographic Information Science* 40(2): 61–77.

Liu X, Derudder B and Wu K. (2016) Measuring polycentric urban development in China: An intercity transportation network perspective. *Regional Studies* 50(8): 1302–1315.

Liu Y, Sui Z, Kang C, et al. (2014) Uncovering patterns of inter-urban trip and spatial interaction from social media check-in data. *PLoS ONE* 9(1): e86026.

Neal ZP. (2010) Refining the air traffic approach to city networks. *Urban Studies* 47(10): 2195–2215.

Neal ZP. (2014) The devil is in the details: Differences in air traffic networks by scale, species, and season. *Social Networks* 38: 63–73.

Neal ZP. (2012) *The connected city: How networks are shaping the modern metropolis.* New York: Routledge.

Poorthuis A, Zook M, Shelton T, et al. (2014) Using geotagged digital social data in geographic research. In: Clifford N, French S, Cope M, et al. (eds) *Key methods in geography.* London: SAGE, 248–269.

Tatem AJ. (2009) The worldwide airline network and the dispersal of exotic species: 2007–2010. *Ecography* 32(1): 94–102.

Wang J, Mo H, Wang F, et al. (2011) Exploring the network structure and nodal centrality of China's air transport network: A complex network approach. *Journal of Transport Geography* 19(4): 712–721.

Watts DJ and Strogatz SH. (1998) Collective dynamics of 'small-world' networks. *Nature* 393(6684): 440.

Wu W, Wang J and Dai T. (2016) The geography of cultural ties and human mobility: Big data in urban contexts. *Annals of the American Association of Geographers* 106(3): 612–630.

Yang H, Dobruszkes F, Wang J, et al. (2018) Comparing China's urban systems in high-speed railway and airline networks. *Journal of Transport Geography* 68: 233–244.

Zhang W, Derudder B, Wang J, et al. (2018) Regionalization in the Yangtze River Delta, China, from the perspective of inter-city daily mobility. *Regional Studies* 52(4): 528–541.

Zhang W, Derudder B, Wang J, et al. (2019) An analysis of the determinants of the multiplex urban networks in the Yangtze River Delta. *Tijdschrift Voor Economische En Sociale Geografie* 3: 1–17. doi:10.1111/tesg.

4 Spatially weighted interaction model of traffic flows on motorway networks

Terry Pulford, Jianquan Cheng, and Cheng Jin

The advent of technologies such as electronic ticketing, social media and mobile phones are providing unprecedented sources of high-volume, highly localised and dynamic flow data in addition to the more typical survey approach. This 'big data' phenomenon associated with mobility also brings with it new challenges to the analysis of spatial interactions. Global models of flows resulting from spatial interactions can fail to reveal important local information about their structure, just as global models of other processes in a landscape do. The geographically weighted modelling method has been employed with success in other areas of study to better explore local variations in relationships. The recently described spatially weighted interaction models (SWIM) framework brings a similar focus to local modelling of spatial interactions.

In this study, the transaction data collected during the process of tax payment at each toll gate have been used to aggregate the flows of traffic to certain spatial and temporal scales, such as one-year flow on county level. Applying the flow-focused method of spatially weighted interaction modelling, this chapter aims to show the spatially heterogeneous socio-economic determinants shaping the spatial pattern of these traffic flows between counties across an economically wealthy province in China. The spatial non-stationarity in the flow determinants reflects the spatial imbalance in the regional development and transformation. The chapter ends with some significant findings on China's transformation and methodological recommendations for future work.

1 Introduction

Rapid urbanisation has stimulated massive and remarkable urban transformation across China in the past decades. For example, flows of internal migrants occurring in modern China (Cheng et al., 2014) have been the largest movement of people in the long history of mankind. In the meanwhile, the advance in sensor, digital and internet technologies has created inspiring opportunity for the development of big data and its analytics. For instance, the transaction data regarding the tax payment at each toll gate enables the collection of traffic flows over motorway networks across Jiangsu province at very high temporal resolutions (Cheng et al., 2016). Flows of intra-city tourists can be collected through a web service, and the user-generated content data with a mixture of text, image and maps can be used to explore the temporal heterogeneity in tourist mobility (Jin et al., 2017). These different categories of flows, as dynamic driving forces for urban transformation, may have demonstrated interesting spatial patterns and processes. The analyses of flow data mentioned need scientific and accurate models of spatial (and temporal) interactions.

Spatial Interactions are the study of the movement of people, goods, information, diseases and socio-economic resources between geographical locations, usually as the result of a decision-making process or policy (Kordi and Fotheringham, 2016). Such processes are highly important to the understanding of complexity inherent in many fields of study including social and economic geography, urban planning and transportation (Cheng and Bertolini, 2013; Vobruba et al., 2016).

Spatial interaction models are mathematical tools used for investigating and analysing spatial movements. The importance of these models has been recognised for many years, from probabilistic, raster-based approaches (Besag, 1974) to more recognisably contemporary models (Wilson, 1967; Batty and Mackie, 1972). Spatial interactions are particularly relevant in the field of mobility. The needs to analyse population movements for access to work, services, migration and education are important factors to understand for planning, disease surveillance, security and economic consequences (Balcan et al., 2009). Modern phenomena such as social media and mobile phone technology add the dimension of low-cost, large-scale data collection, the 'big data' challenge, to these mobility studies (Song et al., 2010; Hasan et al., 2013; Zhong et al., 2016; Zhao et al., 2016).

Generally, much past work on the gravity models has considered a global model of spatial interaction, that is the processes in the study area have been considered to be spatially homogenous, any locally significant variations thus being smoothed out by the model. Logically, this is not the case; hilly or mountainous regions undoubtedly have a different influence on housing density or road (Manhattan) distances to flat plains, for example. These local considerations have influenced many areas of spatial analysis (Fotheringham, 1997; Fotheringham and Brunsdon, 1999). Changes in the geography manifest themselves as changes in the spatial model parameters depending on where the calibration is considered.

The variation in processes and model behaviour across the study area is known as spatial non-stationarity, and it bears some similarities to the modifiable areal unit problem (MAUP) (Fotheringham et al., 2002), particularly when working with aggregated data sources. A global model will not necessarily provide a model correctly fitted to anywhere in the study area (Fotheringham, 1997; Unwin and Unwin, 1998; Fotheringham et al., 2002).

A primary concern in spatial interaction is the modelling of the flow of whatever quantity is being considered between locations in a study area. An early method of exploring non-uniformities in the directions of flow in migration patterns (Fotheringham and Pitts, 1995) used a double-log conversion of a multi-variate, power-interaction model similar to (6) in what follows, to measure the model parameters via the expansion method (Casetti, 1972). This double-log approach to calibration had earlier been cautioned against (Wilson, 1971) because of the local variations in propulsiveness and attractiveness parameters.

Improvements in modelling by considering non-stationarity and refinement of local calibration are not just limited to spatial interactions. In the wider context the loss of information by only considering global models may be problematic. Several techniques have been considered to include local statistics, such as moving window regression (Lloyd, 2011; Lloyd, 2010) and spatially adaptive filtering (Trigg and Leach, 1967; Foster and Gorr, 1986). However, the GWR approach is widely applied and has given rise to the modelling of spatial non-stationarity, one form of spatial heterogeneity, with many variations adapted for specific domains (Nakaya, 2002; Hadayeghi et al., 2010; da Silva and Rodrigues, 2014; Li et al., 2016), including spatial interactions.

The aim of this study was to explore the recently described geographically weighted technique for modelling spatial interactions known as spatially weighted interaction models (SWIM). A program for the flow-focussed approach was developed and employed in a case study to evaluate the method. The case study is based on Chinese traffic flow data derived from toll road metering for counties in the Jiangsu Province in Eastern China in 2014.

Following this introduction section, Section 3 briefly explains spatial non-stationarity and geographically weighted modelling method. Section 3 introduces the study area, data sets and methods of spatially weighted interaction models. Section 4 presents the results from the SWIM modelling methods. The last section ends with the general conclusion and discussion of limitations and recommendations.

2 Spatial non-stationarity and geographically weighted modelling

Creating a mathematical model of a particular problem is one way of trying to understand or predict the properties of one set of observations, the dependent (or response) variable, in terms of one or more independent (explanatory, or predictor) variables. The models are frequently approximated to linear relations between variables, and a closed-form OLS solution defines the model in many cases. A major problem with such a simple linear model is that it ignores the influence of the non-stationarity in the spatial contribution; local variations are 'averaged' out of the results (Fotheringham et al., 2002, p. 211) .

Non-stationarity arises because the relationships in the model are not consistent everywhere (there are variables that the model has not considered), this is in contrast to relationships such as the $E = mc^2$ mass-energy equivalence equation (Fotheringham et al., 2002, p. 9), which are held to be universal. This condition is exacerbated by the size of the data set being considered, and it was long recognised that localised parameters gave better insights than global ones (Fotheringham et al., 2002). One manifestation of this is that the errors between the observed values and those that are predicted by the model for the dependent variable, known as residuals, may not follow a normal distribution and may exhibit heteroskedasity

(Williams, 2015; Bishoff et al., 1991), i.e. the variance of the error term is not constant. Whilst this may be attributed to spatial dependencies, it may be difficult to attribute it as such (Brunsdon et al., 1996; Fotheringham et al., 2002).

The issues with non-stationarity of parameters and the recognition that classical statistical methods were failing with spatial analysis at the global level (Unwin and Unwin, 1998) were drivers behind the development of GWR as a tool for investigating problems at the local level (Fotheringham and Brunsdon, 1997). It was also recognised that local models would facilitate the visualisation of the local variations via mapping (Brunsdon et al., 1996; Fotheringham et al., 2002).

Regression is a mathematical technique for investigating the relationships between a dependent variable and one or more independent variables. Most commonly, the regression is modelled as a linear relationship between the dependent variable and the independent variables, plus some randomised error term. Providing that the distribution of the independent data are normal and independent, the ordinary least squares (OLS) method can be used to obtain a set of estimated regression coefficients for the model that minimise losses (Bishoff et al., 1991; Fotheringham et al., 2002). The resulting model is global and assumes (contrary to Tobler's First Law) that there is no variation in the coefficients across the study area, i.e. the data exhibit spatial homogeneity. The general form for a global linear regression model is given by (Fotheringham et al., 2002; Brunsdon et al., 1996) equation (1):

$$y_i = \beta_0 + \sum_k \beta_k x_{ik} + \varepsilon_i \qquad (1)$$

where y_i, x_{ik} and ε_i *are the dependent, Kth* independent variable and ε_i, the error at *i* respectively. A closed-form solution exists for estimating the coefficients of Gaussian linear regression using OLS, as shown in equation (2)

$$\hat{\beta} = \left(X^T X\right)^{-1} X^T Y \qquad (2)$$

where $\hat{\beta}$ is a matrix of parameter estimates, X, X^T are the matrix of explanatory variables, and its transpose, and Y a matrix of dependent observations.

The underlying GWR premise is that there is an underlying nonstationarity associated with the data, and the linear regression model is adapted to account for this. The model is considered spatially heterogeneous and influenced more by local factors than distant. In GWR, points around the regression point influence the model dependent on their distance from it, so the calibration becomes specific to the point under consideration. From (Fotheringham et al., 2002), equation (1) becomes:

$$y_i = \beta_0(u_i, v_i) + \sum_k \beta_k(u_i, v_i) x_{ik} + \varepsilon_i \qquad (3)$$

and the estimator becomes a weighted least squares (WLS) solution, by incorporating a diagonal (square) matrix of weights $W_{(u_i,v_i)}$:

$$\widehat{\beta}_{(u_i, v_i)} = \left(X^T W_{(u_i, v_i)} X \right)^{-1} X^T W_{(u_i, v_i)} Y \tag{4}$$

Equation (4) is applicable for Gaussian regression (dependent data with a continuous function) (Bishoff et al., 1991), but for discrete quantities count and interval quantities (Fotheringham et al., 2002; Kordi and Fotheringham, 2016; Nakaya et al., 2005), advocate the use of a geographically weighted generalised linear model (GWGLM) and its derivatives. This is based on the generalised linear model (GLM) work of (Nelder and Wedderburn, 1972). The GLMs do not have closed-form solutions because of the discrete (and probabilistic) nature of the data, and therefore require iterative solutions. Examples not using the Gaussian regression model include (Zhibin et al., 2013; Hadayeghi et al., 2010). A negative binomial model has advantages over Poisson under certain circumstances (Kordi and Fotheringham, 2016; da Silva and Rodrigues, 2014) and also has a closed form solution.

Key to the GWR process is calibration of the model parameters separately for each regression point in the model, based on the observations in the near vicinity of the regression point and diminishing the contribution to the model the further away the observation was from this point.

GWR considers a spatial kernel placed around the regression point to generate the weighting matrix, as illustrated in Figure 4.1. The contribution from data points under the kernel is dependent on the magnitude of the observation, the value of the kernel function at the data point and also the number of observations covered by the kernel. The value of the kernel function diminishes, with distance being a maximum at the regression point and decaying with distance from this.

The rate of decay is governed by both the function characteristics and the bandwidth selected, and this value is reflected in the weight generated. Selection of bandwidth has a significant impact on the model. It is suggested that GWR is quite insensitive to kernel selection but not to bandwidth (Fotheringham et al., 2002, p. 211).

Kernels that are Gaussian or Gaussian-like are generally used (Fotheringham et al., 2002; Lloyd, 2010) because they provide a smooth transition with distance to the cut-off point, beyond which the influence of observations is negligible or zero. It is important that the function be continuous to avoid the extreme sensitivity the model would have in response to spatial variations if a step function were to be used (Fotheringham et al., 2002).

Two main strategies are adopted by GWR regarding the application of kernels. The simplest is to select a fixed bandwidth for all of the kernels generated for the model. The other is adaptive bandwidths, where the bandwidth is permitted to vary across the study area.

The fixed-bandwidth approach has the advantage of being simpler to implement but at the expense of some possible loss of information about relationships of interest occurring in the model in areas of high feature densities.

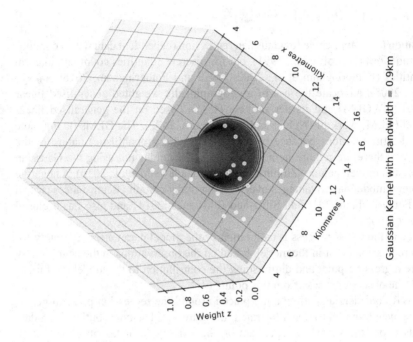

Gaussian Kernel with Bandwidth = 0.9km

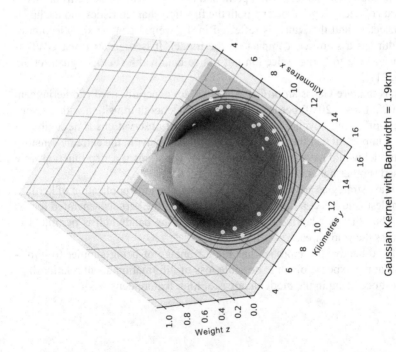

Gaussian Kernel with Bandwidth = 1.9km

Figure 4.1 Spatial kernels

Variable bandwidth modelling seeks to maintain the ability to examine in closer detail high-feature-density areas at the cost of more complexity in realisation. The selection of variable bandwidth kernels has been a long-established subject of study in kernel density estimation (Abramson, 1982; Giné and Sang, 2010), and similar techniques apply to GWR in this respect.

Both fixed- and variable-bandwidth selections are made by a process of optimisation using the model data. Suitable starting places may be estimated using rules of thumb based on density analysis of the study data (Silverman, 1986; Scott, 2012) before applying an iterative process in conjunction with a suitable measure such as cross validation (CV), or Akaike information criterion (Akaike, 1998; Akaike, 1974) (AIC, or AICc, which is adjusted to penalise high degrees of freedom). The process is: select a candidate bandwidth, calibrate the model using it and then assess the results using CV or AIC(c) and rejecting or accepting the selected bandwidth.

With CV, a bandwidth is selected, and each observation is removed in turn and regression done with just the remaining ones. A prediction is then obtained for the excluded observation, and the error between actual and prediction is recorded. This process is repeated for each observation in turn. The bandwidth resulting in the minimum cross-validation loss is the one selected (Lloyd, 2010; Fotheringham et al., 2002).

AICc (Fotheringham et al., 2002) considers the model fit and the degrees of freedom to produce a score that can be used to compare the resulting bandwidths via the models. The lower the value of the score the better, with a difference of 3 indicating significant difference (Fotheringham et al., 2002, p. 96; Akaike, 1974).

Having selected suitable bandwidths and kernel functions, the model can be calibrated for each observation in the data set. From this, statistics are obtained regarding the model's descriptive variables and its goodness of fit (Fotheringham et al., 2002, p. 213). The estimated parameter values and associated statistics may be mapped to visualise the relationships in the data. In a similar way to bandwidth selection, CV and AICc may be used to evaluate its suitability by comparison of losses in the dependent variable.

Although GWR is regarded as a significant tool for investigating local relationships and understanding spatial heterogeneity (Brunsdon et al., 1996; Fotheringham and Brunsdon, 2010; Cheng and Fotheringham, 2013), potential problems have been indicated. Wheeler and Tiefelsdorf, 2005; Páez et al. (2011), reported concerns regarding multicollinearity problems with GWR. These concerns were, however, addressed by (Fotheringham and Oshan, 2016), and (Páez et al., 2011; Wheeler, 2007) provides guidance on avoiding such problems.

The GWR technique has been investigated for application with spatial interaction flow modelling, as noted in (Fotheringham et al., 2002; Nakaya, 2002; Nissi and Sarra, 2011), with various limitations. Significantly, with the SWIM approach (Kordi and Fotheringham, 2016), the modelling emphasis has moved away from the origin and destination points and polygons and been directed at the flow vectors. The technique is described in more detail in the methods section.

3 Data and methods

3.1 Study area

Many social and environmental impacts associated with Chinese economic development are influenced by spatial interactions. Traffic growth is an area in which there is a significant influence in this respect. Jiangsu Province and the proximity of large conurbations such as Shanghai is one particular region that highlights these spatial interaction factors. These and the ready availability of data for this region were the major influences for considering a case study based on this region. The area of interest for the case study is shown below in Figure 4.2.

3.2 Data sets

The data for the case study consisted of three sets of data: toll station counts, station locations and county-based economic data. Place and county names were in Chinese (UTF-8), and so additional administrative spatial data were obtained from www.gadm.org for context and English labelling purposes.

As shown in Figure 4.2, the case study covers the Chinese eastern coastal province of Jiangsu. The flow data for the case study were traffic counts collected from the 334 expressway toll stations in 2014 within the study area. The count data are the aggregate values for that year. The entry and exit counts for the study were keyed with the associated toll station identifiers, forming a 334-square flow matrix of count values. The station identifiers and projected coordinate values were supplied as a table of 334 station identifiers and coordinate values. These data, in the format of spreadsheet files, were originally sourced from the Jiangsu Expressway Network Operation and Management Centre.

The county data were supplied in ESRI Shapefile format, with the county polygon boundaries and their associated economic measures as attributes. The socioeconomic data were originally derived from the Jiangsu Statistical Yearbook for the same period as the toll station data. All of the spatial data were projected values (Xian 1980 – EPSG:2385), and this projection was appropriate for the whole study region. All of the county centroids lay within the boundaries of their respective polygons and were therefore suitable candidates for aggregating the flow data to. An overview of the locations of the toll stations and centroids of the county polygons used for data aggregation purposes is shown in Figure 4.3. As a preliminary step, the spreadsheet toll station and traffic data required pre-conditioning to be suitable for analysis with SWIM. This was done with a combination of QGIS and Postgres/Postgis to convert the spreadsheets into a spatial layer with the station data aggregated and flow vectors re-assigned to the originating and destination county centroids (Figure 4.4). It can be seen that there was one county without any toll stations, and the econometric data for that county was also missing from the shapefile, and it was therefore excluded from the study. One data toll data point was outside of the study area and therefore not considered.

Whilst the files contained various candidate observations for consideration as propulsiveness and attractiveness factors, for the purposes of the case study,

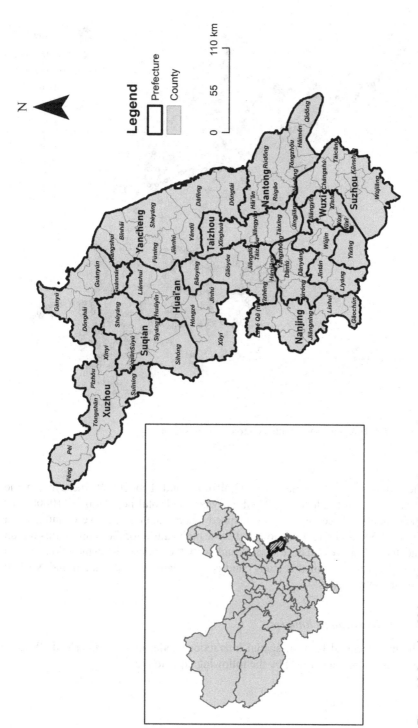

Figure 4.2 Location of the study area and its administrative units

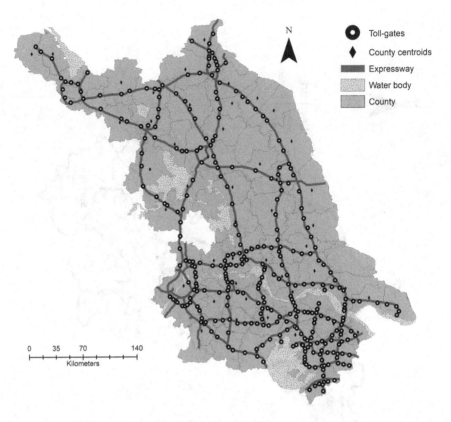

Figure 4.3 Toll gates and county centroids in study area

the two selected variables were GDP100m and Tpop10000, these being the gross domestic product × 100 million yuan, and total population × 100000 for each county. These values were mapped against their respective counties as in Figure 4.5 and Figure 4.6 below and show high values for the south of this region and the north west. These correspond with the Industrial conurbation around Shanghai (not part of this study) and capital Nanjing in the south and Xuzhou City in the northwest.

3.3 Methods and techniques

The most general form of spatial interaction model may be described (Wilson, 1967; Sen and Sööt, 1981) by the following equation (5):

$$T_{ij} = f\left(V_i W_i C_{ij}\right) \tag{5}$$

Aggregated flows overview map

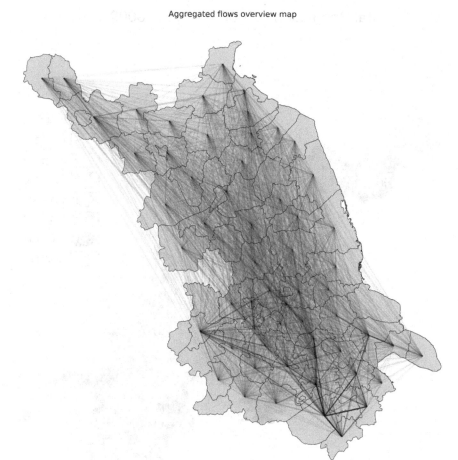

Figure 4.4 Relative flow volumes after aggregation to county centroids

where T_{ij} is the interaction between paired origins i and destination j, V_i is a vector describing the factors driving a flow from i to j (the 'propulsiveness' factors), W_{ij} is a vector of 'attractiveness' factors at the destination j, and C_{ij} is a vector describing the separation (typically distance or impedance) between origin and destination.

The recognition that the strength of interaction was dependent on the size of the propulsiveness and attractiveness factors but diminished by increase in distance (aligned with Tobler's First Law of Geography) led, by analogy, to models incorporating this concept, to be known as 'gravity' models.

Experiences with applying the gravity model to problems indicated that the simple linear dependency model didn't adequately describe the behaviour. Subsequently, developments of modelling coefficients in terms of powers, including

Total Population (x10000) - Tpop10000

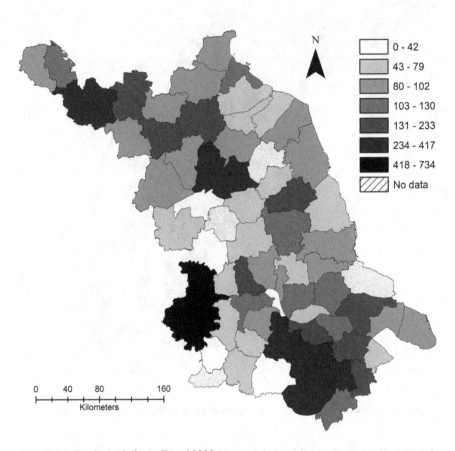

Figure 4.5 Total population – Tpop10000

Newtonian, inverse square distance relationships (Haynes et al., 1984; Roy and Thill, 2004; Sen and Smith, 1995; Ubøe, 2004), led to better tuning of the gravity model. To account for higher importance of factors such as transit mode on distance or cultural influences on propulsiveness or attractiveness, the more familiar power parameters form of the gravity model familiar today evolved:

$$T_{ij} = \kappa P_i^\alpha P_j^\gamma d_{ij}^\beta \tag{6}$$

where T_{ij} is as in (5) above, P_i, P_j are measures of quantities (generally population) at origin i and destination j, d_{ij} the distance between i and j; and κ, α, γ and β are

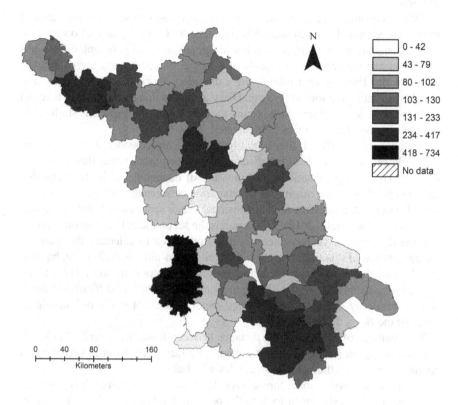

Total Population (x10000) - Tpop10000

Figure 4.6 County GDP – GDP100m

estimates from the model that reflect the contribution to the overall spatial flows made by each of the explanatory variables.

Worthy of note is that the gravity model for spatial interactions was not the only concept adopted from physics. Other researchers (Wilson, 2010) have considered an entropy model based on a Boltzmann statistical mechanics analogy. The entropy models, by nature, consider temporal aspects in addition to spatial, by the fact the origin and destination populations might change over time because of the flows, thus modifying the propulsiveness and attractiveness parameters. Considering the temporal characteristics is not always important to a particular problem, but in cases in which there is a longitudinal study being conducted, for example, this dimension cannot necessarily be disregarded (Huang et al., 2010).

The SWIM, a progression from GWR and on earlier work (Nakaya, 2002), are a new approach (Kordi and Fotheringham, 2016) to modelling spatial interaction, which apply techniques from GWR to examine interactions via locally sensitive analysis of spatial flows. Whereas GWR is driven by the local relationships around point and polygon features, SWIM additionally places emphasis on the relationships between the local flow vectors and the flow between the regions of interest.

SWIM falls into three main categories: origin-focused, destination-focused and flow-focused models (Kordi and Fotheringham, 2016). In the case of origin- and destination-focused models, the calibration points are real geographic locations and flows are weighted on the basis of a kernel placed around the calibration point. In the flow-focused model, the calibration entity is a flow vector, and weights are calibrated for the flows that have an interaction on the basis of a kernel in four-dimensional vector space around the calibration flow. For this study, only the flow-focussed method was implemented.

In flow-focused SWIM, the spatial interactions are considered only in terms of the flows. The measure of the distance is between them rather than related to destinations or origin locations. The measure of distance used in the weighting calculation becomes the magnitude of separation between the calibration flow and other flows in the model in a four-dimensional vector space (Kordi and Fotheringham, 2016; Macdonald, 2010). The kernel is the set on the calibration flow vector and the distances in vector space to other flows used to calculate the weights. Representation of this vector space is difficult in two-dimensional space, but It is this distance that is applied to the kernel weighting function, the kernel now being centred on a calibration flow rather than a point and therefore difficult to visualize, as the decay distance is defined in vector space, not the two-dimensional space of the flows themselves.

Two methods of calculating the distance between flows are described in Kordi and Fotheringham (2016): The four-dimensional Euclidean distance vector, and a spatial trajectory method and these are describe below.

The general gravity-model formula for the flow-focused approach is shown in equation (1) and is similar in form to the other methods despite the difference in distance concept:

$$T_{ij} = \kappa_{ij} v_i^{\alpha_{ij}} \omega_j^{\gamma_{ij}} d_{ij}^{\beta_{ij}} \tag{7}$$

where T_{ij} is the flow between locations i and j, v_i is the origin propulsiveness, ω_j is the destination attractiveness at j and d_{ij} the distance between flows i and j. As before κ, α, β and γ are the model parameters to be estimated by calibration around flow ij.

For a Gaussian model, the calibration in the WLS method is applicable as in equation (8):

$$b_{ij} = \left(X^T W_{ij} X \right)^{-1} X^T W_{ij} T_{ij} \tag{8}$$

A representation of the four-dimensional kernel using colour to represent the four-dimensional vector in Euclidean space, used in the distance calculations (Kordi and Fotheringham, 2016), is shown in Figure 4.7.

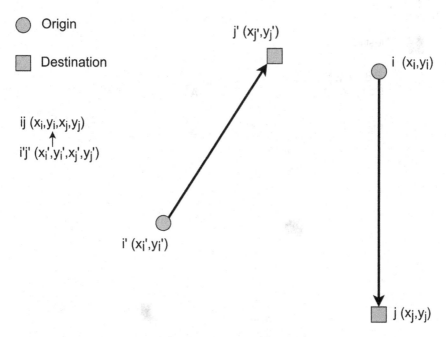

Figure 4.7 Flow-focused SWIM. 4-dimensional vector distance

Source: Kordi and Fotheringham, 2016

The magnitude of this vector between the two flows represents the distance in the kernel weighting calculation and is given by equation (9):

$$d_{(ij)(i',j')} = \sqrt{(x_i - x_i') + (y_i - y_i') + (x_j - x_j') + (y_j - y_j')} \qquad (9)$$

As mentioned, this can give rise to the situation in which the nearest vector may not be the one adjacent in two-dimensional space, as illustrated in Figure 4.8.

Considering flow 1, in two dimensions, flows 1 and 2 have closer proximity to each other than flows 1 and 3. However, in the four-dimension kernel space, flows 1 and 3 are closer (thus more heavily weighted) because the components of the four dimensional vector *AE* and *BF* are less than *AC* and *BD*.

A second distance measure proposed by Kordi and Fotheringham (2016) for SWIM is a directed graph approach described as the trajectory-based distance (Figure 4.9). In this case, the similarity between the two paths is considered in the determination. If the two trajectories are of the same order (same number of vertices or nodes), then one measure of distance may be obtained by considering the distance between the corresponding vertices in each path, as shown in Figure 4.9.

This distance may be Euclidean or some other measure of distance. The overall distance between the trajectories is then obtained by a sum-of-pairs distance

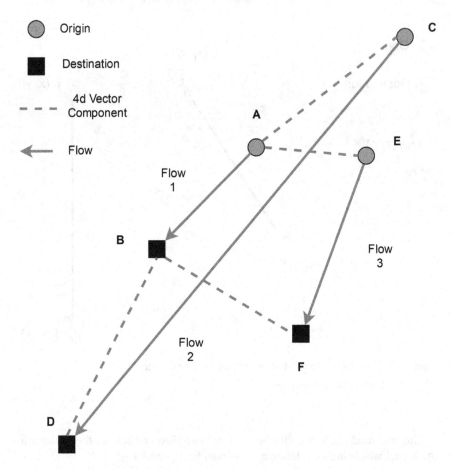

Figure 4.8 Illustration of closest flow in 2D space not the same in 4D space

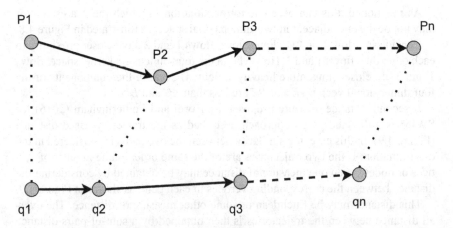

Figure 4.9 Spatial trajectory distance – two trajectories with equal number of nodes

Source: Kordi and Fotheringham, 2016

(*SOP*) (Zheng and Zhou, 2011; Agrawal et al., 1993). The distance may be calculated from equation (10).

$$SOP\,(ij,i'j') = d\,(i,i') + d\,(j,j')\tag{10}$$

where the function $d(q,\,q')$ may be the Euclidean distance between the vertices in the trajectory. Either the four-dimensional kernel or the trajectory distances may be used in SWIM in the same manner for determining the flow relationships, but the distances will be different.

To accommodate the exploratory nature of the program-development environment, finding ways of mitigating the calibration time was a factor in the research. In hand with this was the requirement to easily visualise the results of calibrating a SWIM model. The programming environment choices and model implementation were required to produce maps and graphs of results from the model.

Bounds were set to the development scope to be able to realise the software components and to work with the case study data. A Gaussian model that accepts a fixed bandwidth argument for calibration and avoids the complexity and computational load that the variable bandwidth kernel approach would make was opted for. The calibrated model would be able to produce the parameter estimates and descriptive statistics and to map and visualise the outputs.

The calibrated models provided parameter estimates for the intercept (k), distance (β), propulsiveness (α) and attractiveness (γ) for each calibration flow, as well as calculating the corresponding t-statistics for each of the explanatory variables. The value for adjusted coefficient of determination; r^2 (a measure of goodness of fit) for each flow was generated based on the formula(Fotheringham et al., 2002; Lloyd, 2010) in Equations (11) to (13):

$$r_i^2 = \frac{TSS_i - RSS_i}{TSS_i}\tag{11}$$

where r_i^2 is the coefficient of determination at flow i and:

$$TSS_i = \sum_{j=1}^{n} w_{ij}\left(y_j - \bar{y}\right)^2\tag{12}$$

$$RSS_i = \sum_{j=1}^{n} w_{ij}\left(y_j - \hat{y}_j\right)^2\tag{13}$$

where w_{ij} is the weighting for parameter j and flow i, y is the observed flow, $\bar{y}$ the mean value of flows and $\hat{y}_j$ the estimated value of parameter j for flow i.

The t-statistic will also be computed for each calibrated model in equation (14):

$$t_i = \frac{estimated\ param}{standard\ error\ of\ param}\tag{14}$$

As part of the calibration processing, the AICc value will be calculated as per (Fotheringham et al., 2002, p. 96).

The software will implement a four-dimension distance function described by equation (9) and weighting functions based on equations (15) to (17), which correspond to Gaussian, bi-squared and Gauchy kernel weighting, respectively.

$$w_{ij} = e^{-0.5\left(\frac{d_{ij}}{b}\right)^2} \tag{15}$$

$$w_{ij} = \left[1 - \left(\frac{d_{ij}}{b}\right)^2\right]^2 \; if \; d_{ij} < b = 0 \, otherwise \tag{16}$$

$$w_{ij} = \sqrt{1 + \left(\frac{d_{ij}}{b}\right)^2} \tag{17}$$

The decision was to use Python, as it offers wider possibilities of integration with desktop/open-source GIS and Web applications in the future, has good numerical library support through NumPy and SciPy, and opens the door to eventually parallel processing via PyOpenCL and PySpark. These final points are deemed important to provide scalability. As previously noted, the 'big data' phenomenon is exerting an influence on how analysis of spatial interactions is conducted.

The case study considered a Gaussian regression model as indicated in the previous section. The traffic flow data were in essence discrete counts, and as such, a Poisson (or negative binomial as the data were all positive integer values) regression model might be more appropriate going forward. In order to accommodate the data within the Gaussian model, a log transform was applied (ln(*count*)) to the data to obtain continuous values. Additionally, all observations were incremented by 1 to avoid the degenerate case in which some of the counts could be zero and the logarithm indeterminate. Doing this did not alter the distribution of the data, only provided a minor offset to the values.

The program developed was used to produce a calibrated set of models and to derive statistics for the case study from the model. The intention was to map parameter *t*-scores, r^2 and AICc values for each calibrated flow from the study data and evaluate the results. In addition to the maps, matrix heat maps were also generated for the parameters' values as per (Kordi and Fotheringham, 2016) to see what insights into relationships could be revealed via this visualisation technique.

4 Results

The strategy of SWIM modelling in this study was to implement a simple GWR program as verification of key concepts and then adapt the principles to suit the flow-focused model. A suitable worked example of GWR was found in (Lloyd, 2010, pp. 116–119) and adopted for this purpose.

Allowing for differences in numerical precision (also mentioned by Lloyd), the results were the same for the predictions and the r^2 value obtained and confirmed that the basic method and interpretation was correct. This code was subsequently modified to become test data for the SWIM model class by implementing a 'dummy' distance function that returned appropriate values from the example.

The initial bandwidth was set at the median (four-dimensional) distance value between flows with a view to optimising this via a golden section search as per the GWR method described by Fotheringham et al. (2002), AICc scores are generated when the model is calibrated to support this. However, whilst trying to generate the seeding triplet for this process, it was noted that the minimum AICc score was invariant over a wide range of bandwidths. Consequently, the results presented in this section are all based around the median value of 262 km as bandwidth.

Maps of the *t*-scores for the parameter estimates for each flow in the model are shown in Figure 4.10, Figure 4.11, Figure 4.12 and Figure 4.13. All of these exhibit variability with geographic location. The maps for Tpop10000 and GDP100m variables show better parameter estimates have been obtained for the northwest to southeast areas of the region and less good to the central eastern parts. When compared with the Tpop10000 and GDP100m maps in Figure 4.5 and Figure 4.6, these suggested that estimates were better for higher population and GDP100m values.

The *t*-statistics for the distance parameter show a distinction between the north and south of the region. When compared with the aggregated flows map in Figure 4.4, the better estimates reflect the larger flows of traffic in the south.

The matrix heat maps (Figures 4.17–4.19) are based on those in Kordi and Fotheringham (2016, pp. 1005–1010) and show the value of each parameter estimate for all calibrated flows (between each combination of pairs of centroids) in the study area. The location of counties is shown in Figure 4.2.

Figure 4.16 shows the parameter estimate for Tpop10000 propulsiveness factor α indicates that the population in Qidong is contributing relatively strongly to flows across the region, whereas, Lishui in the southwest is generally contributing much less.

Table 4.1 Global calibration results for study area

	Intercept (κ)	*Distance (β)*	*Tpop10000 (α)*	*GDP100m (γ)*
Co-efficient	6.74674649e+00	−1.01865392e-05	6.38067418e-07	6.60959196e-06
t-statistics	122.6386	−49.2827	31.21405	34.80945

Table 4.2 Summary parameter values for all models at bandwidth = 262 km

	Mean	*Max*	*Min*	*Std. Dev.*
Intercept (κ)	6.77166e+00	7.07724e+00	6.53242e+00	1.04096e-01
Distance (β)	−1.04405e-05	−8.94036e-06	−1.18556e-05	5.12579e-07
Tpop10000 (α)	6.33501e-07	6.83373e-07	5.72850e-07	1.87998e-08
GDP100m (γ)	6.56080e-06	6.90701e-06	6.28821e-06	1.23205e-07
z score – intercept	−5.36836e-16	2.93556e+00	−2.29822e+00	
z score – distance	−5.36836e-16	2.92658e+00	−2.76079e+00	
z score – alpha	−1.10225e-16	2.65283e+00	−3.22613e+00	
z score – gamma	−1.10225e-16	2.81005e+00	−2.21244e+00	

T- statistic values for each calibrated model - Tpop10000

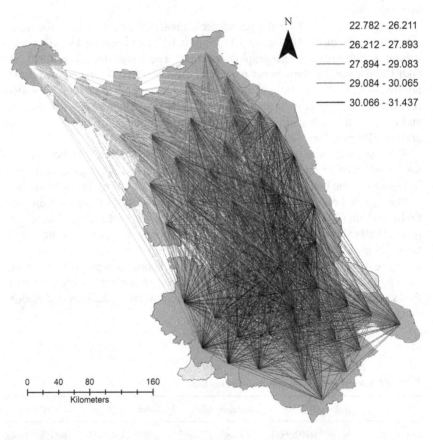

N

	22.782 - 26.211
	26.212 - 27.893
	27.894 - 29.083
	29.084 - 30.065
	30.066 - 31.437

0   40   80   160
Kilometers

Figure 4.10 T-statistics for Tpop1000 parameter α. Bandwidth = 262 km

T- statistic values for each calibrated model - GDP100m

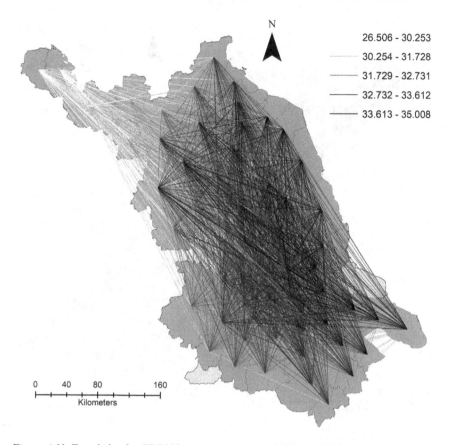

N

26.506 - 30.253
30.254 - 31.728
31.729 - 32.731
32.732 - 33.612
33.613 - 35.008

0   40   80   160
Kilometers

Figure 4.11 T-statistics for GDP100m parameter *γ*. Bandwidth = 262 km

The equivalent is shown for the GDP100m parameter estimates in Figure 4.17. Here Qidong shows high flows to it from most other regions and Lishui attracting lower flow from most other regions.

The distance values are shown in Figure 4.18 and suggest that distance is not as much of a deterrent to flows to or from Shuyang, Siyang and Suining counties from anywhere in the region.

A program to implement and evaluate the SWIM method was successfully developed and was able to produce calibrated models to evaluate the flow-focused SWIM method with a Gaussian kernel and a specified fixed bandwidth.

T- statistic values for each calibrated model - Distance

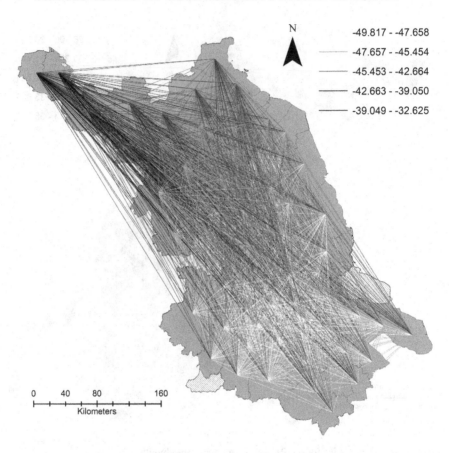

Figure 4.12 *T*-statistics for distance parameter β. Bandwidth = 262 km

The results (Figure 4.10 through Figure 4.15) obtained from the calibrated model proved to be aligned with expectations of spatial non-stationarity in the parameter values being observed and explainable with regards to the two independent variables selected from the sample data.

Similarly, the matrix heat maps (Figure 4.16 through Figure 4.18) of the parameters indicated explainable relationships in the data. These are an interesting schematic way of visualising the relationships between flows and their origin and destination points.

During the bandwidth calibration process, it was noted that the same minimum AICc value was returned for every evaluation of the bandwidth triplet. Starting

T- statistic values for each calibrated model - Intercept

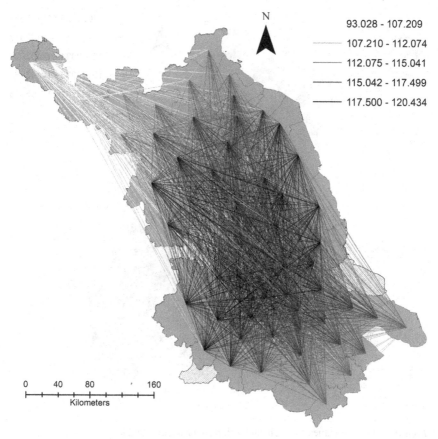

Figure 4.13 *T*-statistics for intercept κ. Bandwidth = 262 km

bandwidths ranging from 10 km to 500 km all resulted in a minimum AICc value of 12096124.

To investigate this, the search process was repeated, with subsets of the calibrated flow data being used in the bandwidth determination (primarily to reduce the calibration processing time), and it was found that the same condition was reached, but with differing values.

The search was again repeated with calibrations at 262 km (the median distance between flows), 10 km, 400 km and 500 km and each result set tested for the flow responsible for the minimum AICc score. In each case the flow was found to be at position 360 in the data. This was mapped as shown in Figure 4.19 against the flow values used in the calibration for all flows. This flow appears to be distant

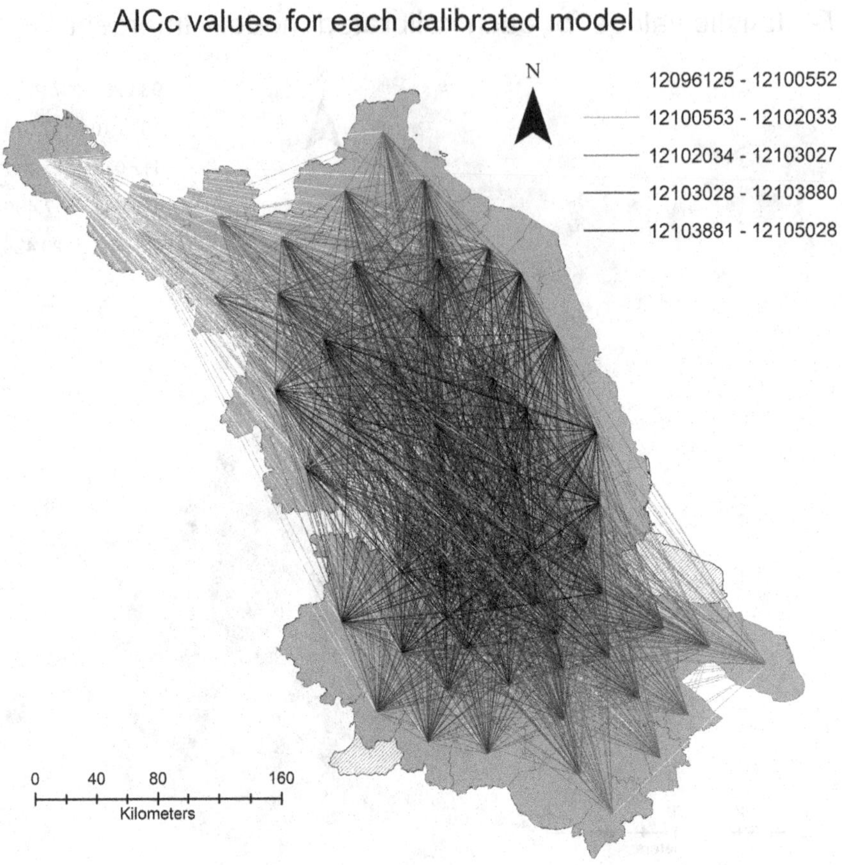

AICc values for each calibrated model

Figure 4.14 AICc values for each calibration. Bandwidth = 262 km

from the others, and those nearby have quite low values, and this is presumed to be the reason why it resulted in a good (low) AICc score. This would appear to be an issue for both CV and especially the AICc bandwidth selection methods with fixed bandwidth selections.

A possible improvement to the situation might be with the use of adaptive kernel selection to ensure that an equal number of observed flows are factored into the bandwidth calculation and avoiding any bias to isolated flows.

5 Conclusions and discussion

The SWIM model developed for this chapter was successfully calibrated using the test case data, and the maps produced did indicate signs of non-stationarity in the flows.

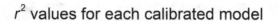

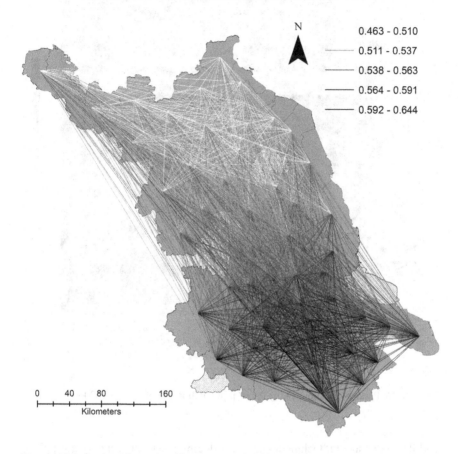

Figure 4.15 r^2 values for each calibration. Bandwidth = 262 km

As could be expected with such a recent study, the literature review mostly revealed GWR material than any directly related to SWIM, with the exception of the (Nakaya, 2002; Nissi and Sarra, 2011) papers. That said, the worked GWR example from (Lloyd, 2010) was extremely helpful in gaining insight into how the process actually works.

As mentioned, further exploration of SWIM, particularly the different models such as Poisson and negative-binomial, would be worthy of further study, in preference to investigating the origin and destination methods of SWIM.

Adaptive kernel bandwidth selection should also be a candidate, particularly in light of the experience with bandwidth optimisation covered here. It would be

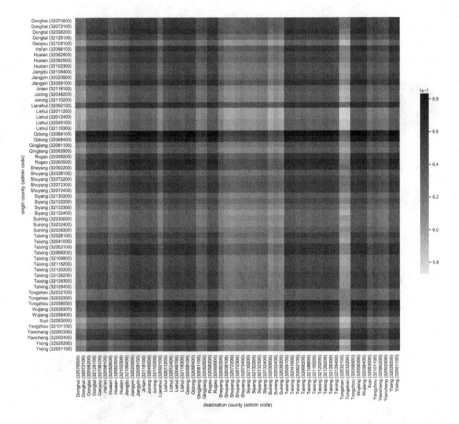

Figure 4.16 Parameter estimates (α) for total population. Bandwidth = 262 km

useful to understand if techniques such as ridge-regression might have an application in finding the minima in bandwidth optimisation.

However, the implementation of a parallel computation approach to this topic
has to be key to its success and wider application. There was a lot of background
information required to commence the programming part of this project; had
this not been the case, a parallel implementation would have been interesting to
pursue.

The potential of SWIM with any substantially sized problems will require a
different approach to its execution based on the evidence from this research. The
aggregated flows were associated with 59 sites, resulting in 3481 interactions to
calculate weights for and to perform the regression on.

It is clear that one of the objectives going forward will be to investigate options
for parallel processing. This process for the Gaussian model has repeated patterns
of calculation that could operate independently and be suitable for solving either
by a distributed (including cloud), map-reduce approach, such as with Apache

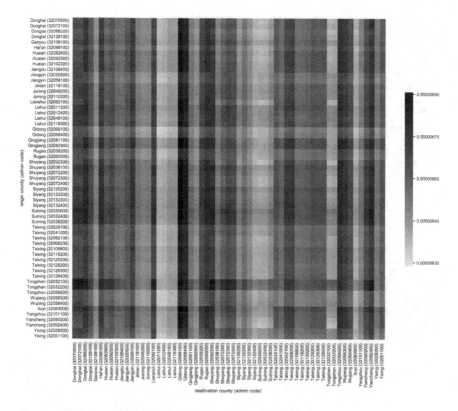

Figure 4.17 Parameter estimates (γ) for GDP100m. Bandwidth = 262 km

Spark (You et al., 2015; Rompf, n.d.; Zaharia et al., 2016), or a GPGPU approach (Zhang, 2010; Zhang et al., 2014).

As mentioned, automated collection of flow data in large volumes is now possible from technological and social changes (Hudson-Smith, 2014; Roth et al., 2011). Analysis of these types of interactions is also going to require parallel and distributed computation.

The SWIM framework in its current form only addresses the spatial dimension of interactions. Many of the new types of data sources vary substantially over short periods of time (for example, commuting flows), and even the more familiar spatio-temporal patterns such as the property market have been assessed in the past based on GWR (Huang et al., 2010). It would seem that SWIM might be investigated to see if it has a role in examining spatio-temporal aspects too.

This research only addressed the flow-focused, Gaussian model. Whilst this was a good starting place, the Poisson or negative binomial regression models are probably appropriate for the counts data, as in the example in the SWIM

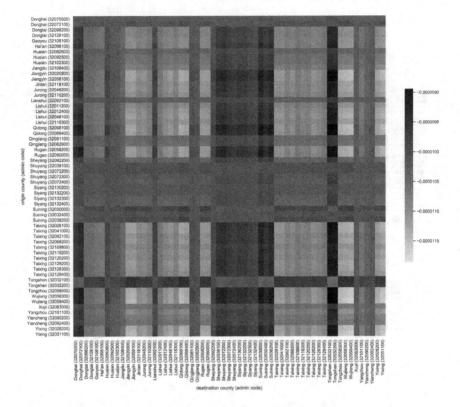

Figure 4.18 Parameter estimates (β) for distance. Bandwidth = 262 km

paper (Kordi and Fotheringham, 2016, p. 1007). As it is, taking logarithms of the flow values was sufficient for the case study. These alternative regression models should be investigated in due course, and implementing a generalised linear model should be considered.

The optimisation of bandwidth, as noted in the results, was problematic and would appear to have been data related to the outlying flow. As further work, it would be interesting to determine if it would still be an issue if an adaptive kernel approach was used and reduced the significance that flow number 360 had. It would also be interesting to verify that the observations made for GWR regarding adaptive kernels also hold true for SWIM (Guo et al., 2008), for example.

Another approach to consider for investigation for resolving this condition would be to calculate the starting triplet at three diverse scales and eliminate any flows from the search that have the same (lowest) AICc value across all bandwidths before continuing the golden section search process.

The visualisation of the flows is a challenge with regard to the display of the high number of flow interactions to show, resulting in a very crowded map, and

Possible Explanation of same best fit AICc across multiple bandwidths - ln(flow values)

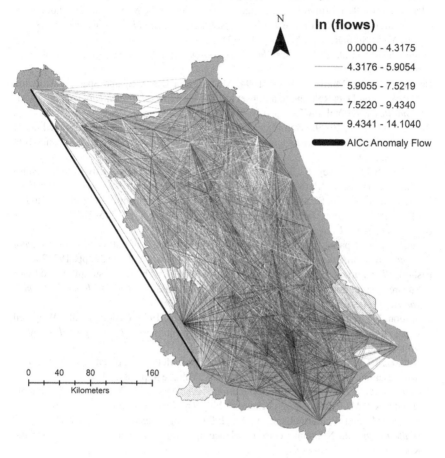

Figure 4.19 Map of flow resulting in lowest AICc value at every bandwidth

the four-dimensional kernel distances between flows are not necessarily easy to represent in map form. The matrix heat maps may be something that has potential for visualising parameter-flow relationships.

Bibliography

Abramson, I. S., 1982. On Bandwidth Variation in Kernel Estimates-A Square Root Law. *The Annals of Statistics*, Volume 10, pp. 1217–1223.

Advanced Micro Devices, 2015. *AMD Accelerated Parallel Processing OpenCL Programming Guide*, s.l.: Advanced Micro Devices.

Agrawal, R., Faloutsos, C. and Swami, A., 1993. Efficient Similarity Search in Sequence Databases. *Foundations of Data Organization and Algorithms*, pp. 69–84.

Akaike, H., 1974. A New Look at the Statistical Model Identification. *IEEE Transactions on Automatic Control*, Volume 19, pp. 716–723.

Akaike, H., 1998. Information Theory and an Extension of the Maximum Likelihood Principle. In: E. Parzen, K. Tanabe and G. Kitagawa, eds. *Selected Papers of Hirotugu Akaike.* New York: Springer New York, pp. 199–213.

Armbrust, M., et al., 2015. *Spark SQL: Relational Data Processing in Spark.* s.l.: s.n., pp. 1383–1394.

Bailey, T. C. and Munford, A. G., 1994. Modelling a Large, Sparse Spatial Interaction Matrix Using Data Relating to a Subset of Possible Flows. *European Journal of Operational Research*, Volume 79, pp. 489–500.

Balcan, D., et al., 2009. Multiscale Mobility Networks and the Spatial Spreading of Infectious Diseases. *Proceedings of the National Academy of Sciences*, Volume 106, pp. 21484–21489.

Balemans, S., Van Hoey, S., Nopens, I. and Seuntjes, P., 2015. Interactive Model Evaluation Tool Based on IPython Notebook. *Geophysical Research Abstracts*, Volume 17.

Batty, M. and Mackie, S., 1972. The Calibration of Gravity, Entropy, and Related Models of Spatial Interaction. *Environment and Planning*, Volume 4, pp. 205–233.

Beazley, D., 2010. *Understanding the Python Gil.* s.l.: s.n.

Besag, J., 1974. Spatial Interaction and the Statistical Analysis of Lattice Systems. *Journal of the Royal Statistical Society. Series B (Methodological)*, Volume 36, pp. 192–236.

Bishoff, W., Cremers, H. and Fieger, W., 1991. Normal Distribution Assumption and Least Squares Estimation Function in the Model of Polynomial Regression. *Journal of Multivariate Analysis*, Volume 36, pp. 1–17.

Brunsdon, C., Fotheringham, A. S. and Charleton, M. E., 1996. Geographically Weighted Regression: A Method for Exploring Spatial Nonstationarity. *Geographical Analysis*, Volume 28, pp. 281–298.

Casetti, E., 1972. Generating Models by the Expansion Method: Applications to Geographical Research. *Geographical Analysis*, January, Volume 4, pp. 81–91.

Chang, W., et al., 2015. *Shiny: Web Application Framework for R, 2015.* [Online] Available at: http://CRAN.R-project.org/package = shiny.Rpackageversion0.11.

Charlton, M. and Fotheringham, A. S., 2009. *Geographically Weighted Regression White Paper.* s.l.: National Centre for Geocomputation, National University of Ireland Maynooth.

Cheng, J. and Bertolini, L., 2013. Measuring Urban Job Accessibility With Distance Decay, Competition and Diversity. *Journal of Transport Geography*, Volume 30, pp. 100–109.

Cheng, J. and Fotheringham, A. S., 2013. Multi-scale Issues in Cross-border Comparative Analysis. *Geoforum*, Volume 46, pp. 138–148.

Cheng, J., Gould, N., Han, L. and Jin, C., 2016. Big Data for Urban Studies: Opportunities and Challenges: A Comparative Perspective. In: *IEEE XPLORE.* Toulouse, France, 18/7/2016. pp. 1229–1234. [Online] Available at: http://ieeexplore.ieee.org/document/7816985/.

Cheng, J., Young, C., Zhang, X. and Owusu, K., 2014. Comparing Inter-migration Within the European Union and China: An Initial Exploration. *Migration Studies*, Volume 2, Issue 3, pp. 340–368.

Cheng, T., Haworth, J. and Manley, E., 2012. Advances in Geocomputation (1996–2011). *Computers, Environment and Urban Systems*, Volume 36, Issue 6, pp. 481–487.

Cho, S., Lambert, D. and Chen, Z., 2010. Geographically Weighted Regression Bandwidth Selection and Spatial Autocorrelation: An Empirical Example Using Chinese Agriculture Data. *Applied Economics Letters*, Volume 17, pp. 767–772.

Dalcin, L., et al., 2010. Cython: The Best of Both Worlds. *Computing in Science & Engineering*, Volume 13, pp. 31–39.

Dale, P., 2014. *Mathematical Techniques in GIS*. 2nd ed. s.l.: CTC Press.

da Silva, R. A. and Rodrigues, T. C. V., 2014. Geographically Weighted Negative Binomial Regression – Incorporating Overdispersion. *Statistics and Computing*, September, Volume 24, pp. 769–783.

Foster, S. and Gorr, W., 1986. An Adaptive Filter for Estimating Spatially-Varying Parameters: Application to Modeling Police Hours Spent in Response to Calls for Service. *Management Science*, July, Volume 32, pp. 878–889.

Fotheringham, A. S., 1983. A New Set of Spatial-interaction Models: The Theory of Competing Destinations. *Environment & Planning A*, Volume 15, pp. 15–36.

Fotheringham, A. S., 1997. Trends in Quantitative Methods I: Stressing the Local. *Progress in Human Geography*, Volume 21, pp. 88–96.

Fotheringham, A. S., 1998. Trends in Quantitative Methods II: Stressing the Computational. *Progress in Human Geography*, June, Volume 22, pp. 283–292.

Fotheringham, A. S. and Brunsdon, C., 1997. Measuring Spatial Variations in Relationships with Geographically Weighted Regression. In: M. Fischer and A. Getis, eds. *Recent Developments in Spatial Analysis: Spatial Statistics, Behavioural Modelling and Computational Intelligence*. Berlin: Springer-Verlag, pp. 60–82.

Fotheringham, A. S. and Brunsdon, C., 1999. Local Forms of Spatial Analysis. *Geographical Analysis, October*, Volume 31, pp. 340–358.

Fotheringham, A. S. and Brunsdon, C., 2010. Local Forms of Spatial Analysis. *Geographical Analysis*, Volume 31, Issue 4, pp. 340–358.

Fotheringham, A. S., Brunsdon, C. and Charlton, M., 2002. *Geographically Weighted Regression*. s.l.: John Wiley & Sons Ltd.

Fotheringham, A. S. and Oshan, T., 2016. Geographically Weighted Regression and Multicollinearity: Dispelling the Myth. *Journal of Geographical Systems*, Volume 18, Issue 4, pp. 303–329.

Fotheringham, A. S. and Pitts, T. C., 1995. Directional Variation in Distance Decay. *Environment and Planning A*, May, Volume 27, pp. 715–729.

Gong, Z., Tang, W., Bennet, D. A. and Thill, J., 2013. Parallel Agent-based Simulation of Individual-level Spatial Interactions Within a Multicore Computing Environment. *International Journal of Geographical Information Science*, Volume 26, Issue 6, pp. 1152–1170.

Guo, L., Ma, Z. and Zhang, L., 2008. Comparison of Bandwidth Selection in Application of Geographically Weighted Regression: A Case Study. *Canadian Journal of Forest Research*, Volume 38, Issue 9, pp. 2526–2534.

Hadayeghi, A., Shalaby, A. and Persaud, B., 2010. Development of Planning Level Transportation Safety Tools Using Geographically Weighted Poisson Regression. *Accident Analysis and Prevention*, Volume 42, pp. 676–688.

Harris, B. and Wilson, A. G., 1978. Equilibrium Values and Dynamics of Attractiveness Terms in Production-constrained Spatial-Interaction Models. *Environment and Planning A*, Volume 10, pp. 371–388.

Hasan, S., Schneider, C. M., Ukkusuri, S. V. and González, M. C., 2013. Spatiotemporal Patterns of Urban Human Mobility. *Journal of Statistical Physics*, Volume 151, pp. 304–318.

Haseman, R., Wasson, J. and Bullock, D., 2010. Real-Time Measurement of Travel Time Delay in Work Zones and Evaluation Metrics Using Bluetooth Probe Tracking. *Transportation Research Record*, Volume 2169, pp. 40–53.

Haynes, K. E., Fotheringham, A. S. and others, 1984. *Gravity and Spatial Interaction Models*. Beverly Hills, CA: Sage.

Huang, B., Wu, B. and Barry, M., 2010. Geographically and Temporally Weighted Regression for Modeling Spatio-temporal Variation in House Prices. *International Journal of Geographical Information Science*, March, Volume 24, pp. 383–401.

Hudson-Smith, A., 2014. Tracking, Tagging and Scanning the City. *Architectural Design*, Volume 84, pp. 40–47.

Jin, C., Cheng, J. and Xu, J. 2017. Using User-Generated Content to Explore the Temporal Heterogeneity in Tourist Mobility. *Journal of Travel Research*. https://doi.org/10.1177/00 47287517714906.

The Khronos Group, 2015. *OpenCL – The Open Standard for Parallel Programming of Heterogeneous Systems*. [Online] Available at: www.khronos.org/opencl/resources/viennacl-linear-algebra-and-iterative-solvers-using-opencl [Accessed October, 2016].

Klöcknera, A., et al., 2012. PyCUDA and PyOpenCL: A Scripting-based Approach to GPU Run-time Code Generation. *Parallel Computing*, Volume 38, Issue 3, pp. 157–174.

Kordi, M. and Fotheringham, A. S., 2016. Spatially Weighted Interaction Models (SWIM). *Annals of the American Association of Geographers*, Volume 106, Issue 5, pp. 990–1012.

Li, X., Huang, B., Li, R. and Zhang, Y., 2016. Exploring the Impact of High Speed Railways on the Spatial Redistribution of Economic Activities – Yangtze River Delta Urban Agglomeration as a Case Study. *Journal of Transport Geography*, Volume 57, pp. 194–206.

Li, Z., Cheng, J., and Wu, Q. 2016. Analyzing Regional Economic Development Patterns in a Fast Developing Province of China Through Geographically Weighted Principal Component Analysis. *Letters in Spatial and Resource Sciences*, Volume 9, Issue 3, pp. 233–245.

Li, Z., et al., 2013. Using Geographically Weighted Poisson Regression for County-level Crash Modeling in California. *Safety Science*, October, Volume 58, pp. 89–97.

Lloyd, C. D., 2010. *Spatial Data Analysis*. s.l.: Oxford University Press.

Lloyd, C. D., 2011. *Local Models for Spatial Analysis*. 2nd ed. s.l.: CRC Press.

Lu, B., Harris, P., Charlton, M. and Brunsdon, C., 2015. Calibrating a Geographically Weighted Regression Model With Parameter-Specific Distance Metrics. *Procedia Environmental Sciences*, Volume 26, pp. 109–114.

Macdonald, A., 2010. *Linear and Geometric Algebra*. s.l.: Alan MacDonald.

Matthews, S. and Yang, T., 2012. Mapping the Results of Local Statistics: Using Geographically Weighted Regression. *Demographic Research*, Volume 26, pp. 151–166.

McKinney, W., 2012. *Python for Data Analysis: Data Wrangling with Pandas, NumPy, and IPython*. s.l.: OŔeilly Media, Inc.

Mittal, S. and Vetter, J. S., 2015. A Survey of CPU-GPU Heterogeneous Computing Techniques. *ACM Computing Surveys*, Volume 47, Issue 4.

Nakaya, T., 2002. Local Spatial Interaction Modelling Based on the Geographically Weighted Regression Approach. *GeoJournal*, Volume 53, pp. 347–358.

Nakaya, T., Fotheringham, A. S., Brunsdon, C. and Charlton, M., 2005. Geographically Weighted Poisson Regression for Disease Association Mapping. *Statistics in Medicine*, September, Volume 24, pp. 2695–2717.

Nelder, J. A. and Wedderburn, R. W. M., 1972. Generalized Linear Models. *Journal of the Royal Statistical Society. Series A (General)*, Volume 135, pp. 370–384.

Nissi, E. and Sarra, A., 2011. Detecting Local Variations in Spatial Interaction Models by Means of Geographically Weighted Regression. *Journal of Applied Sciences*, Volume 11, Issue 4, pp. 630–638.

Oshan, T., 2016a. A Primer for Working With the Spatial Interaction Modeling (SpInt) Module in the Python Spatial Analysis Library (PySAL). *REGION*, Volume 3, Issue 2, pp. R11–R23.

Oshan, T., 2016b. *GitHub – Pysal/Pysal/Contrib/Spint/*. [Online] Available at: https://github.com/pysal/pysal/tree/master/pysal/contrib/spint [Accessed 17 December 2016].

Oshan, T. and Fotheringham, A. S., 2014. *SciPy 2014 – pySI: A Python Framework for Spatial Interaction Modelling*. [Online] Available at: https://conference.scipy.org/scipy2014/schedule/presentation/1716/ [Accessed December 2016].

Páez, A., Farber, S. and Wheeler, D., 2011. A Simulation-based Study of Geographically Weighted Regression as a Method for Investigating Spatially Varying Relationships. *Environment and Planning A*, Volume 43, Issue 12, pp. 2992–3010.

Pedregosa, F., et al., 2011. Scikit-learn: Machine Learning in Python. *Journal of Machine Learning Research*, Volume 12, pp. 2825–2830.

Peng, D., et al., 2012. From CUDA to OpenCL: Towards a Performance-portable Solution. *Parallel Computing*, Volume 38, pp. 391–407.

Pérez, F. and Granger, B. E., 2007. IPython: A System for Interactive Scientific Computing. *Computing in Science & Engineering*, Volume 9.

Qi, J., Wang, Z., Wang, Y. and Li, D., 2015. Visualization and Analysis on the Spatial-temporal Patterns of Flow Direction of Interprovincial Migration in China Based on Origin–destination Matrix. *Procedia Environmental Sciences*, Volume 26, pp. 115–118.

Rey, S. J. and Anselin, L., 2009. PySAL: A Python Library of Spatial Analytical Methods. In: *Handbook of Applied Spatial Analysis*. s.l.: Springer, pp. 175–193.

Rompf, R. Y. T. T., n.d. *On Supporting Compilation in Spatial Query Engines* (Vision Paper).

Roth, C., Kang, S. M., Batty, M. and Barthélemy, M., 2011. Structure of Urban Movements: Polycentric Activity and Entangled Hierarchical Flows. *PLoS ONE*, Volume 6, p. e15923.

Roy, J. R. and Thill, J. C., 2004. Spatial Interaction Modelling. *Regional Science*, Volume 83, pp. 39–361.

Rupp, K., 2012. High-Level Manipulation of OpenCL-Based Subvectors and Submatrices. *Procedia Computer Science*, Volume 9, pp. 1857–1866.

Rupp, K., Rudolf, F. and Weinbub, J., 2010. ViennaCL-a High Level Linear Algebra Library for GPUs and Multi-core CPUs. *International Workshop on GPUs and Scientific Applications*, pp. p 51–56.

Scott, D. W., 2012. Multivariate Density Estimation and Visualization. In: J. E. Gentle, W. K. Härdle and Y. Mori, eds. *Handbook of Computational Statistics: Concepts and Methods*. Berlin and Heidelberg: Springer, pp. 549–569.

Sen, A. and Smith, T., 1995. *Gravity Models of Spatial Interaction Behaviour*. s.l.: Springer-Verlag.

Sen, A. and Sööt, S., 1981. Selected Procedures for Calibrating the Generalized Gravity Model. *Papers in Regional Science*, Volume 48, pp. 165–176.

Silverman, B., 1986. *Density Estimation for Statistics and Data Analysis*. Monographs on Statistics and Applied Probability.

Singleton, A. D., Spielman, S. and Brunsdon, C., 2016. Establishing a Framework for Open Geographic Information Science. *International Journal of Geographical Information Science*, February, pp. 1–15.

Smith, L. S. and Liang, Q., 2013. Towards a Generalised GPU/CPU Shallow-flow Modelling Tool. *Computers and Fluids*, Volume 88, pp. 334–343.

Song, C., Qu, Z., Blumm, N. and Barabási, A.-L., 2010. Limits of Predictability in Human Mobility. *Science*, Volume 327, pp. 1018–1021.

Thissen, D., Steinberg, L. and Kuang, D., 2002. Quick and Easy Implementation of the Benjamini-Hochberg Procedure for Controlling the False Positive Rate in Multiple Comparisons. *Journal of Educational and Behavioural Statistics*, Volume 27, Issue 1, pp. 77–83.

Trigg, D. W. and Leach, A. G., 1967. Exponential Smoothing With an Adaptive Response Rate. *OR*, March, Volume 18, pp. 53–59.

Ubøe, J., 2004. Aggregation of Gravity Models for Journeys to Work. *Environment and Planning A*, April, Volume 36, pp. 715–729.

Unwin, A. and Unwin, D., 1998. Exploratory Spatial Data Analysis With Local Statistics. *Journal of the Royal Statistical Society Series D-The Statistician*, Volume 47, pp. 415–421.

Van Der Walt, S., Colbert, S. C. and Varoquaux, G., 2011. The NumPy Array: A Structure for Efficient Numerical Computation. *Computing in Science & Engineering*, February, Volume 13, Issue 2, pp. 22–30.

Vobruba, T., Körner, A. and Breitenecker, F., 2016. Modelling, Analysis and Simulation of a Spatial Interaction Model. *IFAC-PapersOnLine*, Volume 49, Issue 29, pp. 221–225.

Wheeler, D., 2007. Diagnostic Tools and a Remedial Method for Collinearity in Geographically Weighted Regression. *Environment and Planning A*, Volume 39, Issue 10, pp. 2464–2481.

Wheeler, D. and Tiefelsdorf, M., 2005. Multicollinearity and Correlation Among Local Regression Coefficients in Geographically Weighted Regression. *Journal of Geographical Systems*, Volume 7, Issue 2, pp. 161–187.

Williams, R., 2015. *Heteroskedacity*. [Online] Available at: www3.nd.edu/~rwilliam/stats2/l25.pdf [Accessed 2017].

Wilson, A. G., 1967. A Statistical Theory of Spatial Distribution Models. *Transportation Research*, Volume 1, Issue 3.

Wilson, A. G., 1971. A Family of Spatial Interaction Models, and Associated Developments. *Environment and Planning A*, Volume 3, Issue 1, pp. 1–32.

Wilson, A. G., 2010. Entropy in Urban and Regional Modelling: Retrospect and Prospect. *Geographical Analysis*, October, Volume 42, pp. 364–394.

Wong, P., et al., 2006. Generating Graphs for Visual Analytics Through Interactive Sketching. *Visualization and Computer Graphics*, Volume 12, pp. 1386–1398.

You, S., Zhang, J. and Gruenwald, L., 2015. *Large-scale Spatial Join Query Processing in Cloud*. s.l.: s.n., pp. 34–41.

Zaharia, M., et al., 2016. Apache Spark: A Unified Engine for Big Data Processing. *Commun. ACM*, October, Volume 59, pp. 56–65.

Zhang, J., 2010. *Towards Personal High-performance Geospatial Computing (HPC-G): Perspectives and a Case Study*. Proceedings of the ACM SIGSPATIAL International Workshop on High Performance and Distributed Geographic Information Systems, pp. 3–10.

Zhang, J., You, S. and Gruenwald, L., 2014. Large-Scale Spatial Data Processing on GPUs and GPU-Accelerated Clusters. *ACM SIGSPATIAL*, Volume 6, Issue 3, pp. 27–34.

Zhao, L., et al., 2016. Geographical Information System Parallelization for Spatial Big Data Processing: A Review. *Cluster Computing, March*, Volume 19, pp. 139–152.

Zheng, Y. and Zhou, X., 2011. *Computing with Spatial Trajectories*. s.l.: s.n.

Zhibin, L., Wang, W., Bigham, J. and Ragland, D., 2013. Using Geographically Weighted Poisson Regression for County-level Crash Modeling in California. *Safety Science*, Volume 58, pp. 89–97.

Zhong, C., et al., 2016. Variability in Regularity: Mining Temporal Mobility Patterns in London, Singapore and Beijing Using Smart-card Data. *PLoS ONE*, Volume 11, p. e0149222.

5 Profiling rapid urban transformation through urban mobility data in Shenzhen

Chen Zhong, Zhaoliang Luan, Yao Shen, Xiaoming Li, and Wei Tu

Urban mobility data has been widely used in urban studies in recent years, taking advantage of its fine granularity of location information and wide coverage of population groups. This book chapter explores mobility data applications in Shenzhen – a city in a strategic location that forms part of the Pearl River Delta megalopolis and in the immediate north of Hong Kong. Shenzhen has attracted enormous resources from the government and private investors and consequently has undergone a rapid urban development in recent decades. In response to that, we present a particular application which demonstrates the potential of using big human mobility data as a tool for monitoring urban changes. A set of indices is proposed including cumulative population, temporal distribution, distance to a centre, and intra-inter travel, which allows us to detect functional and structural urban changes. We argue that data-informed methods have great value for urban planning and management in practice. To fully exploit the value, a systematic framework needs to be developed to integrate and analyse multi-source new and conventional urban data to reduce uncertainties and enhance information.

1 Introduction

The type of urban mobility data discussed in this chapter refers to location data automatically generated along people's travel in cities. The most popular data sources are mobile phone data, social media data and smart card data, all of which are available in Shenzhen. Human mobility data records people's daily mobility with finer spatial-temporal granularity at the individual level, promising a better understanding of mobility patterns such as travel behavior at individual level (Liu, Hou et al. 2009), choice of activity locations (Zonghao, Dongyuan et al. 2013; Zhi, Li et al. 2016) and collective effects that reshape function and structure of urban space (Zhong, Arisona et al. 2014; Tu, Cao et al. 2017). The derived information can be used in various urban applications, ranging from improving transit service, informing urban planning and transport planning to supporting public policy making.

Giving mobility data is a goldmine. Researchers from different domains have been attracted and develop methodologies dealing with their respective array of problems, including engineering, planning, social science etc. Our research has a particular interest in urban studies; in particular, we endeavour to comprehend our understanding of citizens' response to fast urban transformation. To that end, the first contribution of this work is to propose a method that detects functional urban changes from smart card data. The work considers Shenzhen as a typical example of cities in rapid urban development. As shown in Figure 5.1, the emerging towers are clear evidence, and the massive construction work is still going on around the city. More information on urban context is given in Section 3. Section 4 details our analysis and reflections on the urban process. Section 5 concludes with an emphasis on limitations caused by data uncertainties. As we realised, even though enormous research progress has been achieved, the reliability of extracted information needs to be verified. Moreover, for practices in urban planning and management, more comprehensive information is required to understand impacts. Therefore,

(a)

(b)

Figure 5.1 Photos of the skyline in Nanshan District, Shenzhen, China, in 2014 (a) and in 2017 (b)

our second contribution is a summary of existing work on urban mobility data applications in Chinese cities (in Section 2) and sharing ideas on research agenda (Section 5).

2 Related work: mobility data for China urban studies

The development of information infrastructure and the advance of sensor technology have generated an enormous amount of data in recent years. Meanwhile, the rise of smart city programs in China has pushed forward the research and applications making use of the generated big urban data. Particularly in the past decade, the amount of related work on China urban studies in this trends has increased significantly.

As mentioned, mobility data refers to the kind of automatically collected human trajectory data that comes in large volume, updates frequently and most importantly with fine granularity. Floating car data could be considered as the first kind that emerged with the popularity of GPS navigation system. Taxi data as one category of floating car data that is available in many cities, such as Beijing (Yuan, Zheng et al. 2012), Shanghai (Liu, Wang et al. 2012), Wuhan (Yue, Wang et al. 2012) etc. Relevant urban applications are mainly about spatial interactions and dynamic urban functions coupling with other data sets. Mobile phone data becomes popular when portable phones and the wireless network become largely affordable. It is as powerful as taxi data for understanding urban space (Yuan, Raubal et al. 2012; Tu, Cao et al. 2017). Moreover, mobile phone data can better identify individuals' difference and has social information embedded. For instance, spatial impacts and social ties have been studied (Shi, Wu et al. 2016). Social media data has become overwhelming in recent years as "self-media" becomes a new phenomenon. Check-in data has been then used to characterise urban space coupling with other datasets (Shen and Karimi 2016; Zhi, Li et al. 2016; Tu, Cao et al. 2017). Smart card data used in this work becomes available only when megacities begin to build extensive subway networks. Most of the published case studies are about Beijing (Long and Thill 2015; Zhong, Batty et al. 2016) and Shenzhen (Liu, Hou et al. 2009; Gong, Lin et al. 2017). Recently, smart card studies have been initiated in Wuhan since its first metro line opened. As mentioned, these cities share the same features: undergoing massive urban infrastructure development. The extracted information help in monitoring the use of public transportation at different stages of urban development (Zhong, Arisona et al. 2014) and under various environment conditions (Zhou, Wang et al. 2017). These available data sets allow us to compare Chinese cities with other world cities, thus to find universal laws and regularity (Ahas, Aasa et al. 2015; Zhong, Batty et al. 2016). Moreover, with the experience learned from case studies, we shall be able to approximate short-term and long-term impacts of urban development.

Our research project takes Shenzhen as an example of cities undergoing a rapid urban transformation. There is a good foundation for this research regarding data availability and scientific achievements. For instance, mobile phone positioning data has been used for approximating residential locations (Ning, Ning et al. 2014). In Zonghao, Dongyuan et al. (2013), mobile billing data has been used to plot an employment distribution map. Coupling with social media data, the integrated data sets have been used for exploring the distribution and dynamics of functional regions (Tu, Cao et al. 2017). As a way of validating detected patterns, Fang, Yang et al. (2017) have developed a model to investigate the stability of convergence and divergence patterns of daily travels. Shenzhen is among the first cities putting smart card data into research usage. The value of smart card data for understanding travel behaviours has been explored in (Liu, Hou et al. 2009) and further verified by variability analysis of intra-city trips in (Gong, Liu et al. 2012). In (Zhou, Wang et al. 2017), weather conditions have been incorporated to understand variations in travel behaviours. Advanced methods such as spatial segmentation (Zhang, Zhao et al. 2016) and clustering-based anomaly detection (Zhao, Qu et al. 2017) were proposed, allowing us to continue improving the quality of data.

3 Shenzhen as an example of rapid urban transformation

Shenzhen's advance of data availability and research innovation resulted from various reasons, rooted in its economic development and policy which promoted the development of innovative industries. We give a brief introduction to the city in this section, with a focus on its rapid urban transformation and extreme dynamics of floating population.

Shenzhen is China's first Special Economic Zone (SEZ). Four decades ago in 1980, Shenzhen was a tiny rural town next to Hong Kong in Bao'an county. In 1985, rural migrants were allowed to register as temporary residents in urban areas. Since then, the city has grown at an astonishing rate (Wu and Webster 2010). Migration undoubtedly played a vital role in the urbanisation process (Wang, Wang et al. 2009). Like many other growing cities in China, rural-to-urban migration is the main factor contributed to the urbanisation process (Zhang and Shunfeng 2003).

Current population density in Shenzhen is about 3,597 per square km, the highest on the Chinese mainland. Among the total population by the year, 2016 is about 11.38 million, among which only 3.55 million are with residence registration, and about 69% of residence belong to the floating population. The floating population are officially addressed as non-registered population, who stay in the city for less than half a year (Shenzhen Statistics Bureau 2016).

A topic closely related to the population growth is 'urban village' (cheng zhong cun), which has quite often been criticised in China studies and significantly contributes to the making of megacities in China, including Shenzhen (Bach 2010). These urban villages develop rapidly and provide low-cost living space for increasing numbers of residents. These urban villages have gone through distinct phases of the urban process, namely, expansion, densification and intensification following the strategic urban planning in Shenzhen (Hao, Geertman et al. 2013), and are still undergoing urban regeneration. Our following analysis will show that the ongoing urban process can be detected from flows of people. We also argue that using frequently updated automatic data can overcome the challenge of monitoring urban population changes caused by high dynamics of floating population and consequently can contribute to a better allocation of public resources in urban development.

4 Profiling fast urban changes from intra-city travels

4.1 Preliminary data processing

In this experimental work, smart card data collected in September 2014 and June 2016 are the main data sets used to profile the dynamic distribution of populations in Shenzhen. Smart card data comes as individual trip records like that introduced in previous studies such as (Liu, Hou et al. 2009). We further processed the data to get in-coming flow defined as $Inflow(i,t)$ and out-going flow defined as $Outflow(i,t)$ at each individual station i in time unit t and origin–destination flow matrix F_{ij} and distance matrix D_{ij}. Other data sources such as annual report of census statistics in Shenzhen (Shenzhen Statistics Bureau 2016) are from open websites and are referred as supplementary data to interpret the analysed results.

4.2 Methods: indices for detecting urban changes

In one of our earlier studies on smart card data analysis (Zhong, Manley et al. 2015), measures have been proposed to quantify the variability of urban flows at different aggregated levels. This research further developed the sort of variability measures incorporating a temporal dimension and applied them to longitude data to profile urban changes. We start from a comparison at the aggregated level looking at overall changes and move into detailed comparisons at more disaggregated levels of individual stations and interactions between stations. Only significant changes are discussed, which are detected as **outliers** adapting the concepts in statistical analysis. Detailed indices are described as follows:

Cumulative population Cum_flow(s,t) of an average weekday is calculated at station level using 1 hour as time interval. Different from in $Inflow(i,t)$ and $Outflow(i,t)$ that profiles how busy one area is, Cumulative population profiles where people stay for regular activities.

$$Cum\_flow(s,t) = Cum\_flow(s,t-1) + Inflow(s,t) - Outflow(s,t) \qquad (1)$$

Therefore, the spatial distribution of the cumulative population is plotted for a visual comparison of overall changes. It is calculated using kernel density estimation of the cumulated counts at stations, assuming people travelling to one station are heading to destinations within a transit catchment area (surrounding areas of 500 meters to a station). Quantile interval is used for colour symbolization. Therefore, we are comparing the distribution and spatial heterogeneity using relative values rather than absolute values. The generated contour map gives a good proxy of the spatial structure of urban regions.

Scaled temporal distribution of trips is plotted using $Z(i,t) = Z\_Sore(Inflow(i,t))$ at each station i. Temporal distribution of flows has a strong relation to land uses in transit catchment areas and is used to detect changes of urban functions. The relations of temporal distribution of flows and urban function can be discussed in many of the reviewed related work. Considering the fast population growth in Shenzhen, we use scaled temporal distribution. Difference between scaled temporal distributions is calculated as

$$flow_{diff(i)} = 1 - Corr\left(Z_{2016}(i) - Z_{2014}(i)\right) \qquad (2)$$

Distribution of travel distance of trips is calculated based on $(Outflow(i,t))$ over time distance $D_{time_{ij}}$. It tells the impact area of a station reflected from where people are from. We aim to propose simple measures which can be adapted to even real-time urban monitoring. Therefore, time-costly algorithms like gamma distribution fitting is opted out; instead, we give a density distribution of flows versus distance from a station. Similar to the comparison of temporal distribution, the differences of 2 years are computed using a correlation measure.

Intra-trips and inter-trips is a combination of multiple network measures. Weighted degree measures how busy is the station; community detection tells the groups of stations with strong interactions with each other. Detailed mathematics foundation and interpretations can be found in (Newman 2003; Barthélemy 2011; Zhong, Arisona et al. 2014).

4.3 Analysis and results

Overview changes: Comparing the overall travels in 2014 and in 2016, there is an increase of 146,695 metro trips per average weekday (exact numbers are shown in Table 5.1). The increased trips were not evenly distributed across space in the temporal dimension, as that reflected in 2 – overall distribution of cumulative populations (calculated using equation (1)) at different periods of a weekday. As it shows, Luohu and Futian districts have the biggest commercial centres and

Table 5.1 Overview of smart card data collected in 2014 and 2016

Categories	2014	2016
Number of Metro trips[1]	1487487	1634181
Number of total stations	118	118
Avg. flow[2] **of people**	25211	27689
Max flow of people	32507	35469
Avg. travel distance (in seconds)	1785	1804
Morning peak hour	8 AM–9 AM	8 AM–9 AM
Evening peak hour	18 PM–20 PM	18 PM–20 PM

[1] Valid recorded on avg. weekday
[2] Summed number of outgoing trips and incoming trips per station on an average weekday

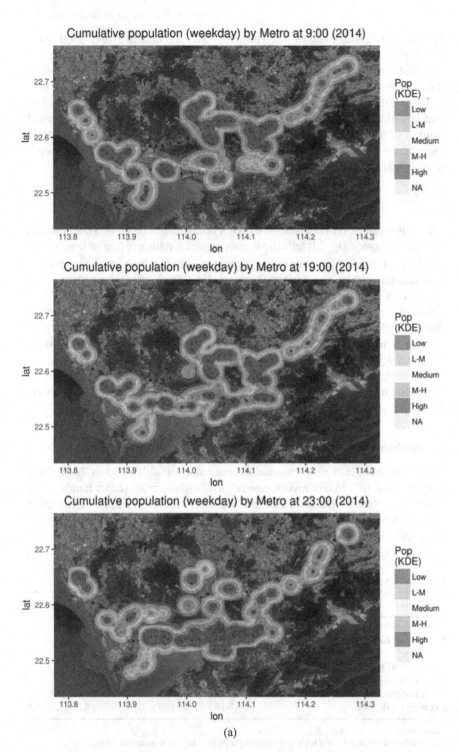

Figure 5.2 Temporal patterns of the cumulative population by Metro in 2014 and 2016
Note: Circles denote areas with comparatively significant changes.

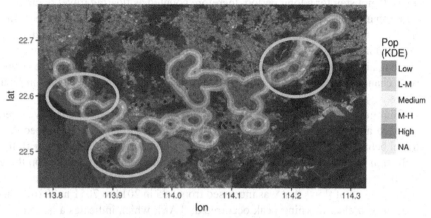

Cumulative population (weekday) by Metro at 9:00 (2016)

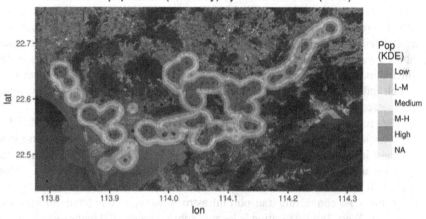

Cumulative population (weekday) by Metro at 19:00 (2016)

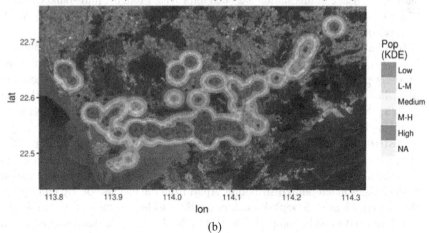

Cumulative population (weekday) by Metro at 23:00 (2016)

(b)

Figure 5.2 (Continued)

are the busiest areas in Shenzhen. However, most of the people travel to these areas do not stay for a long period, therefore counted as floating travel population rather than cumulative population. However, in the evening, there is a clear shift from northern area Longgang and Longhua to the South. There are clear changes revealed in a two-year period, especially, in the areas of Baoan Central, Nanshan-Houhai, and Longgang-Henggang, marked in circles. These three areas are in line with changes detected using other indices and will be further discussed in later sections.

Changes of dominating urban functions in transit service areas have been changed along with recent infrastructure development and reflected by people's travel behaviours. We identify these changes by comparing **scaled temporal distribution** (calculated using equation (2)) as that shown in Figure 5.3 – top three stations with significant changes. Changes in Shenkang station are obvious even in the volume of flows that was increased from 385 in 2014 to 7051 in 2016. Consequently, a clear morning peak occurred at 8 AM, which indicates a large number of residential buildings have been developed in the transit service areas and consequently new residents moved into this area. The major development in this area is a public housing project launched by the government, started in 2009 and completed in 2014 (Shenzhen Government 2014). More than 2700 public rental houses were put on the market in October 2014. The evening peak and smaller fluctuations in 2014 were eliminated by significant large volume in the morning, which indicates that the non-residential functions in these areas are only small businesses that might not be able to support the living of residents.

The second-ranked station is Liyumen station, which is located in Nanshan district, circled in Figure 5.3. Similar to Shenkang station, Liyumen has a significant increase in volume from 2080 per day in 2014 to 13735 in 2016. Liyumen station was underused at its early stage because the roads connecting to this station were still under construction. Therefore the interchange at this station was not convenient. As connecting transport infrastructures were completed, for instance, Shenzhen West Railway Station is located approximately 200 meters south of this station; the usage of this station has been improved. From the third-ranked station and onward, there is no emerging or eliminating of any peaks, and only small changes occur along the fluctuations.

In addition to the volume and temporal distribution of flows, we observed changes of peak hours. Great variability occurs at peak hour, in particular the morning peak (shown in Figure 5.4). Though Table 5.1 tells that peak hours in Shenzhen remain the same, there is a trend that the morning peak hour is shifting from 8 AM to 9 AM at certain stations, indicating the type of industry sectors is changing in some areas. Moreover, the professionals in Shenzhen are changing.

Distribution of travel distance reflects people's choice of locations. Figure 5.5 shows the top three stations with significant changes in the distribution of travel distance to a station. Liyumen station was mentioned as the second-ranked station with changes in temporal distribution. Apart from the increase of trip numbers to this station, Figure 5.5 (top) shows that the share of long-distance trips to this station increased as well, comparing to that in 2014. The same trend was observed

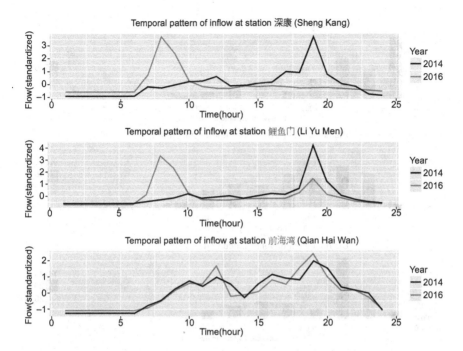

Figure 5.3 Top 3 stations with most significant changes in inflow patterns

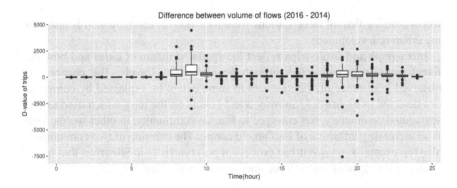

Figure 5.4 Changes of trip numbers comparing data of 2014 and 2016

Note: X-axis – timeline. Y-axis – absolute number of differences between the temporal distribution of trips.

at Pingzhou station, which indicates increasing the attractiveness of surrounding areas, resulting from diverse urban functions and better accessibility. Lingzhi station shows the opposite – that short-distance trips increased and the three peaks (16 minutes, 35 minutes, and 50 minutes) also become even more outstanding. It

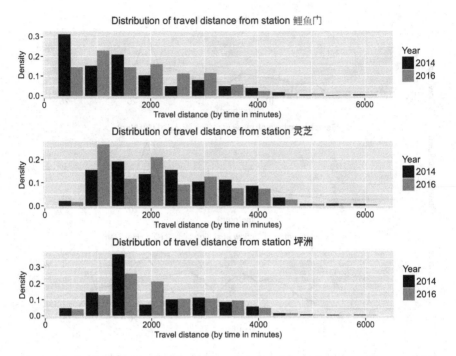

Figure 5.5 Top 3 stations with most significant changes in travel distance

worth noticing that all three stations were near Bao'an centre, which is undergoing urban redevelopment.

Intra-trips and inter-trips reflect the spatial structure of cities and how different areas were connected through people's daily travels. The changes we observed in distance distribution can to some extent be explained by communities detected in Figure 5.7. Subway line 5 (circle on the top), which used to be a segregated community, has emerged to Bao'an community. In other words, there is an increasing influence of Bao'an old centre. The merging of two communities also represents the unique urban process of polycentricity in Shenzhen that spatial structure is shaped along with the transformation of urban villages.

4.4 Discussion: redevelopment and unique decentralisation in Shenzhen

The analysed results show that Shenzhen is still undergoing rapid urban development, as changes were detected in local functions and overall structure even in a two-year interval. In Hao, Geertman et al. (2013), the authors have identified three overlapping stages in Shenzhen's urban process, namely, expansion, densification and intensification. Our results gave more indications on regeneration, which is overlapped with the process of intensification. Rather than identifying urban process from building topology, this work looked into flows of people. Intensification is revealed by the increasing residential population and public transport users. Regeneration process was detected from travel patterns, resulting from changed urban functions in transit service areas like the area nearby Shenkang station. The result also unveils urban issues. For instance, as regarding housing problems, new residential apartments are built; however, whether there is enough supporting facility needs further investigation. Regarding spatial structure, Shenzhen has a unique decentralisation process, unlike the other planned cities or self-organised cities. Shenzhen's polycentricity is shaped along with the process of transforming and merging urban villages, to which the transport infrastructure made great contributions by increasing the connectivity between spatially segmented periphery areas. The changes detected in travel distance to stations in Bao'an district and merging communities both well represent Shenzhen's unique pathway towards polycentricity.

5 Conclusion and outlook

This chapter discussed the use of automatically collected human mobility data for urban studies. A case study of Shenzhen was presented, which profiled urban changes using smart card data of the year 2014 and 2016. We started from an overall profile of temporal changes over days and then zoomed into changes in areas and at individual stations. The analysis presented does not need costly computing power; therefore, it can be applied in any other case studies, even for real-time monitoring of urban changes. The indices we proposed in this chapter reflect urban functional and structural changes but are not exclusive ones. They can be calculated using aggregated data. Therefore, privacy can be well protected. Though the value of mobility data in the various urban applications is the motivation of this chapter, we would like to further discuss the limitations leading to directions of our future work.

Limitations of the presented work are rooted in the uncertainties of the data. Firstly, there are variabilities in detected mobility patterns, which have been addressed in one of our previous studies (Zhong, Batty et al. 2016). Not all trips recorded in smart card data are regular ones that represent routine activities of travellers. The random trips add noises to the data and thus increase difficulties in analysis. To tackle this issue, methods for extracting regular trips and measures for evaluating variabilities have been proposed as that in Manley, Zhong et al. (2016) but need further improvements. Second, coverage of full transport modes cannot be achieved by analysis using smartcard only. In Shenzhen, less than 30% of the overall population is using rail-based public transport. Though significant efforts have been put into building and promoting public transport infrastructure, the use of private cars and taxis is still increasing. To what extent this single transport mode can represent overall changes in Shenzhen needs further investigation. For instance, dynamic distribution of population as that shown in Figure 5.3 is estimated using limited sample points which are the metro stations, which is more like to be the population of metro travel groups. It is fair to use the estimated population to identify changes but not enough to represent an overall population at the single time point. To validate, enhance and scale up the results, our future research will work on the fusion of different mobility datasets, such as mobile phone data and social media data. Finally, coverage of overall socio-economic population is a long-standing issue that lies in all type of mobility data. In most cases, social demographic information is not complete nor comprehend in data records. Though registration of user information is collected in many cities, to protect privacy, the detailed information is not likely to be released. To address this issue, inferring methods to model proxy information from surveyed data could be a solution. From the perspective of research methodology, the approach represents a way to combine conventional survey and interview-based analysis methods and big data–based computational methods. It is highly important, as the qualitative study can supplement missing information such as people's perception of place, cultural identity and the impact of policy, which helps understand the trigger of detected changes. Such research methodology will be framed in our ongoing project on data-informed evaluation methods for urban plans, which partially supported research work in this chapter.

Acknowledgement

This work was supported by the Tsinghua University Open Fund for Urban Transformation Research: [Grant Numbers No. K-17014–01], the Open Fund of Key Laboratory of Urban Land Resources Monitoring and Simulation, Ministry of Land and Resources [Grant Numbers No. 2016–02–010]; and Faculty Research Fund at Kings College London. Last but not least, we are grateful to three anonymous reviewers for their in-depth comments that improve the quality of the manuscript significantly.

References

Ahas, R., Aasa, A., Yuan, Y., Raubal, M., Smoreda, Z., Liu, Y., Ziemlicki, C., Tiru, M. and Zook, M. (2015). "Everyday space–time geographies: using mobile phone-based sensor data to monitor urban activity in Harbin, Paris, and Tallinn." *International Journal of Geographical Information Science* **29**(11): 2017–2039.

Bach, J. (2010). "'They come in peasants and leave citizens': urban villages and the making of Shenzhen, China." *Cultural Anthropology* **25**(3): 421–458.

Barthélemy, M. (2011). "Spatial networks." *Physics Reports* **499**(1): 1–101.

Fang, Z., Yang, X., Xu, Y., Shaw, S.-L. and Yin, L. (2017). "Spatiotemporal model for assessing the stability of urban human convergence and divergence patterns." *International Journal of Geographical Information Science* **31**(11): 2119–2141.

Gong, Y., Lin, Y. and Duan, Z. (2017). "Exploring the spatiotemporal structure of dynamic urban space using metro smart card records." *Computers, Environment and Urban Systems* **64**: 169–183.

Gong, Y., Liu, Y., Lin, Y., Yang, J., Duan, Z. and Li, G. (2012). *Exploring spatiotemporal characteristics of intra-urban trips using metro smartcard records*. 20th International Conference on Geoinformatics (GEOINFORMATICS), IEEE, Hong Kong, China.

Hao, P., Geertman, S., Hooimeijer, P. and Sliuzas, R. (2013). "Spatial analyses of the urban village development process in Shenzhen, China." *International Journal of Urban and Regional Research* **37**(6): 2177–2197.

Liu, L., Hou, A., Biderman, A., Ratti, C. and Chen, J. (2009). *Understanding individual and collective mobility patterns from smart card records: a case study in Shenzhen*. IEEE.

Liu, Y., Wang, F., Xiao, Y. and Gao, S. (2012). "Urban land uses and traffic 'source-sink areas': evidence from GPS-enabled taxi data in Shanghai." *Landscape and Urban Planning* **106**(1): 73–87.

Long, Y. and Thill, J.-C. (2015). "Combining smart card data and household travel survey to analyze jobs – housing relationships in Beijing." *Computers, Environment and Urban Systems* **53**: 19–35.

Manley, E., Zhong, C. and Batty, M. (2016). "Spatiotemporal variation in travel regularity through transit user profiling." *Transportation*: 1–30.

Newman, M. E. (2003). "The structure and function of complex networks." *SIAM review* **45**(2): 167–256.

Ning, X., Ning, Y. and Jinxing, H. (2014). "Detecting residential locations for large samples of mobile phone data [in Chinese]." *Wuhan University information technology* **39**(6): 750–756.

Shen, Y. and Karimi, K. (2016). "Urban function connectivity: characterisation of functional urban streets with social media check-in data." *Cities* **55**: 9–21.

Shenzhen Government. (2014). *Affordable housing in Shenzhen* [in Chinese]. Accessed in November 2017, from www.sz.gov.cn/jzgws/szsjzgws/new/gcjs/200903/t20090311_835240. htm.

Shenzhen Statistics Bureau (2016). *Shenzhen statistical yearbook*, China Statistics Press **26**: 53–56.

Shi, L., Wu, L., Chi, G. and Liu, Y. (2016). "Geographical impacts on social networks from perspectives of space and place: an empirical study using mobile phone data." *Journal of Geographical Systems* **18**(4): 359–376.

Tu, W., Cao, J., Yue, Y., Shaw, S.-L., Zhou, M., Wang, Z., Chang, X., Xu, Y. and Li, Q. (2017). "Coupling mobile phone and social media data: a new approach to understanding urban functions and diurnal patterns." *International Journal of Geographical Information Science*: 1–28.

Wang, Y. P., Wang, Y. and Wu, J. (2009). "Urbanization and informal development in China: urban villages in Shenzhen." *International Journal of Urban and Regional Research* **33**(4): 957–973.

Wu, F. and Webster, C. (2010). *Marginalization in urban China: comparative perspectives*, Springer.

Yuan, J., Zheng, Y. and Xie, X. (2012). *Discovering regions of different functions in a city using human mobility and POIs*, ACM.

Yuan, Y., Raubal, M. and Liu, Y. (2012). "Correlating mobile phone usage and travel behavior – a case study of Harbin, China." *Computers, Environment and Urban Systems* **36**(2): 118–130.

Yue, Y., Wang, H.-d., Hu, B., Li, Q.-q., Li, Y.-g. and Yeh, A. G. O. (2012). "Exploratory calibration of a spatial interaction model using taxi GPS trajectories." *Computers, Environment and Urban Systems* **36**(2): 140–153.

Zhang, F., Zhao, J., Tian, C., Xu, C., Liu, X. and Rao, L. (2016). "Spatiotemporal segmentation of metro trips using smart card data." *IEEE Transactions on Vehicular Technology* **65**(3): 1137–1149.

Zhang, K. H. and Shunfeng, S. (2003). "Rural–urban migration and urbanization in China: Evidence from time-series and cross-section analyses." *China Economic Review* **14**(4): 386–400.

Zhao, J., Qu, Q., Zhang, F., Xu, C. and Liu, S. (2017). "Spatio-temporal analysis of passenger travel patterns in massive smart card data." *IEEE Transactions on Intelligent Transportation Systems*.

Zhi, Y., Li, H., Wang, D., Deng, M., Wang, S., Gao, J., Duan, Z. and Liu, Y. (2016). "Latent spatio-temporal activity structures: a new approach to inferring intra-urban functional regions via social media check-in data." *Geo-spatial Information Science* **19**(2): 94–105.

Zhong, C., Arisona, S. M., Huang, X., Batty, M. and Schmitt, G. (2014). "Detecting the dynamics of urban structure through spatial network analysis." *International Journal of Geographical Information Science* **28**(11): 2178–2199.

Zhong, C., Batty, M., Manley, E., Wang, J., Wang, Z., Chen, F. and Schmitt, G. (2016). "Variability in regularity: Mining temporal mobility patterns in London, Singapore and Beijing using smart-card data." *PLoS One* **11**(2): e0149222.

Zhong, C., Manley, E., Arisona, S. M., Batty, M. and Schmitt, G. (2015). "Measuring variability of mobility patterns from multiday smart-card data." *Journal of Computational Science* **9**: 125–130.

Zhou, M., Wang, D., Li, Q., Yue, Y., Tu, W. and Cao, R. (2017). "Impacts of weather on public transport ridership: results from mining data from different sources." *Transportation Research Part C: Emerging Technologies* **75**: 17–29.

Zonghao, R., Dongyuan, Y. and Zhengyu, D. (2013). "Resident mobility analysis based on mobile-phone billing data." *Procedia – Social and Behavioral Sciences* **96**(Supplement C): 2032–2041.

Part III

6 Modeling land development

Heterogeneity in space, time and context

Guanpeng Dong

In order to capture the heterogeneity in relationships or associations between variables as to dimensions of space, time and attribute, an extended geographically weighted regression (GWR) model that captures the closeness between units in the spatiotemporal and contextual dimensions has been developed. The extended GWR model is called GTAWR. In the proposed methodology, the attribute dimension is defined and measured by characteristics of the context in which each spatial unit is located. The GTAWR model embeds a series of simpler versions of GWR models. The standard GWR (Fotheringham et al. 2002) is a special case of GTAWR assuming away any heterogeneity in the temporal and attribute dimensions, whilst the geographically and temporally weighted regression (GTWR; Huang et al. 2010) model does not take into account the heterogeneity in contextual characteristics. I demonstrate the methodology by exploring the residential land market in Beijing, China, from 2003 to 2009. The results show that there is significant improvement of GTAWR in terms of model fit. More specifically, GTAWR explains 73.2% of the variation in land prices and yields a 55.1% improvement of model fit over an OLS model, a 51.9% improvement over GWR and a 28.7% improvement over GTWR, respectively. This signifies the importance of considering the heterogeneity in housing prices in space, time and contextual attributes simultaneously.

1 Introduction

As an exploratory spatial statistics tool, geographically weighted regression (GWR) has been widely employed to investigate spatial relationships or associations between a response variable and a set of independents variables (Fotheringham et al. 2002). GWR has been applied in a variety of disciplines and studies, aided by the increased availability of geo-referenced data at finer scales, and by an appreciation that global regression models can mask substantively important departures from average trends at local levels. Applications include real estate studies (Fik et al. 2003; Kestens et al. 2006; Bitter et al. 2007; Yu 2007), land use dynamics (Geniaux et al. 2011), environment (Harris et al. 2010), health (Comber et al. 2011; Yang and Matthews 2012) and crime studies (Leitner and Helbich 2011).

At its heart, GWR accounts for spatial heterogeneity in relationships between variables by fitting a series of locally weighted regression models, with spatial weights defined in the pure space dimension. On one hand, it exploits the spatial correlations or dependencies among geographically close observations in the model-fitting process, as indicated by the first law of geography (Tobler 1970). On the other hand, it takes into account the similarities or dissimilarities among spatial entities (geographical proximity) when forming the spatial weights matrix, which plays a key part in model estimation. With the development of smart locating devices and their wide applications in a range of science and social science disciplines, data with fine spatiotemporal granularity are increasingly collected and complied. As such, data with spatiotemporal structures become common in the spatial analysis literature.

With temporal information available from the data, a better measurement of closeness or similarity among observations can be built by combining (dis)similarities of observations in both space and time. Two observations that are close in both space and time dimensions are likely to be more correlated than those that are close in space but distant in time, or close in time but distant in space. This is the idea underlying the geographically and temporally weighted regression (GTWR) modelling approach in Huang et al. (2010). Building upon this idea, they form a spatiotemporal weights matrix that is used in implementing local regression models. Doing this also captures the heterogeneity of data in dimensions of space and time at the same time.

The chapter extends the idea to data with a more complex structure: multiple-scale, spatial and temporal. Many geographical data sets have a multiple-scale structure or a hierarchical structure – for example, houses nested into districts into regions in an urban housing market. Using the language of the multilevel modelling literature (Hox 2002; Goldstein 2003), the finer spatial scale at which outcomes of interest are measured is termed the lower level, and the higher levels are the more aggregate spatial scales such as regions. The assumption of multilevel modelling is that there is both difference between objects at the higher level and some level of group dependence within those objects. In other words, differences between regions and correlations within regions are expected: the outcomes of lower level units in the same region tend to be correlated because they are impacted by the same effects. This is usually described as vertical group dependence. Dong and Harris (2015) further define a horizontal dependence effect – the correlations or dependencies among units at the same spatial scale because of geographical proximity effects. Harris et al. (2013) devised a contextualised GWR (CGWR) for such multiple-scale spatial data, again by defining a spatial weights matrix based on both spatial proximity and contextual similarity, that is presented by a multivariate distance metric of contextual attributes. This model captures potential heterogeneity of data in both space and context.

The proposal in this study is a generalisation of the two important extensions of GWR models: GTWR for spatiotemporal data and CGWR for multiple-scale spatial data. A weights matrix that takes into account the closeness in dimensions

of space, time and context (or attributes) simultaneously is employed to estimate local models, thereby proposing a GTAWR model. The logic of this idea
is intuitive. Given the multiple-scale, spatial and temporal structure, data can be
conceptualised in a three-dimensional space: space, time and context. Taking the
example of hedonic land price models, space simply refers to the geocoordinates
of each house or land parcel, while time is the date and time of the market transaction of a property. Context refers to the contextual environment or attributes
of the place where the property is located, for instance, attributes of the neighbourhood or district. Based on this conceptualisation, the closeness between two
observations is preferably defined by using information from each of the three
axes. The measure of contextual similarity is based on observable contextual
attributes, which will be detailed in what follows. The benefits are at least in two
aspects. First, exploiting similarities simultaneously in the three dimensions will
benefit the measurement of closeness between observations and the construction
of a better weights matrix for model estimation. In fact, as will be shown, our
proposal model significantly outperforms both GWR and GTWR. Second, estimation of the model can reveal the relative importance of the three dimensions,
which is useful for prediction.

The chapter is organized as follows. A brief recap of the standard GWR model
will be provided before detailing our extension of GWR to model data with a
complex multiple-scale, spatial and temporal structure. We then describe the land
price data in Beijing and variables used in our models. Then model estimation
and comparison results will be discussed. Finally, we offer some final thoughts
and observations in the discussions and conclusions.

2 A brief recap of the GWR model

2.1 Model estimation

A detailed description of GWR is provided by Fotheringham et al. (2002).
Here we limit ourselves to reviewing the conceptual functions upon which
our model extension will be built. The specification of a basic GWR model is
denoted as:

$$Y_i = \beta_0\left(u_i, v_i\right) + \sum_k \beta_k\left(u_i, v_i\right) X_{ik} + \varepsilon_i, i \in \{1, 2, \ldots, n\}, \tag{1}$$

where (u_i, v_i) denotes the coordinates of point i in a two-dimensional space,
$\beta_0(u_i, v_i)$ and $\beta_k(u_i, v_i)$ represent the estimated intercept and coefficient for variable
k at point i. The parameters in a GWR model are estimated by using the weighted
least squares approach. The estimation of $\beta_k(u_i, v_i)$ is given by:

$$\hat{\beta}\left(u_i, v_i\right) = \left[X'W\left(u_i, v_i\right)X\right]^{-1} X'W\left(u_i, v_i\right)Y \tag{2}$$

where $W(u_i, v_i)$ is an $n \times n$ matrix with diagonal elements denoting the weights of
observation points for the regression point i and with the off-diagonal elements

being zeros. The weights matrix is calculated for each point i at which parameters are to estimate.

2.2 Weighting scheme

A weighting approach must be chosen to determine the rate of decrease in the weights from the fit point to some threshold distance, known as the bandwidth, at and beyond which the weights are set to zero. A commonly used kernel function is the Gaussian distance decay-based function (Fotheringham et al. 2002):

$$W_{ij} = exp\left(-d_{ij}^2 / h^2\right)$$

(3)

where h is a non-negative parameter known as bandwidth and d_{ij} is usually the Euclidean distance between points i and j, calculated from their geographical coordinates (u_i, v_i) and (u_j, v_j):

$$d_{ij}^2 = \left(u_i - u_j\right)^2 + \left(v_i - v_j\right)^2.$$

(4)

Equations (3) and (4) together define the spatial weights matrix used in the model estimation process. Other commonly used weighting functions include the *bi-square* function (Fotheringham et al. 2002) and the *tri-cube* kernel function (McMillen and Redfearn 2010). A further decision is whether the bandwidth h should relate to physical distance away (be it Euclidean or Great Circle, in either case giving what is referred to as a fixed kernel) or be defined by the nth nearest neighbor (an adaptive kernel). If the latter, the number of observations receiving a non-zero weight is the same around each fit point. The logic of this is to adapt the kernel to the local density of the data collection points, extending it over a larger physical area where the observations are sparsely distributed and containing it to a smaller area where the observations are more closely clustered. The concern is that a fixed-distance approach will smooth out spatial heterogeneity where observations are closely located but lead to estimations based on too narrowly contained samples where the observations are further apart (Páez et al. 2002).

2.3 Choosing an optimal bandwidth

In the process of calibrating a GWR model, the unknown bandwidth parameter h in the spatial weights matrix should be calculated first. This is usually achieved by using a cross-validation procedure that maximises out-of-sample model predictions (Fotheringham et al. 2002). Denote the predicted value of y_i from the local model at location i as $\hat{y}_{\neq i}(h)$, which is a function of h and calculated as the fitted value of y_i by using the local regression coefficients. The optimal bandwidth h can be obtained by minimizing the following equation:

$$CVRSS(h) = \sum_i (y_i - \hat{y}_{\neq i}(h))^2.$$

(5)

3 Extending the GWR model

3.1 Model development

Denote a four-dimensional coordinate system as $[u,v,t,a]$ where the first two consist of the spatial dimension, t for the temporal dimension and a for the context dimension or attribute space. The distance between observations i and j can be expressed as a linearly weighted combination of distances in space, time and attributes:

$$(d_{ij}^{gta})^2 = \gamma(d_{ij}^g)^2 + \delta(d_{ij}^t)^2 + \mu(d_{ij}^a)^2$$

$$= \gamma[(u_i - u_j)^2 + (v_i - v_j)^2] + \delta(t_i - t_j)^2 + \mu(a_i - a_j)^2 \qquad (6)$$

γ, δ, μ represent the relative importance of each dimension. It is clear to see that this general weighting scheme nests the geographical weighting scheme (δ and μ = 0) and space-time weighting scheme (μ = 0). So the GTAWR model proposed here nests GWR models and GTWR models.

The distance in the attribute space can be based on multiple contextual attributes. So a_i is a composite index. Let Z_k represent the contextual attributes used to construct d_{ij}^a using the formation below:

$$(a_i - a_j)^2 = \sum_k (Z_{ik} - Z_{jk})^2. \qquad (7)$$

In cases when large correlations and scale differences between Z_k were found, we can also use Mahalanobis distance for calculation (Lu et al. 2016):

$$(a_i - a_j)^2 = (Z_i - Z_j)' \boldsymbol{\pounds}^{-1} (Z_i - Z_j) \qquad (8)$$

where Σ is variance-covariance matrix of Z.

Based on the distance equation, we are ready to construct weights matrices for model estimation. Using a fixed Gaussian kernel approach,[1] the weight of observation j in estimating regression parameters for observation i can be expressed as:

$$w_{ij} = \exp\left(-\frac{\gamma[(u_i - u_j)^2 + (v_i - v_j)^2] + \delta(t_i - t_j)^2 + \mu(a_i - a_j)^2}{h_{gta}^2}\right)$$

$$= \exp\left(-\left(\frac{[(u_i - u_j)^2 + (v_i - v_j)^2]}{h_g^2} + \frac{(t_i - t_j)^2}{h_t^2} + \frac{(a_i - a_j)^2}{h_a^2}\right)\right)$$

$$= w_{ij}^g * w_{ij}^t * w_{ij}^a \qquad (9)$$

where h_{gta} is the distance decay parameter or bandwidth in the spatial, temporal and attribute space. $h_g^2 = h_{gta}^2/\gamma, h_t^2 = h_{gta}^2/\delta$ and $h_a^2 = h_{gta}^2/\mu$ can be thought of as bandwidth parameters in dimensions of space, time and attributes, respectively. Parameters w_{ij}^g, w_{ij}^t and w_{ij}^a are weights in the three dimensions.

In order to calibrate the GWR models, the bandwidth parameters in the spatial, temporal and attribute space should be decided first. In the case of GTAWR, this is more complicated, as there are three unknown parameters γ, δ and μ, as well as the scale differences in the space-time-attribute metric system. In order to deal with scale differences, the distances between observations in a dimension were first scaled by dividing by the variance of distances in that dimension.

To estimate the unknown dimensional importance parameters γ, δ and μ, Equation (6) can be rewritten as:

$$(d_{ij}^{gta})^2/\gamma = [(u_i-u_j)^2+(v_i-v_j)^2]+\delta/\gamma*(t_i-t_j)^2+\mu/\gamma*(a_i-a_j)^2 \qquad (10)$$

and we have $W'_{gta}(i) = W_{gta}(i)/\gamma$. Multiplying $W(u_i, v_i, t_i, a_i)$ by a constant will not influence local regression coefficient estimation (Huang et al. 2010). Therefore, we only have to estimate the two ratio parameters δ/γ and μ/γ, which represent the relative importance of dimensions of time and attributes to space.

The simplest way to fix the two ratio parameters is, of course, using *a priori* values, but this may not be appropriate if no solid theories were in place. We take the cross-validation approach in Equation (5), which is now a function of bandwidth h_{gta}, as well as δ/γ and μ/γ. We can obtain these three parameters simultaneously by minimizing the CV score. In practice, we need to extend the one-dimensional optimisation procedure in implementing standard GWR models to a multi-dimensional optimisation problem for GTAWR models. More specifically, the Nelder and Mead (1965) optimisation method was used.

Having defined the weights matrix, the GTAWR model can be expressed as:

$$Y_i = \beta_0(u_i,v_i,t_i,a_i)+\sum_k \beta_k(u_i,v_i,t_i,a_i)X_{ik}+\varepsilon_i. \qquad (11)$$

Local coefficients of variable X_{ik}, $\beta_k(u_i, v_i, t_i, a_i)$ for observation i can be estimated as:

$$\hat{\beta}(u_i,v_i,t_i,a_i)=\left[X'W(u_i,v_i,t_i,a_i)X\right]^{-1}X'W(u_i,v_i,t_i,a_i)Y \qquad (12)$$

where $W(u_i, v_i, t_i, a_i) = diag(w_{i1}, w_{i2}, \ldots, w_{in})$ and n is the number of observations. The GTAWR model is coded by using the R language, and the scripts are available upon request.

4 Data and model estimation results

4.1 Study area and data

The metropolitan area of Beijing covers a land area of 16,808 km^2 and is divided into 16 districts. The Beijing government and previous researches often use the term "Ring Roads (No. 2 to No. 6)" to define the urban area of Beijing (Zheng and Kahn 2008; Dong et al. 2011). Following this convention, the study area in this article is defined mainly within the sixth ring road, which covers 132 sub-districts (*Jiedao*). Similar to the term "census-block" in the US context, *Jiedao* is the fundamental census administrative organization in urban China. *Jiedao* is the basic neighborhood unit in this study and their socio-demographic characteristics are proxies for contextual attributes to form the distances in the attribute dimension. The study area, main physical (rivers and green parks) and transport features (ring roads and subway lines) are portrayed in Figure 6.1. Along with these key urban landscape features, the spatial distribution of residential land parcels leased during 2003 and 2009 are also presented in Figure 6.1. Black dots are land parcels whose per-square meter leasing prices exceed the sample mean of 2992 RMB, while grey dots represent land parcels with per square meter leasing prices below the mean.

The beginning of land reform in Beijing started officially in 1992. Since then, real estate developers can purchase the right to buy numerous land parcels from the government, first through negotiation (before 2003) and then through open and competitive auctions – those who bid the highest price obtain the land parcel. Therefore, we choose the land parcels leased during 2003 and 2009 from the Beijing Land Resource Authority (BLRA) as our data to retrieve the hedonic prices of land parcel characteristics and their heterogeneity.

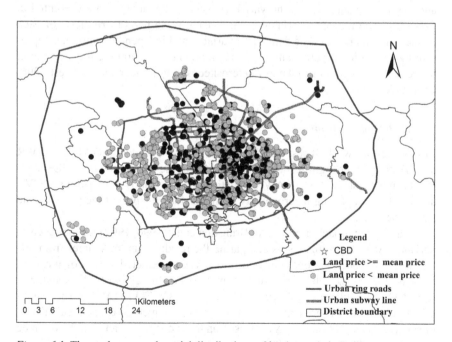

Figure 6.1 The study area and spatial distributions of land parcels in Beijing

This study employs four geo-coded datasets: (a) residential land parcels leasing records from Beijing Land Resource Authority (BLRA), which contain detailed information on the location, price and size of each residential land parcel; (b) *Jiedao* census information from the Fifth Chinese Population Census in 2000, which describes contextual socio-demographic characteristics of each land parcel. These characteristics constitute the attribute space of land parcels in this study. More specifically, we extract for each *Jiedao* the population density (POPDEN), job density (JOBDEN), ratios of residents renting public houses (RatioPUB), median education status (EDU), proportions of houses built before 1949 representing overall physical conditions of buildings (Buildings1949) and crime rates (Crimerate). The third geo-referenced data is on local public goods and amenities in the study area, including subway stations, elementary and high schools, green parks, expressways and rivers. From this, we calculate the proximity of each land parcel to each amenity type: the proximity to nearest subway stations (LogDsubway), to nearest elementary and high schools (LogDele, LogDhigh), to green parks and their sizes (LogDpark, Parksize), to rivers (LogDriver) and to expressways (LogDexpress). In order to analyse land price gradients in Beijing, we also extract a variable LogDcbd denoting the proximity to city centre. Finally, Beijing Economic Units Census data, which geo-coded all the economic units in Beijing in the census year 2001, was used to calculate a series of employment potential indicators for each land parcel: manufacture employment potential (PManu), retail industry employment potential (PTservice) and modern service employment potential (PMservice). Names, definitions and descriptive statistics of the variables used in this analysis are presented in Table 6.1. The response variable is the leasing price per square meter of each residential land parcel. The dependent variable and independent variables representing proximity to public amenities are applied to a natural log transformation to reduce the potential problem of heteroskedasticity (Anderson and West 2006; Cho et al. 2006).

4.2 Model comparisons

In this section, we first test whether the GWR-type models (GTAWR, GTWR and GWR) provide significant better model fit for the data than global OLS models. Then we test whether GTAWR statistically significantly outperforms GTWR and GWR by capturing heterogeneity in dimensions of space, time and attribute simultaneously.

We use the approach proposed in Brunsdon et al. (1996, 1999) for model comparisons. At its heart, the test is comparing the residual sum of squares from different model specifications. For both models, the predicted values of y can be expressed as $\hat{y} = Sy$ where S is the hat matrix. For the global OLS model, $S = X*(X'*X)^{-1}*X'$ and, for GWR-type models, $S = X*(X'*W*X)^{-1}*X'*W)$. The residuals from both models are expressed as $\hat{\varepsilon} = (I - S)y$, which gives the residual sum of squares $\hat{\varepsilon}'\hat{\varepsilon} = y'(I - S)'(I - S)y$. Based on these quantities, an F statistic can be formed as (Brunsdon et al. 1999):

Table 6.1 Variable name, definition, and descriptive statistics

Variables	Definition	Mean	Std. Dev
Dependent Variable			
Logprice	Log (Land parcels' leasing price per square meter (RMB/sq. meter))	7.401	1.067
Land parcel-scale Independent Variables			
Logarea	Log(The area of a land parcel (m²))	7.401	1.067
Square area	Log(The square of the area of a land parcel (m²))	9.368	1.550
LogDcbd	Log(Distance between a land parcel and CBD)	8.999	0.6949
LogDsubway	Log(Distance to the nearest subway station)	7.209	0.957
LogDpark	Log(Distance to the nearest park)	7.760	0.990
LogDriver	Log(Distance to the nearest river)	0.515	0.759
LogDexpress	Log(Distance to the nearest express way)	7.575	0.961
Contextual Variables			
POPDEN	Population density in each Census-Block (thousand people/km²)	1.870	2.637
RatioPUB	Ratio of residents renting public housing	0.327	0.202
EDU	Education median in each Census-Block:1 = junior high school or lower; 2 = high school;3 = university;4 = post graduate	1.738	0.545
Crimerate	Number of reported serious crimes per 1000 people in each Census-Block	5.047	6.070
JOBDEN	Job density in each Census-Block	0.276	0.267
Buildings1949	Ratio of buildings built before 1949 in each Census-Block (%)	0.041	0.107
Year Dummies	Dummies: Residential land parcels leased in each year (base = year 2004)		

$$F = \left[\frac{(y'R_0 y) - (y'R_l y)}{v} \right] \left[\frac{(y'R_l y)}{\delta} \right]^{-1} \tag{13}$$

where $R_z = (I - S_z)'(I - S_z)$, $z \in (0,1)$, $v = Tr(R_0 - R_1)$, $\delta = Tr(R_1)$. The degrees of freedom are $\frac{v^2}{Tr\left[(R_0 - R_1)^2 \right]}$ and $\delta^2 / Tr[(R_1)^2])$. Similarly, we can use this F-test to assess model performances between GTAWR, GTWR and GWR.

The results of model comparisons using our land price data in Beijing are presented in Table 6.2. In this table, the second column lists the residual sum of squares (RSS) of global OLS models, GWR, GTWR, GTAWR and difference between OLS- and GWR-type models. The third column gives the degrees of freedom for each of these models. The fourth column, MS, shows the results of dividing RSS by their respective degrees of freedom. The last two columns show the F-statistic and their corresponding significance level. We first compare

Table 6.2 ANOVA comparison between GWR and OLS models

Source of variations	RSS	DF	MS	F-statistic	p-value
OLS (1) residuals	989.7615	14	70.6973		
OLS (2) residuals	823.8309	20	41.1915		
OLS (3) residuals	789.059	26	30.3484		
GWR residuals	736.9284	1040.9070	0.7080		
GTWR residuals	497.172	1003.794	0.4953		
GTAWR (1) residuals	370.3802	827.2866	0.4477		
GTAWR residuals	354.626	842.6495	0.4208		
GWR/OLS (3) improvement	52.1306	97.0926	0.5369	0.7584	0.9731
GTWR/OLS (3) improvement	291.887	134.2061	2.1749	4.3912	0.0000
GTAWR /OLS (3) improvement	434.433	295.3505	1.4709	3.4951	0.0000
GTWR /GWR improvement	239.7563	37.1135	6.4601	13.0430	0.0000
GTAWR /GWR improvement	382.3024	198.2579	1.9283	4.5820	0.0000
GTAWR/GTWR improvement	142.5461	161.1444	0.8846	2.1019	0.0000
GTAWR/GTAWR (1) improvement	15.7543	−15.3629	−1.0255	−2.4367	0.0000

GWR-based models with global OLS models. The OLS models have three speci-fications, and each of them has a different set of independent variables: OLS (1) with all land parcel-scale variables in Table 6.1; OLS (2) further with year dummy variables; OLS (3) with contextual attribute variables. From the first three rows of Table 6.2, we can see that OLS (3) performs better than OLS (2) and OLS (1) in terms of RSS reduction. So OLS (3) is selected our baseline global model for further comparisons with GWR-type models. From the eighth row, we can see that though GWR model reduces the RSS by 52.13 comparing OLS (3), this reduction is not statistically significant even at the 10% significance level ($p = 0.9731$), whilst rows 9 and 10 shows that GTWR and GTAWR models signifi-cantly outperform OLS (3) at the 0.001 significance level. Comparing the GTWR and GTAWR models to GWR, it clearly shows that there is significant improve-ment in model fit. This implies that hedonic prices of land parcel characteristics vary both in time and context, such as the value of proximity to subway stations being different in different years, and also varies across contexts (or in different attribute space).

4.3 Estimate results from global models

Table 6.3 reports the estimates on regression coefficients of variables from three global OLS models. OLS (3) can explain about 38.6% of the variations in land prices. In OLS (1), size of land parcels and its squared term are not significant, but after controlling time trends in OLS (2) and neighborhood attribute effects in OLS (3), both of them have significant impacts on land price. Size of land parcels has a nonlinear effect, first increasing then decreasing with the size of land parcels. Land price appears to decrease significantly with increasing distance to the CBD. Evaluated at the mean distance to CBD and the mean land price, the marginal

Table 6.3 Hedonic global model (OLS) parameter estimate results

	OLS (1)		OLS (2) + year dummies		OLS (3) + neighborhood attributes	
	Coefficient	t-statistic	Coefficient	t-statistic	Coefficient	t-statistic
Constant	10.5577***	11.097	8.4325***	9.316	9.7431***	9.681
Logarea	0.0965	0.638	0.6701***	4.529	0.5004***	3.345
Square area	−0.0052	−0.61	−0.0366***	−4.397	−0.0284***	−3.396
LogDcbd	−0.1795***	−3.135	−0.1854***	−3.537	−0.303***	−4.873
LogDsubway	−0.2128***	−5.924	−0.1893***	−5.742	−0.1621***	−4.752
LogDele	0.0119	0.313	0.0033	0.094	−0.0118	−0.338
LogDhigh	−0.0085	−0.191	−0.0022	−0.053	0.0056	0.13
LogDpark	−0.1340**	−2.294	−0.1782***	−3.307	−0.14***	−2.621
Parksize	−0.0609	−1.524	−0.0452	−1.232	−0.0468	−1.24
LogDriver	0.0896***	2.82	0.0522*	1.781	0.0633**	2.139
LogDexpress	−0.0517*	−1.887	−0.0598**	−2.374	−0.0452*	−1.802
PManu	4.3259**	2.395	6.0406***	3.635	5.2924***	3.156
PTservice	3.2255**	2.075	4.0649***	2.855	0.2270	0.147
PMservice	1.2784**	2.016	1.2103**	2.084	2.9527***	4.708
Year_dummies	no		Yes		Yes	
POPDEN					0.0221*	1.84
RatioPUB					−0.0059	−0.043
EDU					−0.0227	−0.389
Crimerate					−0.0012	−0.257
JOBDEN					0.5173***	2.982
Buildings1949					−2.0335***	−5.668
Diagnostic information						
R square		0.2526		0.3779		0.4042
Adjusted R square		0.2362		0.3594		0.3858
Residual standard error		0.8607		0.7201		0.6934
Residual sum of squares		989.76		823.83		789.06

Note: Symbols "***", "**" and "*" represent significance levels at 1%, 5% and 10%, respectively.

value of decreasing the distance to CBD by 1000 meters yields about 112 RMB (OLS (3) estimates) increase in per-area land price, indicating a negative land price gradient moving away from city centre.

Proximity to nearest subway stations, parks, rivers and express roads also has significant impacts on land price. According to OLS (3), reducing distance to nearest subway stations, parks, rivers and express roads by 1%, the land price increases by about 0.16%, 0.14%, 0.06% and 0.05%, respectively. Surprisingly, the proximity to elementary and high schools does not have significant influence on land price, as opposed to findings in many other land price studies in Western countries (e.g. Anderson and West 2006; Cho et al. 2006). However, this might be due to the fact that the global model did not capture the potential heterogeneity effect in these associations.

4.4 Estimation results from the GWR, GTWR and GTAWR models

Tables 6.4 and 6.5 report model estimation results from GWR, GTWR and GTAWR models. The bandwidths in GWR, GTWR and GTAWR models are 0.6361, 0.8662 and 1.2597, respectively. The relative weights or importance of the temporal and attribute dimensions to space are 2.7655 and 0.7767 in GTAWR, respectively. It might be tempting to conclude that the temporal dimension is more important than space and context in measuring correlations or closeness among observations. This might be true for this specific data, but the generalisation might not necessarily be true.

Tables 6.4 and 6.5 summarise the distributions of local regression coefficients for each variable. It is clear that there is large variability or heterogeneity in the associations between land parcel characteristics variables and land prices. Statistical comparisons between GWR-based models are also provided. It is useful to note that the percentage of explained variations in land prices has increased from 38.6% in OLS (3) model to 44.4% in the GWR model, 62.5% in the GTWR model and 73.2% in the GTAWR model. The AIC also experiences a large reduction from 2974.87 in GWR to 2572.13 in GTWR and 2513.28 in GTAWR. All these indicate that GTAWR outperforms GTWR and GWR by considering potential heterogeneity of the data in spatial, temporal and attribute dimensions.

Looking at Table 6.5 the varying effects of many variables are evident. Taking the distribution of the coefficients of distance to CBD as an example, the coefficient at the lower quartile ($\beta_{Logdcbd} = -0.3505$) is more than two times larger than that at the upper quartile ($\beta_{Logdcbd} = -0.1448$). Putting this in perspective, reducing the distance to CBD by 1000 meters is associated with an increase of land prices as high as 130 RMB in some places, while it is only associated with an increase of about 53 RMB in other places, evaluated at the mean distance to CBD and mean land price.

Figure 6.2 illustrates the spatially varying associations between proximity to CBD and land prices. The break points correspond to the lower quartile, median and upper quartile of the coefficients, with darker colour indicating stronger impacts of CBD. It clearly shows two areas that are strongly influenced by CBD. The first is the area immediately surrounding CBD, which is easy to understand, as this area is more likely to be directly influenced by the spillover effects of CBD. Another area is the east of CBD, the new Tongzhou financial subcenter, which benefits a lot from the transfer of financial industries from CBD because of the new master plan of Beijing Metropolitan Area. Figure 6.3 depicts places where the impacts of distance to CBD on land price are significant at the 5% significance level with dark colour. Interestingly, nearly all the areas where the proximity to CBD has relative stronger impacts on land price are coincident with areas where these effects are significant at 5% level. As Beijing Metropolitan Area is experiencing a gradual decentralization process and the polycentric urban

Table 6.4 GWR and GTWR parameter estimate results

	GWR (bandwidth = 0.6361)					GTWR (bandwidth = 0.8662, δ/γ = 1.0921)				
	Minimum	Lower Quartile	Median	Upper Quartile	Maximum	Minimum	Lower Quartile	Median	Upper Quartile	Maximum
Constant	−46.076	8.084	9.993	12.854	129.839	−14.946	7.834	9.077	10.522	35.92
Logarea	−4.3112	−0.2597	0.2836	0.6505	2.9347	−3.8596	0.3446	0.7241	1.0031	2.8854
Square area	−0.1649	−0.036	−0.0155	0.0132	0.2333	−0.158	−0.0616	−0.0486	−0.024	0.2055
LogDcbd	−6.9168	−0.3017	−0.2228	0.0354	4.2275	−3.1454	−0.2944	−0.2344	−0.1387	1.0583
LogDsubway	−1.0902	−0.2911	−0.2096	−0.1398	0.3171	−0.9408	−0.2101	−0.1833	−0.1473	0.219
LogDele	−0.5488	−0.0974	−0.0005	0.0655	2.1162	−0.8978	−0.0910	−0.0224	0.0692	0.3183
LogDhigh	−5.7064	−0.0792	0.0013	0.051	1.5839	−0.4907	−0.1179	−0.0234	−0.0067	1.283
LogDpark	−1.5182	−0.2148	−0.1741	−0.0239	2.0395	−1.0401	−0.224	−0.1585	−0.024	0.4261
Parksize	−0.5998	−0.2375	−0.0969	0.0042	3.0972	−1.1024	−0.2017	−0.0813	0.0061	1.5787
LogDriver	−0.5578	0.0072	0.0569	0.12	1.0237	−0.2193	−0.0024	0.0672	0.1009	0.631
LogDexpress	−0.555	−0.1034	−0.0306	0.0038	0.5757	−0.6062	−0.0679	−0.0155	0.0174	0.3982
PManu	−116.791	2.6390	6.2880	10.0330	52.893	−30.8260	2.199	5.098	7.258	37.146
PTservice	−167.1525	−1.7571	2.1286	6.4403	62.3665	−58.213	1.466	2.745	5.96	25.281
PMservice	−27.2612	0.1296	0.9255	1.7107	138.9954	−6.8325	0.5182	0.9108	1.2408	35.7568

Diagnostic information

R square	0.4435					0.6246				
Residual standard error	0.706					0.4953				
Residual sum of squares	736.92					497.17				
AIC	2974.87					2572.13				

Table 6.5 GTAWR parameter estimate results

	Minimum	Lower Quartile	Median	Mean	Upper Quartile	Maximum
Constant	−14.177	9.404	10.663	10.567	12.044	43.629
Logarea	−3.132	−0.0551	0.3175	0.2664	0.5909	2.9875
Square area	−0.1821	−0.0391	−0.0239	−0.0189	−0.0028	0.1672
LogDcbd	−2.855	−0.3505	−0.2267	−0.2593	−0.1448	0.7404
LogDsubway	−1.159	−0.2185	−0.1503	−0.1689	−0.1161	0.6987
LogDele	−1.1424	−0.0906	0.0264	0.0133	0.12	0.8963
LogDhigh	−0.9822	−0.0999	−0.023	0.0002	0.0384	1.8164
LogDpark	−1.4272	−0.2585	−0.1597	−0.1452	−0.0528	2.6912
Parksize	−5.5108	−0.1166	−0.0498	−0.0684	0.0431	1.5845
LogDriver	−0.321	0.0056	0.0735	0.0804	0.1356	2.2027
LogDexpress	−0.5932	−0.0741	−0.0302	−0.0305	0.0196	0.2466
PManu	−254.157	2.892	4.833	3.845	6.251	49.249
PTservice	−91.565	1.851	3.827	2.851	6.419	20.942
PMservice	−18.0787	0.7196	1.1681	1.3854	1.648	45.0656

Diagnostic information

R square	0.7322
Residual standard error	0.4208
Residual sum of squares	354.626
AIC	2513.2772

Note: bandwidth = 1.2597, δ/γ = 2.7655, μ/γ = 0.7767

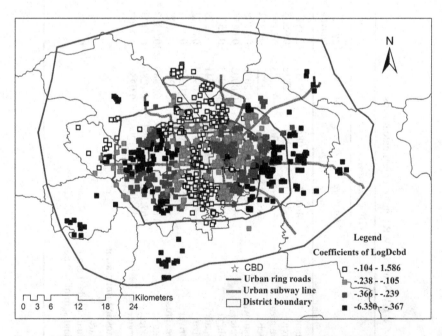

Figure 6.2 Spatial variations in the coefficients of distance to CBD in GTAWR

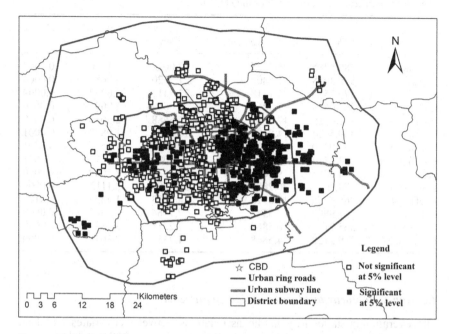

Figure 6.3 Statistical significance of the local coefficients of distance to CBD

spatial structure is emerging, the land price gradient from CBD is not expected to be observed in the whole study area.

4.5 Test the significance of variables in GTAWR

As the effects of each variable on land prices are varying, an obvious question is whether this variable has significant impacts on land price across the study area. In order to answer this question, we adopt the approach proposed by McMillen and Redfearn (2010), which tests the significance on variable effects through comparing the residual sum of squares of an unrestricted (i.e. the model with all the variables) and a restricted (after one or a group of variables deleted) model specifications. This is the same F- test described above.

Table 6.6 presents the results. The second column of Table 6.6 gives the RSS of the restricted models by deleting the variable in the first column. The second and third columns are the differences in RSS, degrees of freedom between unrestricted GTAWR and restricted GTAWR models. The fourth and fifth columns report F-statistics and the associated p-values. It is clear that all of the land parcel structural characteristics have significant impacts on land price. It is useful to note that proximity to elementary and high schools, the size of the nearest park and the job potentials of traditional services are capitalised into land prices, while the global OLS models in table 6.3 do not capture these effects.

Table 6.6 Significance test of variables in GTAWR

	Restricted RSS	Unrestricted RSS Improvement	Freedom Difference	F-statistic	P-value
Constant	380.8785	26.2525	12.0022	5.1980	0.0000
Logarea	376.3068	21.6808	21.7520	2.3687	0.0000
Square area	379.7578	25.1318	22.7412	2.6262	0.0000
LogDcbd	362.0523	7.4263	6.0659	2.9094	0.0000
LogDsubway	371.6519	17.0259	17.5688	2.3030	0.0000
LogDele	369.5634	14.9374	17.8487	1.9888	0.0001
LogDhigh	362.9210	8.2950	10.0899	1.9537	0.0001
LogDpark	363.4717	8.8457	12.6090	1.6672	0.0031
Parksize	364.0884	9.4625	10.7039	2.1008	0.0000
LogDriver	374.9069	20.2809	22.8287	2.1112	0.0000
LogDexpress	366.3236	11.6976	18.7533	1.4823	0.0143
PManu	361.9802	7.3542	7.1664	2.4387	0.0000
PTservice	365.2128	10.5868	7.2218	3.4837	0.0000
PMservice	359.2128	4.5868	4.7354	2.3019	0.0000

4.6 Non-stationarity test for regression coefficients

The overall non-stationarity in the associations between covariates and land prices has been proven through a series of F-test between GTAWR, global OLS models, GTWR and GWR models in Table 6.2. This section will test the statistical significance on the heterogeneity in the capitalisation effects of each covariate. Following Leung et al. (2000), we test the non-stationarity for each variable by using their *F*-statistics. Table 6.7 lists the *F*-statistics and the associated p-values. It can be found that there is statistically significant heterogeneity in the capitalisation effects of the size of land parcels and its squared, distance to CBD, distance to nearest elementary and high schools and the size of nearest parks.

5 Conclusion and discussion

This study develops an innovative extension of the standard GWR model. The proposed GTAWR model significantly outperforms the standard GWR model and the GTWR model in our hedonic land price models. In terms of model fit, the proposed GWR extension can explain about 73% of the land price variations. In contrast, 44% and 62% of the variations in land prices are accounted for in the GWR and GTWR models. The differences in model fit between GTAWR, GWR and GTWR have been found to be statistically significant. This demonstrates the benefit of constructing a spatial weights matrix by explicitly exploiting (dis)similarities in dimensions of space, time and attribute. On one aspect, the proposed approach is theoretically appealing, as it conceptualises and presents observations in a three-dimensional coordinates system – space, time and context – and measures the closeness among observations in each dimension simultaneously. In contrast, traditional GWR models only capture closeness or correlations between

Table 6.7 Non-stationarity test of GTAWR parameters

	Constant	Logarea	Square Area	LogDcbd	LogDsubway
F-statistic	0.3824	2.8257	1.5519	1.9772	0.9059
P-value	0.9773	0.0000***	0.0386**	0.0071***	0.5797
	LogDele	LogDhigh	LogDpark	Parksize	LogDriver
F-statistic	1.7215	2.5437	0.5412	4.9228	0.7215
P-value	0.0138**	0.0000***	0.7874	0.0000***	0.6619
	LogDexpress	PManu	PTservice	PMservice	
F-statistic	1.1489	0.4377	1.2473	0.8124	
P-value	0.2028	0.8009	0.2460	0.5635	

Note: Symbols "***", "**" and "*" represent significance levels at 1%, 5% and 10%, respectively.

observations in a pure space dimension and therefore are exposed to potential confounding effects from other dimensions of the data such as temporal and contextual differences. On the other aspect, the proposed GTAWR model reflects heterogeneity of the data and heterogeneity in the relationships or associations between variables in multiple dimensions.

In essence, the proposal here is elaborating the key element in local spatial model estimation – the weights matrix. In a pure cross-sectional spatial data setting, it is without any question to construct the weights matrix by exploiting the closeness or dependencies among observations in the spatial domain or dimension. With increasing availability of data with rich information in multiple dimensions such as time and context, building weights matrices using spatial information only would be ineffective or even erroneous sometimes. The principle of local spatial model estimation is to assign larger weights to observations that are close to a focal point and smaller weights to observations that are distant. The measure of closeness among observations in multiple dimensions is a challenging task. In the context of spatial data becoming increasingly complex, fine-grained, dynamic and unstructured, Tobler's first law of geography still holds, but the definition and measurement of "near things" must be considered carefully.

The final remark is on the exploratory nature of GWR models. GWR-type models are useful tools to investigate the heterogeneity or variability in associations or relationships between variables, but great caution needs to be exercised if the research purpose is on statistical inference (Waller et al. 2007; Wheeler and Waller 2009; Harris et al. 2013). In the presence of a multi-scale, spatial and temporal data structure, there has been surging interest in developing innovative Bayesian methodologies for modelling heterogeneity in relationships and complex dependency structures underlying data (e.g. Gelfand et al. 2003; Finley 2011; Dong and Harris 2015; Dong et al. 2016; Ma et al. 2017). Future work will focus on developing methodologies to model spatial heterogeneity and hierarchical dependence effects simultaneously within the Bayesian framework.

Note

1 In short, there are two reasons we choose a fixed Gaussian kernel in this chapter. The first is that the land parcels sample are distributed relatively even in the study area, as will be illustrated in Figure 6.1. We do use the adaptive kernel to estimate the GWR-based models, but we do not find a statistically significant difference in model fit between the use of a fixed kernel and an adaptive kernel for each model. As such, all the GWR-type models are estimated by using the fixed-kernel approach.

References

Anderson S T and West S E. 2006. Open space, residential property values, and spatial context. *Regional Science and Urban Economics* 36, 773–789.

Bitter C, Mulligan G and Dall'erba S. 2007. Incorporating spatial variation in housing attribute prices: A comparison of geographically weighted regression and the spatial expansion method. *Journal of Geographical Systems* 9, 7–27.

Brunsdon C, Fotheringham A S and Charlton M. 1996. Geographically weighted regression: A method for exploring spatial nonstationarity. *Geographical Analysis*, 28, 281–298.

Brunsdon C, Fotheringham A S and Charlton M. 1999. Some notes on parametric significance tests for geographically weighted regression. *Journal of Regional Science* 39(3), 497–524.

Cho S H, Bowker J M and Park W M. 2006. Measuring the contribution of water and green space amenities to housing values: An application and comparison of spatially weighted hedonic models. *Journal of Agricultural and Resource Economics* 31, 485–507.

Comber A J, Brunsdon C and Radburn R. 2011. A spatial analysis of variations in health access: Linking geography, socio-economic status and access perceptions. *International Journal of Health Geographics* 10. Available from: www.ij-healthgeographics.com/content/10/1/44 [Accessed 6 July 2012].

Dong G P and Harris R. 2015. Spatial autoregressive models for geographically hierarchical data structures. *Geographical Analysis* 47, 173–191.

Dong G P, Ma J, Harris R and Pryce G. 2016. Spatial random slope multilevel modeling using multivariate conditional autoregressive models: A case study of subjective travel satisfaction in Beijing. *Annals of the American Association of Geographers* 106(1), 19–35.

Dong G P et al. 2011. Spatial heterogeneity in determinants of residential land price: Simulation and prediction. *Acta Geographica Sinica* 66(6), 750–760.

Fik T, Ling D C and Mulligan G. 2003. Modeling spatial variation in housing prices: A variable interaction approach. *Real Estate Economics* 31, 623–646.

Finley A O. 2011. Comparing spatially-varying coefficients models for analysis of ecological data with nonstationary and anisotropic residual dependence. *Methods in Ecology and Evolution* 2, 143–154.

Fotheringham A S, Charlton M E and Brunsdon C. 2002. *Geographically weighted regression: The analysis of spatial varying relationships*. Chichester, John Wiley and Sons.

Gelfand A E, Kim H, Sirmans C F, and Banerjee S. 2003. Spatial modelling with spatially varying coefficient processes. *Journal of the American Statistical Association* 98, 387–396.

Geniaux G, Ay J S and Napoleone C. 2011. A spatial hedonic approach on land use change anticipations. *Journal of Regional Science* 51, 967–986.

Goldstein H. 2003. *Multilevel statistical methods*, third edition. London, Arnold.

Harris R, Dong G P and Zhang W Z. 2013. Using contextualized geographically weighted regression to model the spatial heterogeneity of land prices in Beijing, China. *Transactions in GIS* 17, 901–919.

Hox J. 2002. *Multilevel analysis: Techniques and applications*. Mahwah, NJ, Lawrence Erlbaum Associates.

Huang B, Wu B and Barry M. 2010. Geographically and temporally weighted regression for modelling spatio-temporal variation in house prices. *International Journal of Geographical Information Science* 24(3), 383–401.

Kestens Y, Theriault M and Des Rosiers F. 2006. Heterogeneity in hedonic modelling of house prices: Looking at buyers' household profiles. *Journal of Geographical systems* 8, 61–96.

Leitner M and Helbich M. 2011. The impact of hurricanes on crime: A spatio-temporal analysis in the city of Houston, Texas. *Cartography and Geographic Information Science* 38, 213–221.

Leung Y, Mei C and Zhang W. 2000. Statistical tests for spatial nonstationarity based on the geographically weighted regression model. *Environment and Planning A* 32, 9–32.

Lu B, Charlton M, Brunsdon C and Harris P. 2016. The Minkowski approach for choosing the distance metric in geographically weighted regression. *International Journal of Geographical Information Science* 30, 351–368.

Ma J, Chen Y and Dong G P. 2017. Flexible spatial multilevel modelling of neighbourhood satisfaction in Beijing. *The Professional Geographer*, 1, 1–11.

McMillen D P and Redfearn C L. 2010. Estimation and hypothesis testing for nonparametric hedonic house price functions. *Journal of Regional Science* 50(3), 712–733.

Nelder J A, and Mead R. 1965. A simplex algorithm for function minimization. *Computer Journal* 7, 308–313.

Paez A, Uchida, T and Miyamoto, K. 2002. A general framework for estimation and inference of geographically weighted regression models, 1: Location-specific kernel bandwidths and a test for local heterogeneity. *Environment and Planning A* 34, 733–754.

Tobler W R. 1970. A computer movies simulating urban growth in the Detroit region. *Economic Geography*, 46, 234–240.

Waller L, Zhu L, Gotway C, Gorman D and Gruenewald P. 2007. Quantifying geographic variations in associations between alcohol distribution and violence: A comparison of geographically weighted regression and spatially varying coefficient models. *Stochastic Environment Research and Risk Assessment* 21, 573–588.

Wheeler D and Waller L. 2009. Comparing spatially varying coefficient models: a case study examining violent crime rates and their relationships to alcohol outlets and illegal drug arrests. *Journal of Geographical Systems* 11, 1–22.

Yang T C and Matthews S. 2012. Understanding the non-stationary associations between distrust of the health care system, health conditions, and self-rated health in the elderly: A geographically weighted regression approach. *Health and Place* 18, 576–585.

Yu D. 2007. Modelling owner-occupied single-family house values in the city of Milwaukee: A geographically weighted regression approach. *GIScience and Remote Sensing* 44, 267–282.

Zheng S Q and Kahn M E. 2008. Land and residential property markets in a booming economy: New evidence from Beijing. *Journal of Urban Economics* 63, 743–757.

7 A big data-based characterisation of the residential rental market in Shanghai

Weijiang Zhu, Wenqiang Wu, and Yiming Wang

1 Introduction

The contemporary society sees more and more data readily accessible and obtainable in an enormous amount, hence 'big data', especially by deploying state-of-the-art information and computer technologies (ICT). Nevertheless, one may argue that big data is not an entirely new phenomenon; the information underpinning big data, arguably, has always existed, for example, in such traditional media as newspapers. In this vein, the easy access to and lower cost of acquiring data are arguably the key factors that distinguish big data from the traditional counterparts (Batty, 2013).

Alongside its many successful applications, big data informatics has been deployed increasingly for commercial purposes. For example, many real estate companies nowadays rely on the insights from big data analysis to guide portfolio diversification as an investment strategy (Du et al., 2014). Reinforcing such exercise is the use of geographical information system (GIS) as an ICT tool to visualise and analyse big data related to the pricing of real estate assets.

This chapter is intended to showcase an inquiry of similar nature. Studying a set of big data containing the asking rents advertised upon online letting websites, we aim to characterise the Shanghai rental housing market with regard to the correlation between rents and the rental properties' relative locations to key urban amenities. We firstly deploy ArcGIS as a GIS software package-to investigate the geographical distribution of observed rental prices across the municipal boundary of Shanghai. Secondly, we examine the sample properties' relative locations to such urban amenities as schools, parks, hospitals, and metro stations. Thirdly, we conduct an explorative hedonic-pricing analysis, with a view to unravel some essential determinants of rental price in Shanghai.

The remainder of this chapter-is-organised as follows. Section 2 reviews the extant literature with respect to big data analytics and its potential applicability to real estate research. Section 3 introduces the empirical context of this inquiry in terms of the private rental housing market in Shanghai. Section 4 presents the research method, on top of the specific procedures of data collection and data mining. Section 5 reports and discusses the results of our big data analysis before we conclude the chapter in section 6.

2 Big data and real estate

Many scholars have applied big data analysis in the field of real estate research. For example, Powe (1997) estimated the house price premiums of access to woodland in Southampton, UK, by combining in GIS more than 872 sample observations that contain the locations of residential properties and their nearby amenities. Likewise, Ottensmann et al. (2008) investigated the relationship between urban locations and house prices in Indiana, USA, based upon 8772 home sale transaction records and the properties' specific locational information. Adopting a similar big data approach, Zheng et al. (2015) have-identified the effect of school quality with regard to the resale and rental values of housing properties in Beijing, China.

However, big data is not tantamount to better data. Boyd and Crawford (2012), for instance, find in their study of Twitter users that big data often involves neither random nor independent sampling and thus may not represent the presumed underlying population (e.g. Twitter users as a biased sample of all voters). The same problem can further lead to the issue of spurious correlation, due mainly to the increasing size of dataset rather than reflecting the actual connectedness between the intended factors (Leinweber, 2007).

The aforementioned issues associated with big data analysis in general are also relevant to its particular application in the field of real estate. The problems can, however, be addressed through more careful data mining and explorative statistical analysis, with a view to better understand the dataset with reference to the specific local context of application.

3 The residential rental market in Shanghai

As the largest city in China, Shanghai features one of the most dynamic private rental housing markets within the nation. Numerous local rental properties have been advertised upon online letting websites, yielding a tremendous volume and variety of information which is constantly posted, viewed, shared, and updated by a myriad of market actors, such as renters, landlords, and estate agents. In this vein, the residential rental market in Shanghai provides a well-suited empirical setting to study the application of big data analysis for housing research.

As mentioned above, the big data generated by the online letting websites need to be understood with reference to the specific local market conditions in Shanghai.

Like other major cities in China, the housing market in Shanghai also features a very high price-to-rent ratio (Wu et al., 2012). Intuitively, a price-to-rent ratio of 40, for example, implies that the amount of funds one needs to purchase a property equals 40 years of rent payable for the same residence. Figure 7.1 and 7.2, respectively, illustrate the resale price index versus the rental price index in Shanghai from the years 2006 to 2016. The resale price index shows a clear upward trend, while the rental price index is relatively stable compared with its resale counterpart, partly explaining why Shanghai has witnessed a steady rise in terms of the price-to-rent ratio.

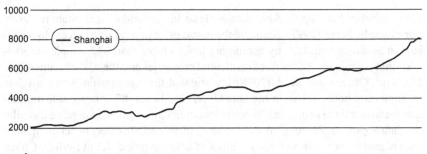

Figure 7.1 Resale price index for condominiums in Shanghai

Source: China Real Estate Index System and fdc.fang.com.

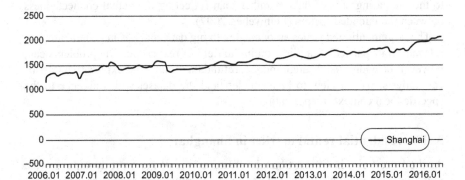

Figure 7.2 Resale price index for condo apartments in Shanghai

Source: China Real Estate Index System and fdc.fang.com.

4 Data and method

4.1 Data collection and mining

We accessed the raw dataset via Leixury Real Estate Market Research and Consulting Co., Ltd (referred to as Leixury hereafter). Leixury had obtained a large amount of data based upon online asking rents posted between December 2012 and January 2013 on two of the largest rental advertising websites in China (www.haozu123.com and www.fang.com). In the data collected by Leixury, two-bed-one-bathroom (2b1b) condominium apartments appear to be the most frequently observed type of housing properties. This resonates with the key findings from the latest Shanghai Census (i.e. the 6th Census in 2010), which indicates that most of the families in Shanghai tend to live in two-bedroom apartments sized between 80 and 100 square meters (Yang et al., 2015). To control for the heterogeneity of different property types with regard to average asking rent, Leixury had further produced a sub-sample that contains only 2b1b apartments. All of the selected 2b1b condominiums were then grouped into 2575 residential complex communities (or *xiaoqu* in Mandarin Chinese). For every *xiaoqu*, the asking rent for all of the 2b1b apartments therein was averaged by their aggregate floorage in square meter, essentially producing a rental price index showing the average rent per square meter (ARSM) for each of the 2,575 communities.

Leixury had also collected the specific longitudes and latitudes for amenities around the communities, such as 46 state-owned hospitals, 159 primary and secondary public schools, 531 parks, and 643 metro station entrances. The original geographical data allowed us to further calculate, using ArcGIS, the Euclidean distance between each *xiaoqu* and its nearest school, hospital, park, as well as the community's distance to the centroid of People's Square construed as the city centre of Shanghai. Unlike some existing studies, which tend to measure transport accessibility based on Euclidean distance between a property and its nearest transport facility (Wang et al., 2016; Sun et al., 2015; Hess and Almeida, 2007), we chose to count the number of metro stations within 1000 meters of each *xiaoqu*. Also included in the final dataset were a couple of additional variables, such as the age of each community since it was initially built and the percentage of green space within every *xiaoqu*.

4.2 Explorative hedonic analysis

We set up an explorative hedonic pricing model, with a view to identify the potential determinants of rental price in Shanghai. Inspired by Rosen's (1974) seminal work, equation (1) specifies a multivariate regression model with a log-log function form, which assume as per equation (2), that the relative variance in rent as the response variable depends upon the relative change in a series of housing attributes as measured by the multiple independent variables. Specifically, r in equation (1) denotes average rent per square metre (ARSM), while $v_1 \sim v_n$ stand for a series of independent variables, each corresponding to a specific housing attribute, and ε is the error term.

$$\log(r) = b_0 + b_1 \times \log(v_1) + b_2 \times \log(v_2) + \cdots + b_n \times \log(v_n) + \varepsilon \tag{1}$$

$$b_k = \frac{\frac{\partial r}{r}}{\left(\frac{\partial v_k}{v_k}\right)} (k = 1, 2, \cdots, n-1, n) \tag{2}$$

We take the following steps to test the regression model specified in equation (1):

Step 1: We test the model in Eviews, using a conventional ordinary least square (OLS) approach.

Step 2: We conduct both the Breusch-Pagan test and White's test to examine whether the OLS results involve any heteroskedasticity issues. According to Wooldridge (2009), if there is a significant presence of heteroskedasticity, OLS does not generate the best linear unbiased estimator (BLUE).

Step 3: Wald test is also exercised to check if insignificant variables as per OLS are jointly significant at specific significance level. If they are not jointly significant, some individually insignificant variables should be excluded from the model to form new models until remaining insignificant variables become jointly significant.

Step 4: We not only apply the above tests to all of the 2575 sample communities but also divide the sample observations into three sub-samples by ARSM (average rent per square meter) in terms of the most expensive 25%, least expensive 25%, and the remaining 50% of the sample *xiaoqu*. We run the same set of tests as mentioned above with regard to each of the three sub-samples.

5 Results

5.1 Descriptive statistics

Table 7.1 shows all of the variables in our research, with the corresponding summary statistics displayed in Table 7.2.

Table 7.1 Variable definition

Variable	Definition	Unit
Rent	Average Yearly Rent per square meter	¥, Chinese Yuan
Age	Age of Community	Year
Green	Percentage of Green Space within Community	%
Centre	Euclidean distance to City Centre	Meter
Hospital	Euclidean distance to Nearest Hospital	Meter
School	Euclidean distance to Nearest School	Meter
Park	Euclidean distance to Nearest Park	Meter
Metro	No. of Metro Entrances within 1000 m radius of the property	–

Table 7.2 Descriptive statistics

	Mean	*Maximum*	*Minimum*	*Std. Dev.*
Rent	551.942099	2320.704102	133.333206	228.898191
Age	11.833790	108	0	6.008242
Green	35.39%	78%	1.4%	9.86%
Centre	10704.190000	57889.865320	36.837096	8021.907000
Hospital	4626.899864	30033.260530	13.821185	5493.163941
School	2075.009000	26660.921740	27.609925	3086.080000
Park	1095.014000	12462.945410	17.06326712	1182.747000
Metro	3.248544	43	0	4.801089

Note: Sample Size: 2575

5.2 Visualization

Visualization can be defined as a process of using information and computer technology to produce more interactive and dynamic visual representations of data, with a view to enhance human cognition (Meyer and Cook, 2000). In the same spirit, we undertake to produce some graphics which are intended to characterise the Shanghai residential rental market.

Figure 7.3 maps the locations of all hospitals, parks, schools, and metro stations which are included in our sample data. According to the figure, we notice that most of the amenities are concentrated around the urban centre of Shanghai, which is marked as a red star in the figure.

Figure 7.4 illustrates the locations of all 2575 residential communities included in our dataset. About 1537 residential communities, which amount to 60% of the *xiaoqu* included in our sample, seem to be located within 10 km of the city centre.

Compiled in ArcGIS, Figure 7.5 illustrates the geographical distribution of rental price with regard to all of the 2575 sample communities across Shanghai. As shown in Figure 7.5, every pillar represents the communities' annual ARSM. In this panoramic view, it's not difficult to tell that the closer a residential community gets to the city centre, the higher the average rent is in the *xiaoqu*. Additionally, the colours (i.e., yellow, amber, red) of the pillar represent three rental price classifications – the top 25% in red, the middle 50% in amber, and the bottom 25% in yellow.

5.3 Hedonic model results

Tables 7.3 and 7.4 illustrate the key results of our hedonic pricing analysis. As suggested by Table 7.3 the *p* values of the Breusch-Pagan tests are rather small, significantly confirming the potential presence of heteroskedasticity. To address the problem, we adapt the usual ordinary least square (OLS) test by including the White heterosekdasticity-robust standard errors. The regression results, after the model adjustment, are presented in Table 7.4.

The coefficient estimates for all of the independent variables included in Table 7.4 are all statistically significant at the 5% level of confidence. Specifically, the distance from a *xiaoqu* to the city centre and various amenities, as well as the age of community, appear to be related negatively to the change in ARSM. In the meantime, the percentage of internal green space and the number of metro stations near every *xiaoqu* are both positively correlated with ARSM, indicating that the renters are significantly willing to pay for green space and accessibility to public transport.

As a comparison, estimation coefficients for every explanatory variable with coloured bars are also reported in Figure 7.5, where distance to city centre seems to account for the largest part of difference in ARSM. Given that both dependent and independent variables are logged, the statistical results seem to suggest that an increase by 1% in terms of the distance to city centre is associated with a 0.14% decrease in the ARSM.

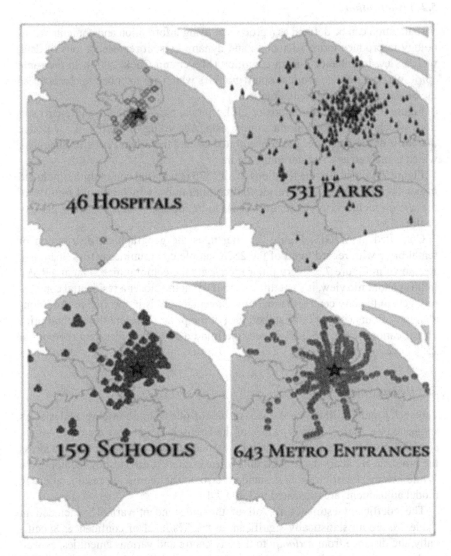

Figure 7.3 Hospitals, parks, schools and metro stations in sample data

To examine the determination of rent within different segments of the local rental housing market, we undertake to further classify the 2575 sample communities into three sub-samples, in terms of top 25%, medium 50%, and lowest 25% by ARSM. Each of the sub-samples is tested respectively, using the same specification as of the full-sample OLS. However, as indicated by the Wald statistics included in Table 7.5, the regressors included in the full sample model are not jointly significant in any of the three sub-sample–based models, suggesting that some independent variables can be removed from the subordinate tests.

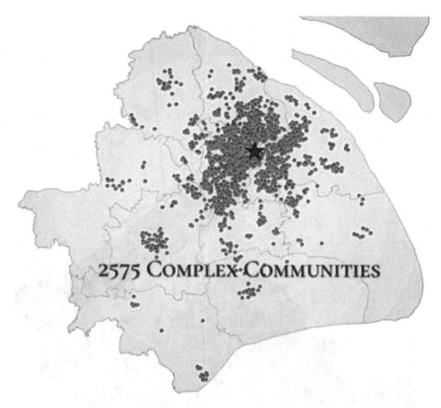

Figure 7.4 Locations of 2575 residential communities in Shanghai

The results of three subordinate models are presented in Tables 7.6, 7.7, and 7.8, indicating some additional findings. For instance, according to Table 7.6 renters at the higher end of the market seem to be more sensitive to the age of residential community and distance to the nearest hospital. In contrast, proximity to the schools and the number of metro stations around a community, according to Table 7.8, appear to be more desired by those renting properties which are priced at the lower end of the market. Difference in the magnitudes of coefficients is further illustrated in Figures 7.8, 7.9, and 7.10 with respective reference to the three subordinate hedonic models.

6. Discussion and conclusion

This chapter demonstrates a characterisation of the residential rental market in Shanghai, based upon an explorative big data analysis which contains data mining, visualisation and hedonic modelling. The study's implication is twofold. First, the empirical findings suggest that the Shanghai residential rental

Figure 7.5 Rental price distribution based on sample observations

market seems to feature a clear monocentric geographical pattern, since distance to the Shanghai city centre proves to be the most important determinant of rental price for local housing properties in Shanghai, albeit with the exception of the most expensive 25% of rental properties (see Table 7.9). In this vein,

Table 7.3 Heteroscedasticity tests

Model	F-test Prob.	Heteroscedasticity
All	0.0000	Yes
Top 25%	0.0014	Yes
Middle 50%	0.0033	Yes
Bottom 25%	0.0000	Yes

* For the Breusch-Pagan test, we are using 5% significance level as a benchmark.
*H_0 = no heteroscedasticity

Table 7.4 OLS results based on the full sample

Variables	Coefficient	Standard Errors	T-test Prob.
Constant	9.155975	0.119827	0.0000
Age	−0.031370	0.013402	0.0193
Green	0.049078	0.017353	0.0047
Centre	−0.144490	0.018262	0.0000
Park	−0.035244	0.007580	0.0000
Hospital	−0.119579	0.009317	0.0000
School	−0.039927	0.006992	0.0000
No. of Metro Entrance	0.003847	0.000440	0.0000

R-squared = O.576845
No. of Observations: 2575

Table 7.5 Joint significance tests

Model	F-test Prob.	Jointly Significant
Top 25%	0.7875	No
Middle 50%	0.1446	No
Bottom 25%	0.6668	No

* For this Wald test, we are using 5% significance level as a benchmark.
* H_0 = no jointly significant

Table 7.6 Estimation output of top 25% model

Variables	Coefficient	Standard Errors	T-test Prob.
Constant	7.251060	0.102500	0.0000
Age	−0.069166	0.017284	0.0001
Hospital	−0.056608	0.012486	0.0000

R-squared = 0.272750.

* No. of Obs: 644

Table 7.7 Estimation output of middle 50% model

Variables	Coefficient	Standard Errors	T-test Prob.
Constant	7.028601	0.054101	0.0000
Centre	−0.052316	0.007836	0.0000
Hospital	−0.029057	0.004178	0.0000
School	−0.010717	0.004263	0.0121
No. of Metro Entrance	0.001018	0.000267	0.0001

R-squared = 0.235516.

* No. of Obs: 1288

Table 7.8 Estimation output of bottom 25% model

Variables	Coefficient	Standard Errors	T-test Prob.
Constant	8.098609	0.211796	0.0000
Age	−0.037976	0.013268	0.0043
Centre	−0.153043	0.027865	0.0000
Park	−0.036546	0.009691	0.0002
Hospital	−0.036925	0.017847	0.0390
School	−0.037595	0.009556	0.0001
No. of Metro Entrance	0.002008	0.000695	0.0040

R-squared = 0.302505.

* No. of Obs: 643

Table 7.9 Key determinant of asking rent in Shanghai

Model	Most attributable housing characteristics to rent
Full	Distance to City Centre
Top 25%	Distance to Hospital
Middle 50%	Distance to City Centre
Bottom 25%	Distance to City Centre

the supply of affordable rental housing should not involve price-based policy interventions, but also spatial planning strategies in terms of how to encourage the development of major urban infrastructures and amenities in the periphery of Shanghai.

Apart from its policy implications, the inquiry reported in this chapter is also expected to shed some light on the future application of big data for real estate research. As illustrated, real estate big data, such as asking rents posted online, are readily available and easily accessible nowadays on the internet. However, real estate big data collected from the websites may involve issues such as biased sampling and heteroskedastic residuals in regression analysis. Although attentive data

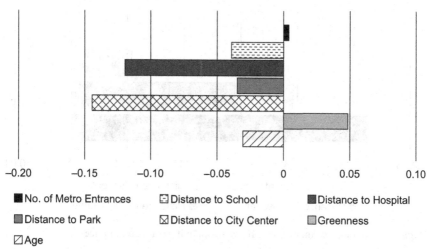

Figure 7.6 Hedonic estimations based on 2,575 observed rental communities

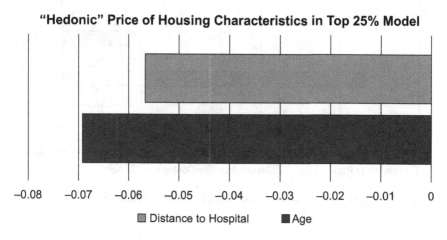

Figure 7.7 Hedonic estimation for most expensive rental communities

mining and explorative inferential statistical tests can help address some of the inherent problems associated with big data, these must be done with a conscious reference to the specific local context in which the big data analysis is applied. In a nutshell, big data analytics must be context sensitive.

"Hedonic" Price of Housing Characteristics in Middle 50% Model

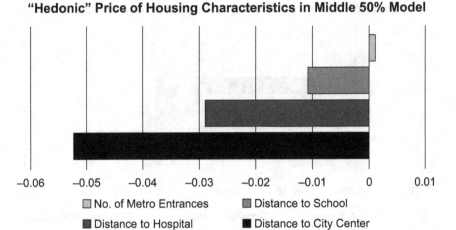

Figure 7.8 Hedonic estimations for rental communities of medium price

"Hedonic" Price of Housing Characteristics in Bottom 25% Model

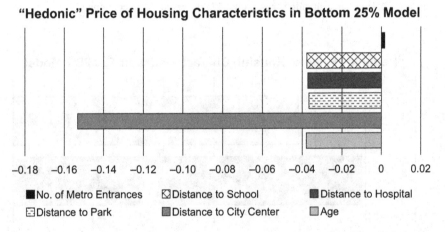

Figure 7.9 Hedonic estimations for least expensive rental communities

References

Batty, M. (2013). Big data, smart cities and city planning. *Dialogue in Human Geography*, 3(3), pp. 274–279.

Boyd, D. and Crawford, K. (2012). Critical question for big data. *Information, Communication & Society*, 15(5), pp. 662–679.

Du, D., Li, A. and Zhang, L. (2014). Survey on the applications of big data in Chinese real estate enterprise. *Procedia Computer Science*, 30, pp. 24–33.

Hess, D. and Almeida, T. (2007). Impact of proximity to light rail rapid transit on station-area property values in Buffalo, New York. *CURS*, 44(5), pp. 1041–1068.

Leinweber, D. (2007). Stupid data miner tricks: Overfitting the S&P 500. *The Journal of Investing*, 16(1), pp. 15–22.

Meyer, R. and Cook, D. (2000). Visualization of data. *Current opinion in biotechnology*, 11(1), pp. 89–96.

Ottensmann, J., Payton, S. and Man, J. (2008). Urban location and housing prices within a hedonic model. *Journal of Regional Analysis and Policy*, 38(1), pp. 19–35.

Powe, N. (1997). Using a geographic information system to estimate a hedonic price model of the benefits of woodland access. *Forestry*, 70(2), pp. 139–149.

Rosen, S. (1974). Hedonic-prices-and-implicit-markets: Product-differentiation-in-pure competition. *Journal-of-Political-Economy*, 82(1), pp. 34–55.

Sun, W., Zheng, S. and Wang, R. (2015). The capitalization of subway access in home value: A repeat rentals model with supply constraints in Beijing. *Transportation Research Part A: Policy and Practice*, 80, pp. 104–115.

Wang, Y., Feng, S., Deng, Z. and Cheng, S. (2016). Transit premium and rent segmentation: A spatial quantile hedonic analysis of Shanghai Metro. *Transport Policy*, 51, pp. 61–69.

Wooldridge, J. M. (2009). On estimating firm-level production functions using proxy variables to control for unobservables. *Economics Letters*, 104(3), pp. 112–114.

Wu, J., Gyourko, J. and Deng, Y. (2012). Evaluating conditions in major Chinese housing markets. *Regional Science and Urban Economics*, 42(3), pp. 531–543.

Yang, S., Wang, M. and Wang, C. (2015). Socio spatial restructuring in Shanghai: Sorting out where you live by affordability and social status. *Cities*, 47, pp. 23–34.

Zheng, S., Hu, W. and Wang, R. (2015). How much is a good school worth in Beijing? Identifying price premium with paired resale and rental data. *The Journal of Real Estate Finance and Economics*, 53(2), pp. 184–199.

8 Evaluating polycentric spatial strategy of megacities

Qiwe Ma, Zhaoya Gong, Changcheng Kan, and Anrong Dang

Polycentric spatial strategy plays an important role in lessening the pressure on central cities, driving the development of suburban areas, and supporting the reform of urban structure and the optimization of urban space, which makes it a common choice of many megacities all around the world. At the same time, there are also important problems emerging in the field of urban research and planning on how to measure the degree of development of sub-centers and the effect of polycentric policies. Existing researches are mainly based on traditional socioeconomic surveys or census data. Because of the drawbacks in spatial and temporal resolutions, the research results may not be able to depict the development level of polycentric megacities accurately. Big data has advantages in the wide coverage of population across geographic areas and high spatial and temporal resolutions, which makes it a novel alternative for this type of research. Based on big data sources provided by Baidu Map, we propose an improved composite index for the measurement of centrality of places. We further apply this measure to the study of centrality of places in Beijing and Shanghai and further demonstrate how it can be used with polycentric density models to assess the performance of sub-centers in the two cities as an evaluation of the implemented polycentric spatial strategy.

1 Introduction

Megacities in the world have developed rapidly in recent decades with the expanding capacity of urban infrastructures, the conglomeration of opportunities, and the advancement of information and communication technologies. They have become the most important pulling magnet for population, economy, and culture, playing a crucial role in the development of human society. On the other hand, with the progressive increasing returns to scale, the external diseconomies of megacities cannot not be overlooked. Traffic congestion, declining environmental quality, and public security issues have plagued many megacities. For cities in China, these issues are even more prominent. Over the past few decades, China has undergone an extremely rapid process of urbanization. The populations of urbanized and urbanizing areas have agglomerated at an incredible rate, which has spawned a number of megacities. In the context of drastic urban agglomeration, urban policies are lagged to accommodate changing spatial structures of megacities. Consequently, massive populations are concentrated in a few sub-areas of cities, especially in central business districts (CBDs), causing a series of urban problems. Around a half decade ago, many cities in China began to implement the polycentric spatial strategy to distribute developments to planned secondary centers and promote more sustainable growth led by megacities such as Beijing, Shanghai, Guangzhou, and Shenzhen. After years of implementation, it is time to evaluate the effectiveness of these polycentric strategies in order to provide a reliable basis for the formulation of follow-up urban development policies.

In this research, we view (sub-)centers (central places) within a city as a complex concept that encompasses a compound of linking elements that can be reflected by measured indicators. They are commonly conceived as bounded areas, such as CBDs, having strong vitality, diversified functions in terms of land uses, and concentration of employment (Jacobs 1961; Alexander 1964), even though their boundaries are usually fuzzy. Areas purely focusing on certain specific functions such as "sleeping city", "corporate city", or city village area are not within the scope of (sub-)centers. Along this line, the centrality of places can be characterized by three major aspects: (1) the intensity of human activity or the use of space, (2) employment concentration, and (3) the diversity of human activity or land uses. From the perspective of activity intensity, according to the theories of urban economics (Alonso 1964), the closer to the city center, the higher the cost of space is; the smaller the per-capita floor area is, the more intensive the use of space is. From the perspective of employment concentration, areas with agglomerated employment opportunities are mainly areas with economic vitality, which are the city (sub-)centers. From the perspective of activity diversity, central places are areas characterized by diversified functions with a high degree of mixed types of land uses serving various human activities.

As big data flourishes with new technologies to generate and process data (e.g. location-aware mobile devices, social media, and cloud computing), digital information is ubiquitously embedded in our daily life, which produces the inextricable interweaving of online and offline human activities in the virtual and physical worlds. It presents new opportunities via novel data sources by sensor networks, user-shared content, and volunteered geographic information to study the interaction of human activities and the physical world under phenomena of interest (e.g. pedestrian and vehicular navigation, disease diffusion, and disaster evacuation). Undoubtedly, the study of centrality can be supported by big data sources that are able to capture the three major aspects above characterizing the centrality of places, such as mobile device positioning for the locations of users who carry out activities or digital map searches for locations of interests (e.g., restaurants). However, few studies have utilized these sources for the measurement of centrality in the literature.

There have been different methodological approaches to the measurement of the centrality of places within a city. Many existing studies only put emphasis on one of a set of centrality indicators such as population density, diversity, employment distribution, or commercial density. Only a few studies made an effort of combining these factors to depict the polycentric structure of cities in more comprehensive and accurate ways (Thurstain-Goodwin and Unwin 2000). For example, Zhong et al. (2017) proposed a composite centrality index combining the density and diversity of human activity through a convolution method. However, its diversity-based measure is lacking the account of both the demand and supply sides for functional activities, and the convolution method is wrongly applied for the construction of a composite index with a mis-specified formulation.

This study, as a response to the identified gaps above, aims at (1) utilizing novel big data sources provided by Baidu Map to the study of centrality, (2) proposing an improved approach to the construction of a composite measure that overcomes the defects of the diversity-based measure and accounts for local spatial associations in indicators, and (3) evaluating the effectiveness of the implemented polycentric spatial strategy for two megacities (Beijing and Shanghai) in China based on our proposed measure of centrality.

The rest of this chapter is outlined as follows. We first review the background and the latest progress of the research. Then the research methodology is described before we introduce the study areas and big data sources and characteristics. After that, we present our results with discussions and suggestions. Finally, conclusions are drawn based on our findings.

2 Related work

Polycentric cities have always been the hot spot of academic research (Kloosterman and Lambregts 2001; Meijers 2008; Burger et al. 2014). A large number of studies mainly focus on the measurement of the polycentricity of cities. They can be divided into three directions: (1) measurement based on spatial form; (2) measurement of functional connection; and (3) measurement based on compound dimensions. Based on the measurement of the polycentricity, some studies further review and examine the urban spatial development strategy.

The measurement based on the spatial form mainly recognizes the polycentricity of cities from the spatial distribution of population, economy, employment, and culture in the city. McDonald (1987) viewed a city's sub-centers as local peaks in the distribution of the urban spatial density. Then (McDonald and Prather 1994) he proposed to identify sub-centers of a city by establishing a functional relationship between the density and the spatial distance. The spatial density can include a single indicator or multiple indicators. Thurstain-Goodwin et al. (2000) superimposed indicators of the retail outlet density and the spatial diversity to identify the center of the city. Some nonparametric methods, including smoothing density functions, are also used to reveal the spatial structure of cities (McMillen 2001). Taking Sydney as a case study, Pfister et al. (2000) measured the development level of the city centers through detailed data analyses. They found that there were two parallel processes in cities: on one hand, many areas were constantly spreading, and their centrality is reduced. On the other hand, some areas have also achieved "re-centralization". Based on the data of the three censuses in Beijing, Feng et al. (2009) conducted a study on the evolution of the spatial structure in Beijing by taking the population density distribution as a measure. According to the conclusions, Beijing's spatial structure is experiencing the evolution of "single center", "dual center", and "multiple center". Zhong et al. (2017) comprehensively considered the urban population density and functional diversity of Singapore. Zhong integrated them into the "centrality indicator" by using the convolution method and then examined the spatial evolution of this indicator over time.

The measurement method based on functional connections believed that the relationship between functions and activities of different centers should be considered and the polycentricity should be investigated systematically. Green et al. (2007) analyzed the economic and social connections among centers in Cornwall with the help of the commuter survey data and mail sending and receiving data. By comparing polycentricities of different centers, Green finally evaluated the performance of the urban development strategies. Shearmur et al. (2007) studied the relationship between the distribution of employment centers and the development and decline of urban areas in several megacities in Canada over time. Taylor et al. (2008) proposed a method called "Interlocking Network Model", which evaluates the centrality of cities and regions in local-area networks based on the business relationships among firms. Using the fine-grained commuter survey data, Vasanen (2012) examines the strength of the connections between cities and the overall urban network in Finland to measure the centrality. Hanssens et al. (2014) proposed that a network system can be constructed by using transactional relations among producers to examine the centrality of nodes in the central region of Belgium, which ultimately proved that the region was in the initial stage of network development. The connections between cities and regional centers are often diverse. In recent years, some studies have tried to interpret the centrality from the perspective of diversity. Burger et al. (2014) constructed the connection network of city centers in many aspects, such as commuting, shopping, and company business, and examined the centrality from different perspectives. Their research showed that with different measurement indicators, the centrality of cities may be different.

In recent years, some researchers have attempted to relate the measure based on the spatial form with the measure based on functions. For example, with Netherlands as the research object, Burger and Meijers (2012) measured and compared the centrality of each city according to the form and function. This study showed that the morphological centrality tended to be stronger than the functional centrality.

In sum, there are two clear trends of researches: one is that it changes from the measurement based on the single indicator to the measurement integrating multiple indicators; the other is that the research is started from the perspective of the overall urban development pattern. At the same time, there are some weaknesses in the existing researches. Firstly, the measurement of the centrality by using single indicators (such as employment, diversity) is still the mainstream; secondly, many studies use traditional census and statistical data. They may be inadequate in terms of the sample size, coverage, and timeliness, restricting the space-time precision of the centrality research in megacities; thirdly, a large amount of work is concentrated on the identification of polycentric structures. However, it is not enough to evaluate the effect of urban polycentric spatial development strategies and put forward substantive planning suggestions.

3 Methodology

3.1 A composite index for the measurement of centrality

3.1.1 Density-based versus diversity-based measures for centrality

A density-based measure is commonly defined as the concentration of a certain spatial phenomenon $Den_{x,y}$ indicating the centrality for a given location or spatial unit (x, y):

$$Den_{x,y} = \frac{n_{x,y}}{A \sum_B n_{x,y}} \tag{1}$$

where $n_{x,y}$ is a quantification of the phenomenon (e.g. population, people's visits, employment) occurred at a location, A is the area of location (x,y), and $\sum_B n_{x,y}$ is the aggregation of quantified phenomena across all locations B.

The functional diversity is commonly measured by an entropy-based quantification that reflects the degree to which various human activity types are mixed (Zhong et al. 2017). Specifically, it is defined as follows for a location (x, y):

$$Div_{x,y} = \frac{-\sum_{i=1}^{N}(I_i \log I_i)}{A \log N} \tag{2}$$

where I_i is the importance of activity i, A is the area of location (x, y), and N is the number of the activity types serviced at location (x, y). Particularly, when $N = 1$, $E_i = 0$.

The importance of an activity type I_i at a location (x, y) is traditionally calculated as the relative activity frequency AF_i (Equation 3) indicating the proportion of activities demanding a particular activity type i at location (x, y). AF_i, as approximate of I_i, only emphasizes the relative importance of an activity from a service demand side, while the consideration of supply side is missing here.

$$AF_i = \frac{f_i}{\sum_N f_i} \tag{3}$$

where f_i is the amount of activities demanding a particular activity type i at location (x, y) where N activity types are served.

To consider the service supply side, we are inspired by the concept of TF-IDF statistic widely applied in the information retrieval domain. TF-IDF statistic is to indicate the importance of a word to a document in a corpus by weighting the word frequency in the document by the word specificity in general, which refers to the fact that some words, e.g. *the*, appear more frequently than others but are not specifically meaningful to a document. In line with central place theory, we recognize the fact that functional services provided in central places are not only more diverse but also at higher levels within a hierarchical structure in the sense that high-level services such as financial services are only provided at fewer central places, while low-level services such as retail stores are more widely available at all hierarchy of places. We thus develop a measure to reflect the scarcity of a higher level function serving a particular type of activity at location (x, y). This inverse location frequency measure ILF_i (Equation 4) is defined as an inverse function of the number of locations where a function is supplied to serve activity type i.

$$ILF_i = \log \frac{|B|}{\left|\{(x,y) \in B : i \in (x,y)\}\right|} \tag{4}$$

where the nominator is the total number of all locations B in the city and the denominator is the number of locations that supplies a particular function to serve activity type i.

Then we can define I_i, the importance of activity type i, based on the relative activity frequency AF_i weighted by the inverse location frequency ILF_i of this activity to incorporate both demand and supply sides for a location (x, y) serving various activities:

$$I_i = Norm\left(AF_i * ILF_i\right) \tag{5}$$

where $Norm()$ is the normalization function to ensure the value of I_i is within the range of $[0,1]$. To this end, for activity type i at location (x, y), the more it is demanded and the less it is supplied, the higher importance it has.

3.1.2 A composite index of centrality

In this study, we propose a composite index of centrality that combines both density- and diversity-based measures and take into account the spatial association in the driving indicators of centrality of a location. We construct this composite index by employing the local G statistic, which measures the degree of local spatial association resulting from the concentration of certain spatial phenomenon with nonstationary process (Getis and Ord 1992). In other words, the local G statistic is able to detect the local pockets of hot spots, which can serve as an indication of central places.

The original local G statistic is developed for a univariate version, which cannot be applied directly to the multivariate situation here. We thus extend the original local G statistic $G^*_{x,y}$ for a location (x, y) to incorporate multiple indicators by taking the product of all variables (Equation 6). The resulting $G^*_{x,y}$ is served as the constructed composite index of centrality $C(x,y)$.

$$C(x,y) = G^*_{x,y} = \frac{\sum_B w_{x,y} V_{x,y}}{\sum_B V_{x,y}}, V_{x,y} = \prod_S v_{x,y} \tag{6}$$

where $v_{x,y}$ is the value at location (x, y) for one of the indicators that constitute a set S that is used to construct the composite index and can include various indicators taking either density- or diversity-based measures. To eliminate the effect of value ranges for different indicators, $v_{x,y}$ is rescaled to the range of [0, 1] before taking the product. $W_{x,y}$ is a distance-based weight matrix that defines the extent of spatial association according to a neighborhood concept. For example, $w_{x,y}$ could identify only adjacent locations as associated with (x, y) via a binary (1 vs. 0) linkage, or it could also specify distance-decay effects on spatial association through numeric weighting schemes. As a result, the centrality of a location is not only affected by its own density- and diversity-based measures but is also closely related to those measures for the surrounding locations.

3.2 Evaluating polycentric spatial strategy

In planning practices, the polycentric spatial strategy for a city usually defines the main center and the sub-centers within a city. The main center, usually CBD, is conceived as an economic powerhouse having a dominant influence on the other places of the city. Playing a secondary and facilitating role, sub-centers take on a share of all high-level functions concentrated in the main center with some specialized attractiveness to pull local developments over the surrounding areas. More importantly, they serve a purpose to relieve the high pressure on the main center in terms of the capacity to supply and the diseconomies due to over-concentration, and further to achieve more distributed and sustainable urban growth. The latter is a main objective of the polycentric spatial strategy. In this section, based on the improved measurement of centrality of places proposed in section 3.1, we then focus on assessing the performance of identified sub-centers by accounting for the effects of the main center in order to evaluate the effectiveness of the implemented polycentric spatial strategy.

In order to assess the performance of sub-centers, we examine their influences on the centrality of their surrounding and remote places. We assume that two basic types of effects are in play. First, the distance decay effect. That is, the influences of (sub-)centers decline with the distance to a place. Second, the accumulative effect. That is, the centrality of a place is influenced by both the main center and the closest sub-center from this place (we assume that the influences of other sub-centers are negligible). This produces an accumulative effect, which is a natural product resulting from the divisions of different levels of functions facilities supplied respectively in the main center and the sub-centers. In general, the main center supplies a range of high-level service functions, while sub-centers only facilitate a few specialized high-level functions and provide services at a lower level. From a perspective of urban economics, the effect of the distance to a (sub-)center reflects the travel cost or accessibility to the (sub-)center, and a place enjoys functional offerings at different levels from both the main center and the nearest sub-center discounted by their accessibilities respectively. Along this line, we use a polycentric density model to describe these features:

$$C(x,y) = ae^{-b_1 r_1} e^{-b_2 r_2} \tag{7}$$

Take logarithms on both sides and get:

$$logC(x,y) = loga - b_1 r_1 - b_2 r_2 \tag{8}$$

where $C(x, y)$ is the centrality at location (x, y), r_1 is the distance from the location to the main center, and r_2 is the distance from the location to the nearest sub-center, a, b_1, b_2 are model parameters.

Since r_1 and r_2 are distance measures in the same unit, their coefficients b_1 and b_2 can be used for a comparison of how different the influences of the main center and the sub-center are. Based on the comparison, three scenarios can be identified as follows. First, when b_1 is far greater than b_2, areas around the sub-center are mainly affected by the main center, which means that the sub-center is underdeveloped. Second, when b_1 and b_2 are similar, it means that the sub-center is well developed, effectively facilitating and jointly providing functions with the main center. Third, when b_1 is far less than b_2, the sub-center dominates the influences, with a restricting influence exerted by the main center.

4 Study areas and data

In this research, our study areas include the two cities of Beijing and Shanghai for a comparison purpose. The area in Beijing covers its entire administrative jurisdiction, excluding four counties including Yanqing, Miyun, Huairou, and Pinggu. The area in Shanghai covers the main part of the city, excluding Chongming Island. Since the excluded suburban counties are remote and disconnected from the corresponding city centers, their developments are rather independent and receive little influence from the city centers. Therefore, the exclusion of these areas does not have a significant impact on the results of this study. For convenience, we apply a gridding scheme to each study area with a uniform spatial unit of 1 km × 1 km for analysis. In total, there are 9,500 units in Beijing and 5,855 units in Shanghai. Thus, a location in our study is defined by one spatial unit here.

One of the highlights in this research is utilizing the individual-level big data sources for the measurement of centrality. Our data are from the data products of Baidu Map, one of the largest big data venders providing spatial data, mapping, and analytics services in China. In 2017, Baidu Map's geolocation data covers

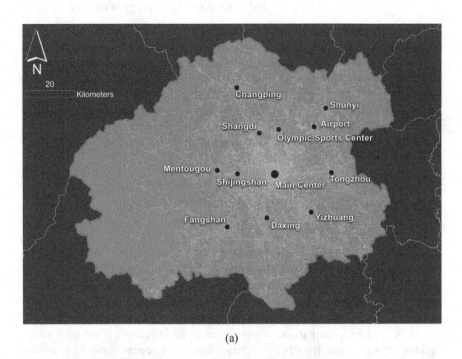

(a)

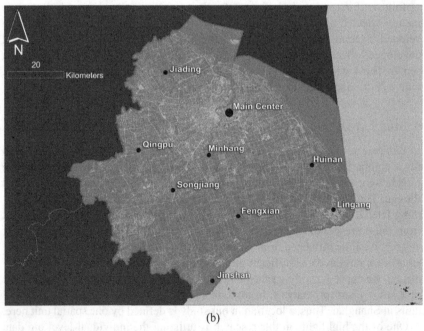

(b)

Figure 8.1 Study areas and the locations of the existing main center and the planned sub-centers
Note: (a) Beijing; (b) Shanghai.

0.6 billion mobile devices with averagely 80 billion times of positioning requests. Its Point of Interest (POI) dataset contains nationally 48 million point locations, which users may find useful or interesting for certain types of activities and usually reflect features such as land uses, building types, or businesses at those locations. Specifically, we have used three types of datasets as follows.

(1) Activity intensity data

This data is averaged daily activity intensity that covers 24 hours on a weekday. It indicates the daily spatial distribution of individuals with their mobile devices' geolocation capability enabled when they conduct certain activities at a place, which can also reflect the intensity of use of space. Given this data, we can derive the amount of activities for each location in the study areas. The sample covers Beijing and Shanghai.

(2) Employment data

The estimated number of employment at each location is provided by Baidu Map, which is obtained by mining the daily commuting patterns between the work and residential places identified based on information from the temporal dimension over a long period. Although it is estimated data for employment and may underrepresent the entire population, it will also be very useful to indicating the centrality of places.

(3) POI popularity data

This data contains two components to represent the supply of and the demand for POIs, respectively. The supply side is represented by the spatial distribution of POIs falling into 13 main categories. Thus, we can obtain the number of locations that supply each category of POIs that serve certain types of activities for Equation 4. The demand side is represented by the number of searches for each POI at different locations. Thus, the aggregated number of daily searches for each type of POIs at a location can be derived and used as the input for f_i in Equation 3. The POI popularity data for Beijing and Shanghai mainly covers the core areas.

To measure centrality, datasets (1) and (2) are used as two density-based measures, and dataset (3) is used as a diversity-based measure. Then $V_{x,y}$ is the product of these three measures according to Equation 6. Further, given our gridding configuration, we apply a contiguity-based spatial weighting specification with 3×3 queen criterion to account for the spatial association within an area of 3×3 km^2 based on an empirical judgement. Technically, it mimics a moving window-smoothing process, which filters out the local sporadic and small-scale "surges" and makes larger scale phenomena more prominent. Other weighting schemes will be further explored in future work.

5 Results and discussions

The three indicators and the results of centrality are shown in Figures 8.2 and 8.3 for the two study areas, respectively. They show that Beijing and Shanghai

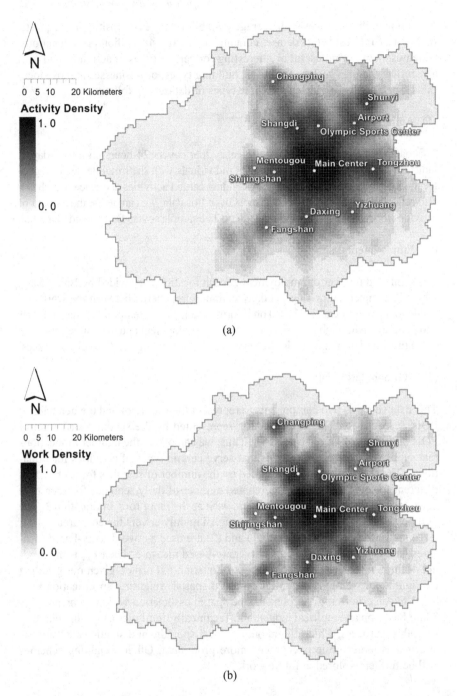

Figure 8.2 Indicators and centrality for Beijing: (a) distribution of activity intensity; (b) employment concentration; (c) activity diversity; (d) centrality

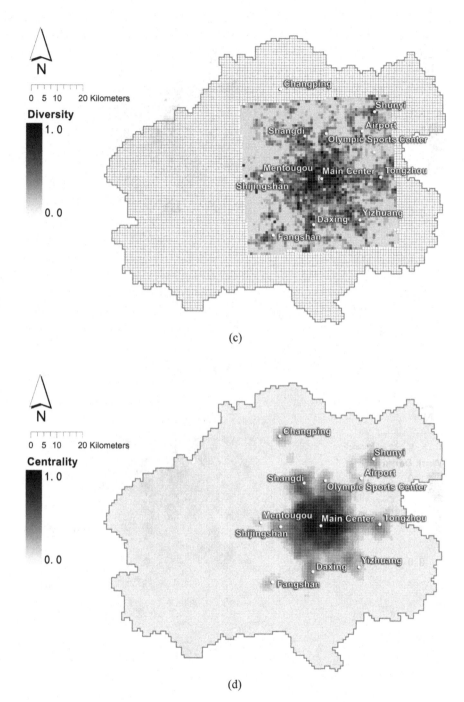

Figure 8.2 (Continued)

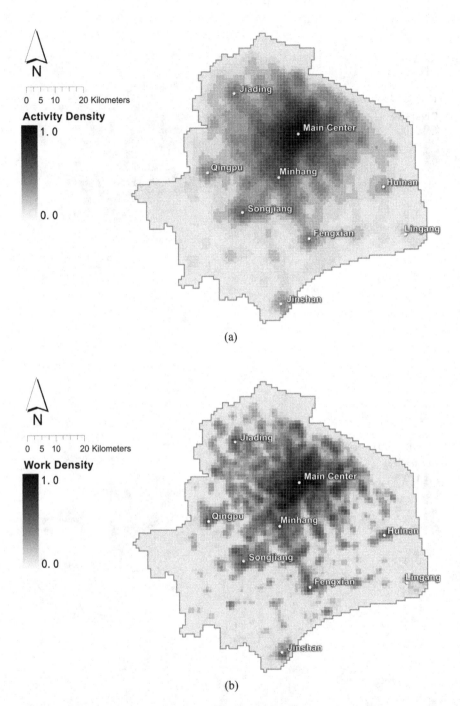

Figure 8.3 Indicators and centrality for Shanghai: (a) distribution of activity intensity; (b) employment concentration; (c) activity diversity; (d) centrality

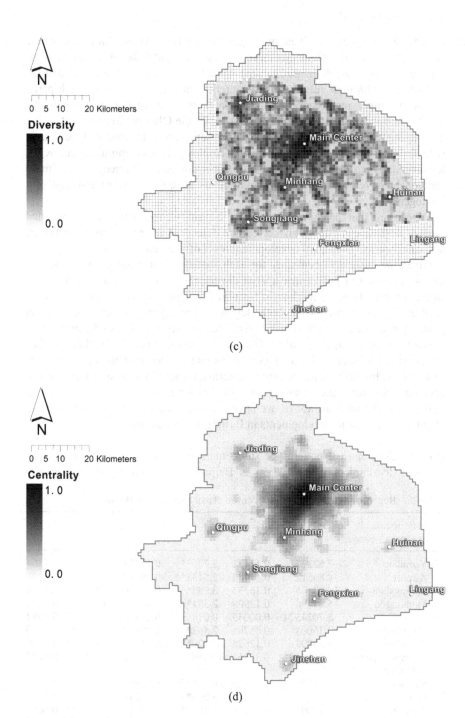

Figure 8.3 (Continued)

have formed polycentric development patterns with the existing influences of the main center. They also show that three indicators exhibit different spatial patterns for the two study areas. In Beijing, the spatial distribution of activity density is a star shape with high values for sub-centers on the north, east, and south parts. As for the employment concentration and activity diversity, relatively lower values are found for Shunyi, airports on the north, the Olympic Sports Center, and the Daxing on the south comparing to other sub-centers. In Shanghai, compared with the distribution of activity density, employment concentration and activity diversity both exhibit more compact cores due to the influence of the main center. The developments of surrounding areas are quite scattered and relatively homogeneous.

We can find that the composite index of centrality constructed by our extended local *G* statistic can effectively correct the defects of single indicators and more accurately reflect the actual development level of sub-centers.

Given the calculated centrality for each spatial unit in Beijing and Shanghai, the performance of polycentric spatial development strategy is assessed for the two cities based on the method in Section 3.2. One polycentric density model is fitted for each sub-center in both Beijing and Shanghai. The estimated model parameters and the main diagnostic results are presented in Tables 8.1 and 8.2.

Based on the comparison of coefficients b_1 and b_2, we apply the three scenarios discussed in Section 3.2 to classify sub-centers in terms of their performance (Table 8.3). In addition to the three scenarios, a fourth scenario is identified to accommodate sub-centers that are yet to be developed.

Based on the analysis above, we have the following common understandings about the polycentric developments in Beijing and Shanghai:

(1) The development patterns of sub-centers in these two cities are distinct. The distribution of sub-centers in Beijing can be roughly described as a

Table 8.1 Regression results of the polycentric density models for Beijing

Id Subordinate center/sub-center	a	b_1	t_1	b_2	t_2	R_2
Yizhuang	7.62227	0.14121	2.770**	0.17624	2.427*	0.4464
Airport	9.86512	0.21784	5.513***	0.29717	4.977***	0.5207
Shijingshan	10.50476	0.36733	3.982***	0.38426	2.892**	0.4202
Mentougou	5.64196	0.12909	2.391*	−0.01609	−0.262	0.4644
Shunyi	5.7024374	0.00045	0.014	0.21306	5.594***	0.4982
Changping	7.36008	0.08705	2.362*	0.30119	7.224***	0.5536
Fangshan	3.30297	−0.12628	−3.120**	0.23267	4.991***	0.3296
Olympic Sports Center	9.365660	0.33864	10.489***	0.00833	0.158	0.8432
Shangdi	9.54750	0.24026	6.819***	0.25656	4.530***	0.7635
Daxing	8.20529	0.17658	3.264**	0.17234	2.469*	0.7542
Tongzhou	8.13094	0.12781	4.100***	0.15310	3.618***	0.6691

Note: "***" indicates that it is significant at 0.001, "**" indicates that it is significant at 0.01, "*" indicates that it is significant at 0.05, "." Indicates that it is significant at 0.1 level.

Table 8.2 Regression results of the polycentric density models for Shanghai

Serial No.	Subordinate center/sub-center	a	b_1	t_1	b_2	t_2	R_2
	Qingpu	8.72174	0.22591	6.316***	−0.01406	−0.233	0.4158
	Lingang	8.78135	0.17784	1.940	0.20224	2.086*	0.05578
	Minhang	8.83424	0.19853	8.248***	0.10791	3.963***	0.6836
	Fengxian	8.6992	0.1966	6.781***	0.1783	4.014***	0.4063
	Jiading	12.82642	0.32042	5.819***	0.66366	11.670***	0.6185
	Huinan	16.35494	0.54111	7.657***	0.61381	8.116***	0.4479
	Jinshan	10.08088	0.21104	4.365***	0.19752	4.454***	0.3302
	Songjiang	7.07266	0.07837	2.126*	0.15111	2.758**	0.457

Note: "***" indicates that it is significant at 0.001, "**" indicates that it is significant at 0.01, "*" indicates that it is significant at 0.05, "." Indicates that it is significant at 0.1 level.

Table 8.3 Classification table of sub-centers in Beijing and Shanghai

Type	Definition	Statistical feature	Sub-center
Driven by the main center	Areas around the sub-center are mainly affected by the main center.	Significant and $b_1 > b_2$	Beijing: Tongzhou, Olympic Sports Center Shanghai: Qingpu, Minhang
Balance-driven	Areas around the sub-center are equally affected by the main center and the sub-center.	Significant and $b_1 \approx b_2$	Beijing: Shijingshan, Yizhuang, Airports, Shangdi, Daxing Shanghai: Fengxian, Huinan, Jinshan
Driven by the sub-center	Areas around the sub-center are mainly affected by this center.	Significant and $b_1 < b_2$	Beijing: Shunyi, Changping, Fangshan Shanghai: Jiading, Songjiang
Initial development	The sub-center has not yet formed, and it is located in remote areas. The main center and the sub-center have small influences on the surrounding areas.	Not significant	Beijing: Mentougou Shanghai: Lingang

"concentric-ring pattern", which means sub-centers close to the main center are more influenced. In contrast, the distribution of sub-centers in Shanghai is a "partition pattern", with different types of sub-centers mainly located on the different directions from the main center. Different patterns may indicate different development processes: the structure of Shanghai is more like a "network" in which the development of every sub-center is based on its own feature, while that of Beijing is more in line with the characteristics of a "sprawled city", where the distance of sub-centers to the main center matters

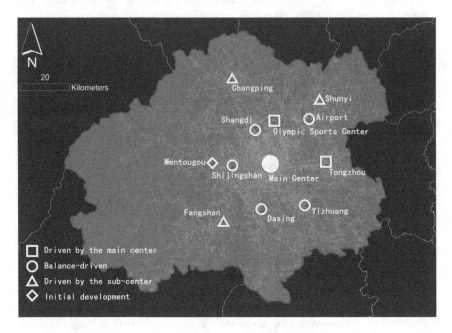

Figure 8.4 Distribution of four types of sub-centers in Beijing

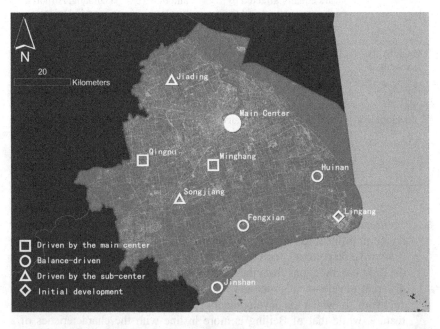

Figure 8.5 Distribution of four types of sub-centers in Shanghai

a lot. Therefore, these patterns suggest that Beijing acts more as a monocentric city, while Shanghai acts more as a polycentric city.

(2) The polycentric strategies implemented by both cities have made some achievements. Most sub-centers have enjoyed a good momentum of development, supporting the purpose to relieve the pressure on the main center in terms of the capacity to supply and the diseconomies due to over-concentration.

(3) There is room for the more balanced and sustainable development of sub-centers in both cities. In particular, sub-centers like Mentougou in Beijing and Lingang in Shanghai need to be further strengthened.

(4) Judging from the status quo, the effectiveness of the polycentric development strategy in Beijing is more obvious. Most sub-centers have had considerable influences. The polycentric development in Shanghai has more potentials, and there is sufficient space for development.

On the other hand, we make the following suggestions on the future urban development:

(1) For a long time, Tongzhou was planned to be the most important sub-center, which will greatly alleviate the pressure of the main center. But from the result of our analysis, the units around Tongzhou sub-center are still mainly influenced by the main center, which implies that the functions of Tongzhou still need to be reinforced. Meanwhile, as there has been an integrated development trend between Tongzhou and the main city, in order to protect the future good urban living environment and efficiency, the development mode must be altered. That means the scale of development should be controlled appropriately, and the special functions should be highlighted and planned to ease the urban functions in a larger region.

(2) Due to the spatial distance and effect of hot spots such as Hongqiao and Xinzhuang, the development level of new towns in Shanghai suburbs is relatively lower than that of Beijing. However, the buffer zone and open space between the main center and the sub-center in Shanghai are relatively adequate, which proves that the concept of "urban circles" proposed by the new general planning of Shanghai is correct. In the future, the cultivation of the "second circle" such as Qingpu and Minhang should be strengthened to avoid the "subsidence areas" for development.

6 Conclusions and further work

In this research, we have employed novel big data sources in the study of centrality of places within cities and demonstrated their utility with examples of two megacities. In addition, we have proposed an improved approach to the construction of a composite measure that overcomes the defects of the diversity-based measure and accounts for local spatial associations in indicators of centrality. We further apply this measure to the study of centrality of places in Beijing and Shanghai and assess the performance of identified sub-centers by accounting for the effects of the main center in order to evaluate the effectiveness of the implemented polycentric spatial strategy. The result shows that the polycentric strategy works better in Beijing for now. But the city needs to adjust its policy and reallocate its functions in a larger region, considering the trend of land use connection between the main center and some sub-centers. On the other hand, the potential of sub-centers in Shanghai are higher, although the development degree is comparatively lower. The results and methodology of this study can be useful for the future planning and development in Beijing and Shanghai, as well as for other cities facing similar problems. In future research, we may consider other types of measure of centrality such as those based on network structures. We may also refine our polycentric density model to account for the attractiveness of (sub-)centers.

References

Alexander, C. (1964 [1965]). A city is not a tree. *Architectural Forum* **122**(1): 58–62.

Alonso, W. (1964). *Location and land use: Toward a general theory of land rent*. Cambridge: Harvard University Press.

Burger, M. and E. Meijers (2012). "Form follows function? Linking morphological and functional polycentricity." *Urban studies* **49**(5): 1127–1149.

Burger, M. J., B. Van Der Knaap and R. S. Wall (2014). "Polycentricity and the multiplexity of urban networks." *European Planning Studies* **22**(4): 816–840.

Feng, J., F. Wang and Y. Zhou (2009). "The spatial restructuring of population in metropolitan Beijing: Toward polycentricity in the post-reform era." *Urban Geography* **30**(7): 779–802.

Getis, A., & Ord, J. K. (1992). The analysis of spatial association by use of distance statistics. In *Perspectives on spatial data analysis* (pp. 127–145). Berlin, Heidelberg: Springer.

Green, N. (2007). "Functional polycentricity: A formal definition in terms of social network analysis." *Urban Studies* **44**(11): 2077–2103.

Hanssens, H., B. Derudder, S. Van Aelst and F. Witlox (2014). "Assessing the functional polycentricity of the mega-city-region of Central Belgium based on advanced producer service transaction links." *Regional Studies* **48**(12): 1939–1953.

Jacobs, J., 1961. *The death and life of great American cities*. New York: Random House.

Kloosterman, R. C. and B. Lambregts (2001). "Clustering of economic activities in polycentric urban regions: The case of the Randstad." *Urban studies* **38**(4): 717–732.

McDonald, J. F. (1987). "The identification of urban employment subcenters." *Journal of Urban Economics* **21**(2): 242–258.

McDonald, J. F. and P. J. Prather (1994). "Suburban employment centres: The case of Chicago." *Urban studies* **31**(2): 201–218.

McMillen, D. P. (2001). "Nonparametric employment subcenter identification." *Journal of Urban economics* **50**(3): 448–473.

Meijers, E. (2008). "Measuring polycentricity and its promises." *European Planning Studies* **16**(9): 1313–1323.

Pfister, N., R. Freestone and P. Murphy (2000). "Polycentricity or dispersion?: Changes in center employment in metropolitan Sydney, 1981 to 1996." *Urban Geography* **21**(5): 428–442.

Shearmur, R., W. Coffey, C. Dube and R. Barbonne (2007). "Intrametropolitan employment structure: Polycentricity, scatteration, dispersal and chaos in Toronto, Montreal and Vancouver, 1996–2001." *Urban Studies* **44**(9): 1713–1738.

Taylor, P. J., D. M. Evans and K. Pain (2008). "Application of the interlocking network model to mega-city-regions: Measuring polycentricity within and beyond city-regions." *Regional Studies* **42**(8): 1079–1093.

Thurstain-Goodwin, M. and D. Unwin (2000). "Defining and delineating the central areas of towns for statistical monitoring using continuous surface representations." *Transactions in GIS* **4**(4): 305–317.

Vasanen, A. (2012). "Functional polycentricity: Examining metropolitan spatial structure through the connectivity of urban sub-centres." *Urban studies* **49**(16): 3627–3644.

Zhong, C., M. Schläpfer, S. Müller Arisona, M. Batty, C. Ratti and G. Schmitt (2017). "Revealing centrality in the spatial structure of cities from human activity patterns." *Urban Studies* **54**(2): 437–455.

9 Multi-criteria locational analysis for retail development in small towns

ChengHe Guan and Peter G. Rowe

1 Introduction

The study of location analysis with regard to urbanization has a long and extensive history (Current, Min, & Schilling, 1990). In the realm of economic geography, there are at least three periods. Beginning in the first part of the 19th century, the German school of von Thunen, Christaller, and Losch was followed in the middle of the 20th century by American spatial applications and most recently by the new economic geography of location by the likes of Paul Krugman (Brandeau & Chiu, 1989; Barnes, 2003; Wey, 2015). In the philosophy of science literature, there are two divergent approaches to locational analysis. One argues that geographical and historical contexts have no bearing. As Peter Haggett stated, the term *locational analysis* refers to the logically and mathematically rigorous investigation of the spatial arrangement of phenomena and related flow patterns (Chorley & Haggett, 1965). The idea is that there is a deep-seated universal principle that guides theoretical development (Barnes, 2001). Such an interpretation is also known as 'internalism', as opposed to the position of 'externalism', the belief that knowledge is intimately associated to the local context in which it develops (Shapin, 1998). Indeed, internalism, or the affiliated rational position, has been criticized consistently on the ground that formal logic itself is an entirely local character (Barnes & Bloor, 1982; O'Sullivan & Manson, 2015). These arguments have a common reliance on the definition of locality as stagnant with clear boundaries. However, the evolving knowledge on rapid urbanization has demonstrated that locality is not only fluctuating but also has blurry margins. We argue that the fluid nature of locality creates an extended circle in which local knowledge shares certain commonalities and follows similar regulations. Also, rational models produce analogous outcomes using comparable parameters. In this sense, the encompassing of locational analysis refers to the geographical domain to which knowledge applies, not the conditions in which knowledge is produced. In other words, we use locational analysis as a decision-making procedure aimed at identifying the most suitable location without a pre-established extent, site searching for a specific purpose, or within an agreed area of site selection. We examine quantitative aspects of 20 small pilot towns using locational analysis for both site searching and site selection of the most appropriate retail locations.

2 Retail locational considerations

Prior to embarking on a retail development project, it is usual to conduct a retail market study to determine the feasibility and cost benefits of the potential enterprise. Literature on the topic of retail market analysis is well developed and with broad agreement on the general framework in which study can be undertaken (Kahr & Thomsett, 2005; Brett & Schmitz, 2009; Peiser & Hamilton, 2012). Such a framework is based on analysis of the trade area of the potential project, including factors such as demographics and daytime population measures, time or cost-distance accessibility analyses, barriers, psychographics, competition, and site selection techniques. What follows is an overview of the factors to be considered in such a study (SURBA, 2015).

2.1 Trade area demographics and daytime population measures

The core demographic data of the trade area population, including measures of density, population size, number of households, average household size, age structure, gender composition, per-capita income, household income, educational attainment, ethnic composition, and occupational classification can determine the scale and type of retail to be developed in an area of interest. Specifically, the purchasing power of the trade area can be derived by multiplying the per-capita income and population numbers (Peiser & Hamilton, 2012; Kahr & Thomsett, 2005). Some scholars and practitioners have also argued that residential population size, however, should not necessarily be the sole measure of a community's consumer base and retail potential (Brett & Schmitz, 2009; Kahr & Thomsett, 2005). Depending on the economic and civic activities of the trade area, the daytime population may increase substantially due to the flows of the workforce population, for instance, and can be a predictor of retail attraction and expansion opportunities. Accounting for daytime population increases is significant, particularly for restaurant operators. The additional daytime population can include school-going children, employees, tourist or business visitors, individuals who leave home for activities like shopping and social trips, as well as special attractors such as universities, hospitals, entertainment centers, and regional shopping centers.

2.2 Trade area time–distance accessibility

According to established scholars, the location, ideally, ought to be central for targeted markets and should enjoy easy regional access and convenient local ingress and egress to the site (Kramer, 2008; Brett & Schmitz, 2009). For commodity goods, shoppers will tend towards the largest collection of retail facilities of a given type that fit their desired price or convenience preference. Good access by road or rail will ordinarily allow for a more expansive trade area, and this can be measured through a time–distance accessibility analysis. Apart from good access, the roads must have adequate capacity to avoid congestion during periods of peak traffic. Here, good visibility will also help to improve a center's accessibility, such that shoppers can be directed clearly to the location with appropriate signage. It should be noted that while traffic flow attracts retail business, a site located near a heavily built-up highway with a series of competing distractions, including signs, is in fact less accessible (Peiser & Hamilton, 2012). A rule of thumb indicates that retail customers will travel between 1.6 km and 2.6 km (1 to 1.5 miles), or up to 8 minutes, to reach a neighborhood commercial center (Kahr & Thomsett, 2005). In addition, street network configuration that considers pedestrian mobility can also improve sales performance (Kang, 2016).

2.3 Trade area barriers

These can assume the form of physical or socio-economic and/or cultural barriers. Trade area barriers essentially impede the flow of potential customers and thus significantly influence the size and attraction of a trade area. Physical barriers can include natural and constructed impediments, whether it be rivers and mountains or infrastructure such as expressways, railroads, and large public facilities like train stations and airports. In this regard, the location should have a workable topography, good drainage, minimal complications in the subsoil, and acceptable environmental impact. The site for commercial property development should generally be regular in shape and configured as a contiguous piece, as this will lend itself best to an efficient layout. If an irregularly shaped site is the only type available, then the site should have adequate frontage for visibility. If the development concept is for a town center or street-front retailing, dedicated streets might bisect the site, and traffic through the site should not impede the flow of pedestrians or complicate the movement of cars in the parking area (Kramer, 2008). A rule of thumb for suburban retail development is to build approximately 800 square meters per hectare, and typically for a one-story building with a floor area ration (FAR) of 0.25. Where land availability is not highly constrained, as in the case of suburban areas, the ideal shopping center site should be a regular and unified shape. In urban infill projects, the FAR could reach 1.0 with 100 percent coverage and include no on-site parking requirements (Peiser & Hamilton, 2012). In terms of socio-economic and/or cultural barriers, these include variations in population and neighborhoods because of differences in income, tastes, and/or needs.

2.4 Trade area psychographics

Psychographic analysis uses a system of lifestyle clusters to represent different household lifestyles by demographic, income, and consumption characteristics. By identifying certain lifestyle cluster groups, target populations and criteria can be set, affording the researcher a useful means of screening (Peiser & Hamilton, 2012). Psychographics are especially important for mixed-use and lifestyle retailers, and recent evidence suggests that the strongest market segments for lifestyle retail centers and mixed-use projects in urban settings are young single professionals, couples without children, and older empty nesters. By analyzing and classifying the lifestyle clusters, retail developers would be able to determine the type of tenants that would be best suited for their projects, ensuring that the retail trade area for a proposed location fits the profile of the existing customer base (Kramer, 2008). In this regard, Chinese consumers are avid shoppers, enjoy socializing in malls, are conscious of global brands, and are generally aspirational buyers (Urban Land Institute, 2016).

2.5 Trade area competition, including intercepting locations

In addition, trade area barriers should also take into account 'intercept' locations along the way. Location indications will require an assessment of the relative site of a subject property and its competitor. In an analysis of competing sites, both existing and planned, location is a primary factor. Besides that, amenities, scope of retail offerings, such as types of anchor tenants, structural features, such as enclosed indoor malls versus exterior-access, and types of parking etc. also determine whether other locations are truly competitive. Important amenities include attractive restaurants, food court, cinemas, night clubs, live entertainment. Likewise, well-known and popular stores are likely to bring in a volume of shoppers. Apart from anchor tenants, specialized stores also add to the overall market share, including sports outlets, jewelry stores, discount outlets, and others like bookstores, toys, and gifts. It is important for a competitive analysis to be undertaken, as it may be possible that two seemingly similar retail areas are not actually competitive for the same markets, for example, older downtown districts versus outlying newer malls. Competition can also be defined by shopping patterns and preferences, thereby affecting the visibility, level of prestige, center size, and tenant mix (Kahr & Thomsett, 2005).

3 Study area

In this study, 20 small towns were chosen in Zhejiang Province in the eastern coast of China. Zhejiang Province has the highest GDP per capita among China's provinces and municipal cities (Statistical Bureau of China, 2015). The economic strength is not only concentrated in the large cities but distributed among small towns, especially to the northern part of the province (Zhejiang Statistical Bureau, 2014). Although this region has experienced rapid townization, the varying degrees of available urban infrastructure among the small towns are high (Long, Zou, & Liu, 2009).

In a recent government statement on urban development strategies, small pilot towns were prioritized in terms of favorable growth policies (Guan & Rowe, 2016). Among the policies providing convenience, lifestyle and better commercial services were stressed. With China's economy entering a slow growth period, the so-called new normal of commercial developments that can improve small-town dwellers' quality of life was to be emphasized (Zhang, Li, Hui, & Li, 2016; Guan & Rowe, 2016). Among the selected towns, relatively high household income and high disposable income create a strong consumer market. However, the current retail and commercial centers are falling behind. According to government-issued statistical data, the per capita retail space in small towns in Zhejiang Province is far below standard (Urban Land Institute, 2016). To respond to the imbalance between strong purchasing power and the shortage of retail, communities and life-style service space, a state-owned enterprise (SOE)-backed development strategy was to be implemented. The aim was to create a place of shopping, as well as civic activities and related life-style services referred to as an 'urban living room' (ULR). In collaboration with the Township Development Data Research Institute (TDDR), a local NGO, the data collection process included field surveys, digital information collections, and data extrapolations for existing retail businesses. The results are shown in Table 9.1. It included the current and projected population, total number of retail business and occupied business area, average retail area, and vacancy rates. The numbers reveal that the per-capita supply of retail community and life-style services was low for the towns under investigation.

4 Methodology

4.1 Locational analysis and site selection techniques

Closely bound up with locational considerations are various forms of location analysis and site selection techniques. In well-developed circumstances like North

Table 9.1 Summary of the town survey data for 20 selected towns

Town	Total No. of Retail Business	Total Retail Area (m²)	Average Retail Area (m²)	Vacancy Rate (%)	Retail Area per Person	Population (2010)	Population (2020)
1 Longgang	*4,854*	274,483	56.5	*45.0*	0.69	396,000	471,877
2 Zeguo	*1,691*	106,982	63.3	*31.3*	0.56	192,558	217,274
3 Guali	1,236	104,924	84.9	*21.8*	0.72	191,429	393,895
4 Zhili	*3,441*	181,587	53.0	5.1	0.97	186,609	178,816
5 Zhouxiang	1,371	88,805	64.8	9.2	0.6	151,778	233,612
6 Fotang	1,093	87,475	*80.0*	*10.7*	0.76	115,511	136,078
7 Chong'fu	1,315	71,261	54.2	*13.2*	0.63	112,860	259,873
8 Wangjiangjing	835	44,748	53.6	8.4	0.4	111,121	158,199
9 Chang'an	845	129,805	*153.0*	*10.6*	1.18	110,352	114,931
10 Qianqing	727	29,112	40.0	*16.8*	0.27	107,821	107,437
11 Qiandaohu	*2,029*	129,225	63.7	6.0	1.25	103,396	131,349
12 Shipu	*1,903*	151,620	*79.7*	6.8	*1.64*	92,542	105,251
13 Lianshi	876	135,469	*154.6*	*13.8*	*1.54*	87,765	89,047
14 Chumen	994	139,192	*140.0*	*23.1*	*1.64*	85,047	89,778
15 Tangqi	1,253	63,216	50.5	*13.1*	0.79	79,980	77,368
16 Simen	1,207	98,119	*81.3*	*12.8*	*1.24*	78,975	81,065
17 Xikou	1,400	92,290	65.9	*15.3*	*1.25*	73,756	105,323
18 Xindeng	1,251	79,488	63.5	3.3	1.13	70,580	71,059
19 Xinshi	915	44,377	48.4	8.6	0.65	68,646	77,828
20 Fenshui	1,188	83,591	*70.4*	9.3	*1.52*	55,049	79,371
Average	1,577	NA	*70.4*	10	1.23	NA	NA

Note: Underlines denote values at or above the average.

America and the U.S., they are routinely put to use by governmental jurisdictions for the purposes of making estimates of market values of properties, for instance, as well as determining preferable locations for public facilities (U.S. Department of Housing and Urban Development, 1992). Among private-sector users, they are deployed to help make a variety of capital investment decisions, including for commercial and related property developments germane to this study (Kim, O'Connor, & Han, 2015). In these regards, many adhere to 'highest and best use' doctrines of market analysis, which attempt to secure locations that offer the most physical, financial, legal, and productive possibilities for particular uses. Here, the general notion of 'location' is often used as a proxy for 'highest and best use' (Peiser & Hamilton, 2012). Over time, approaches and techniques have become increasingly more sophisticated from earlier hunch-driven decision making in the direction of systematic, rational, and data-driven site selection processes (Rabianski, DeLisle, & Carn, 2001). Although different in many particulars, most model a step-wise sequence from the decision to seek a site through a 'must and need' list of criteria to evaluate competitive locations, on to site selection (Meyer, 1988). In play are usually data about the size of retail outlets, ancillary requirements like parking, trade area extent, minimum trade area populations, access requirement, and demographic and income characteristics. Most, in fact, attempt to model or otherwise represent most aspects of the locational considerations.

4.2 The application of geographic information system (GIS) and spatial analysis

Geography plays an important role in the establishment of a new retail development (García-Palomares, Gutiérrez, & Latorre, 2012). The success of many future applications for retail site locational analysis may be closely linked to GIS and spatial information acquired (Church, 2002; Church & Murray, 2009; Roig-Tierno, Baviera-Puig, Buitrago-Vera, & Mas-Verdu, 2013). GIS are capable of dealing with large quantities of spatial data and can generate visualizations of data, which make them indispensable tools in the retail development decision making (Ozimec, Natter, & Reutterer, 2010; Roig-Tierno et al., 2013; Guan & Rowe, 2017). As alluded to earlier, spatial data collection used in this study included site surveys, township-level controlled detail plans, statistical yearbook searches, and digital library and satellite image processing. The data were projected to ArcGIS for retail locational analysis.

4.3 A multi-parameter process

Location of potential sites for ULR facilities generally involved a multi-step process. In this research, the process included four consecutive steps listed here in sequential order: accessibility analysis to narrow down search areas; site analysis to identify potential sites; risk analysis to recommend the relative size of facilities development; and future plan analysis to adjust and reevaluate search areas and potential sites.

The first step involved spatially identifying a reasonably narrow 'search area' based on relative time costs, or accessibility to new and planned commercial locations, employment sites, administrative centers, and major routes out of town. The underlying logic was relatively straightforward. In the absence of other guiding features, prime locations for ULRs should be accessible and even visible in relationship to routes in and out of town, close to major employment centers, like industrial complexes, and to administrative centers with sizeable workforces. They should also, when possible, be relatively contiguous with existing or planned commercial concentrations. By describing time-cost accessibility gradients in relationship to centroids of the above concentrations, deployed for automobile use with regard to the townships' roadway systems, separate graphic depictions were produced. For instance, in this study, time distances of 2.5, 5, and 10 minutes were used to differentiate such areas, based on reasonable rates or speeds of travel. Each depiction was then converted into a digitized spatial description in the form of grid points, located at 250-meter intervals, or roughly comparable to a typical megaplot in most town developments. A Boolean search was then conducted across the field of points, or grid cells, to find those with the highest combined accessibilities across all four locational parameters. Rated on a scale of 0 to 4, these areas were then re-mapped over the township's roadway network to yield a reasonably well-defined search area for a potential ULR site.

Once a 'search area' was identified within each township, a more precise potential location for a potential ULR facility was isolated with the use of seven rank-ordered criteria, as described in Table 9.2. These ranged from availability of property of appropriate size and geometry within the search area to walkable circumstances adjacent to prime residential sites. In some instances, the initial location of the search area was defined sufficiently, as at Guali. The seven further locational criteria were then used as a check or clarification of the efficacy of the location. Again, in Guali's case, property was available, the potential address of the ULR was propitious vis-à-vis visibility, and there was close proximity to a major administrative center – the new city hall. The location was also something

Table 9.2 Seven criteria for site selection within a search area

	Priority	Criteria
1	Availability of property of appropriate size and geometry	Site
2	Location along one of the visual axes and/or main non-residential streets of the township	Location
3	Close proximity or adjacency to administrative facilities with relatively large employment	Location
4	Good access to main routes in and out of the township	Location
5	Some agglomeration with other commercial, community, and lifestyle centers of activity	Competition
6	Separation, or not, from competitive outlets	Competition
7	Walkable circumstances to prime residential areas	Demographic

Note: Numbers 1 through 7 denote criteria to be given priority.

of an extension to the north of the existing commercial concentration. It was separated from any competitive outlet locations, and it was within walking distance of a new residential district of considerable scale. Of course, in making many of these judgements, there is no substitute for field reconnaissance. Also, the availability or not of potential sites is a matter of discussion with local officials. Nevertheless, exercise of the seven criteria can narrow the range of preferred sites significantly.

Also of interest, the relative size of a potential ULR facility within a particular town profile could also be made as a nominal guide for development. This took the form of the following array, plotting the relative risk associated within a town for the development of ULRs and the relative suitability of a 'search area' or 'site location' within the town. Here, for instance, a relatively unsuitable 'area' or 'site' within a very risky town would probably indicate no ULR development. By contrast, high-priority 'areas' or 'sites' within low-risk towns may warrant development of very large ULRs. The demand and supply matching model is shown in Figure 9.1.

The last step was to further study the future plans for town development. In Zhejiang Province, town master plans and detail controlled plans were produced by the local planning agencies under the supervision of the Bureau of Development and Reform. Revisions were made every five years or so in order to guide the growth and infrastructure layout. The plans were also used to attract investors, both public and private.

5 Results

The results of the accessibility exercise for Chang'an, used here as an example, yielded two prime search areas situated approximately 2 kilometers apart along the main road through the town from the two main east–west traffic arteries leading into and out of town. As shown in Figure 9.2, some sites in between and to the south near the southern east–west artery were somewhat less prime locations.

Against this locational background, the next step involved focusing in, within the identified prime search areas and, through a stepwise process of elimination, further narrowing down the spatial search for potential sites. This process was conducted according to seven criteria for site location within a search area defined earlier. In many if not most cases, this process also required on-ground field familiarity with the township and the search areas under scrutiny. At the very least, use was made of township maps developed during the course of the study to describe and record field survey information. In the case of Chang'an, the larger prime search area towards the northern end of the main road through the town was ruled out because of the lack of property potentially available. It is presently an area well occupied by existing buildings, whereas the site 2 kilometers or so south was not. It also seemed likely from the accessibility analysis that movement of future development south rather than north along the main road would likely ensue, driven by both available land and broader concentrations of relatively better accessible properties, also represented in Figure 9.2

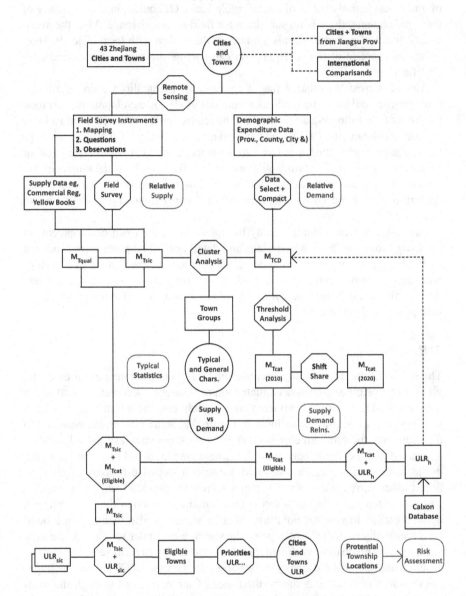

Figure 9.1 Consumer service demand and supply matching model for risk analysis

It turned out that the two competing developments mentioned earlier in Chang'an were also located adjacent to the prime search area. The one disadvantage was their location farther to the west of the main intersection between the main north–south road through the town and an east–west crossing street.

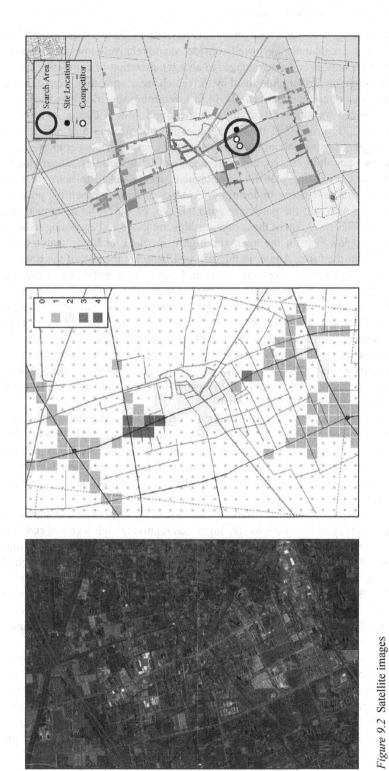

Figure 9.2 Satellite images

Note: Downloaded from Google Maps (left); accessibility analysis to identify the search area: 4 means higher access score and 0 means low (middle); site location using the multi-criteria process and competitors (right) (Chang'an, 2015).

Notwithstanding, what has already been said regarding risks associated with ULR development, except under very well-considered and relatively low-scale circumstances, there may even be advantages to an agglomeration of competing facilities. This might be further underlined by the search areas separation from existing concentrations of commercial activity. In fact, returning specifically to the seven criteria outlined for site location, the site identified now in Chang'an satisfies numbers 1, 2, 3, 4, and 7 of those criteria, while not meeting 5 or 6 regarding existing agglomerations of commercial activity or competitive outlet locations.

Then, as a penultimate step, the relative scale of ULR facilities, already incorporated into the existing plan for development, was matched to both the risks associated with developing or locating in a town and the competitive position of the search area and the particular potential site, or sites. The accompanying matrix identifies a version of these relationships, rank-ordered according to high, medium, and low risk for the town and highly, medium, or lowly search areas and/or sites in the town. Again, in the case of Chang'an, the risk of the town as a location for a ULR was very low in the early round of qualification. Based on survey data, however, particularly with regard to existing scales of commercial, community, and lifestyle service, as well as a low 'net composite score', a relatively small ULR might be recommended if any was to be deployed there at all. In other words, from the prior estimation of absorption capacity, Chang'an ranks very low, making it potentially a risky proposition. If, on the other hand, the existing still-vacant competition is viewed as relatively non-threatening, then the prior net composite score would rise above the qualifying threshold, making Chang'an a reasonable candidate for ULR location.

In some cases, a further future locational analysis was performed in the same manner but based on additional infrastructural and land use deployments. This information was obtained from master plans, or similar, for each town. For the case of Chongfu, another of the small towns, two search areas were identified; one is based on existing condition and the other based on projected master plan, as shown in Figure 9.3.

The risk analysis shows, for instance, in the case of the town of Chang'an, where closer site survey-aided data strongly suggested relatively high levels of risk and potential for a relatively small-scale ULR. This process of risk analysis was diagrammed in the manner described by the decision tree shown in Figure 9.4. Actual tabulations of the risks associated with all towns followed the form shown in Table 9.3. Branches of the nodes and links through the decision tree also implied that relatively low risk only accompanies one particular sequence. By contrast, such a level can also be associated with some less favorable though not disqualifying outcomes along the way.

Locational analysis results for the remaining townships are presented graphically in Table 9.3. There, both a 'search' area and a potential 'site location' for each is represented. In addition, modifications to each by way of new infrastructure, primarily roadway improvements and re-deployment of various land use functions, are also reflected in additional analyses for each town. Overall, among the 20 sample towns, 13 of them had well-defined 'search areas' in the

Chongfu, Tongxiang 2012-2030

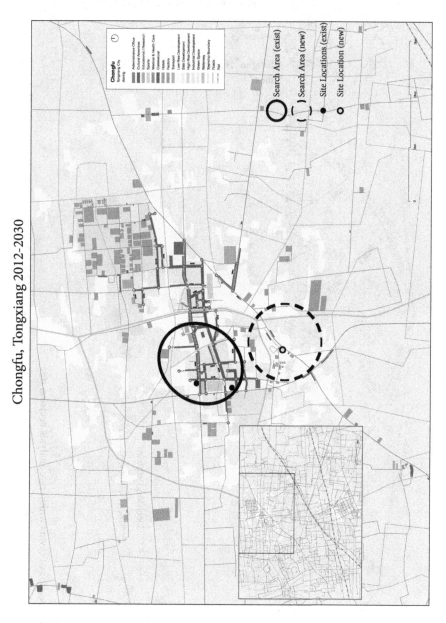

Figure 9.3 Chongfu, 2015–2030

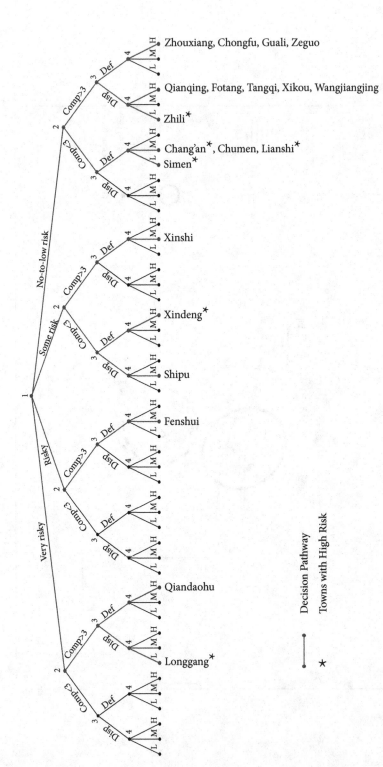

Figure 9.4 Location of towns within risk analysis decision tree

Table 9.3 Tabulation through four steps in risk analysis for 20 towns

	1. Initial Qualification	2. Composit Field	3. Search Area	4. Quality of Potential Location	
Towns	Level of Risk	Data Score	Defined or Dispersed	High, Medium, Low	
Chang'an	No-to-Low Risk	1.2	Defined	5 out of 7	Medium*
Qianqing	No-to-Low Risk	5.6	Dispersed	6 out of 7	High
Zhouxiang	No-to-Low Risk	12.3	Defined	6 out of 7	High
Chongfu	No-to-Low Risk	14.2	Defined	6 out of 7	High
Fotang	No-to-Low Risk	5.5	Dispersed	6 out of 7	High
Guali	No-to-Low Risk	21.3	Defined	6 out of 7	High
Wangjiangjing	No-to-Low Risk	4.0	Dispersed	6 out of 7	High
Simen	No-to-Low Risk	2.2	Defined	4 out of 7	Low*
Zhili	No-to-Low Risk	4.1	Dispersed	4 out of 7	Low*
Chumen	No-to-Low Risk	1.3	Defined	5 out of 7	Medium
Tangqi	No-to-Low Risk	3.1	Dispersed	7 out of 7	High
Xikou	No-to-Low Risk	3.9	Dispersed	6 out of 7	High
Lianshi	No-to-Low Risk	1.3	Defined	5 out of 7	Medium*
Zeguo	No-to-Low Risk	9.0	Defined	6 out of 7	High
Xindeng	Some Risk	0.7	Defined	6 out of 7	High*
Shipu	Some Risk	2.8	Defined/ Dispersed	5 out of 7	Medium
Xinshi	Some Risk	4.9	Defined	5 out of 7	Medium
Fenshui	Risky	4.3	Defined	5 out of 7	Medium
Qiandaohu	Very Risky	7.2	Defined	6 out of 7	High
Longgang	Very Risky	14.9	Defined/ Dispersed	4 out of 7	Low*

Note: Composite Score Coeff $\geq$ 3.0; Quality of Potential Location High = 7, Medium = 5, Low 5; ULRS = 20,000 m², ULRM = 30,000 m², ULRL = 40–50,000 m², ULRVL = 50–60,000 m².

* Relatively risky propositions.

accompanying locational analysis. Among those, 11 also involved future developments. In these regards, Longgang, for instance, moved from dispersed 'site area locations', where there were typically several zones of equally high combined accessibility values to defined 'site area' locations, where there were just one or two obvious concentrations with the highest combined accessibility values. In contrast to Longgang, Shipu moved in the opposite direction from defined to dispersed site locations. In all cases, however, a ranking of 2 or more, indicated that reasonably well-prescribed 'site areas' within the towns were available to seek potential location of ULRs.

Bibliography

Barnes, T. J. (2001). In the beginning was economic geography: A science studies approach to disciplinary history. *Progress in Human Geography*, *25*, 521–544.

Barnes, T. J. (2003). The place of locational analysis: A selective and interpretive history. *Progress in Human Geography*, *27*(1), 69–95.

Barnes, B., & Bloor, D. (1982). Relativism, rationalism and sociology of knowledge. In M. Hollis & S. Lukes (Eds.), *Rationality and relativism* (pp. 21–47). Cambridge, MA: MIT Press.

Brandeau, M. L., & Chiu, S. S. (1989). An overview of representative problems in location research. *Management Science, 35*(6), 645–674.

Brett, D. L., & Schmitz, A. (2009). *Real estate market analysis: Methods and case studies.* Washington, DC: Urban Land Institute.

Chorley, R. J., & Haggett, P. (1965). Trend-surface mapping in geographical research. *Transactions of the Institute of British Geographers,* 47–67.

Church, R. L. (2002). Geographical information systems and location science. *Computers & Operations Research, 29,* 541e562.

Church, R. L., & Murray, A. T. (2009). *Business site selection, location analysis and GIS.* Hoboken, NJ: John Wiley & Sons.

Current, J., Min, H., & Schilling, D. (1990). Multiobjective analysis of facility location decisions. *European Journal of Operational Research, 49*(3), 295–307.

Davis, P. (2006). Spatial competition in retail markets: Movie theaters. *The RAND: Journal of Economics, 37*(4), 964–982.

García-Palomares, J. C., Gutiérrez, J., & Latorre, M. (2012). Optimizing the location of stations in bike-sharing programs: A GIS approach. *Applied Geography, 35*(1–2), 235–246.

Guan, C., & Rowe, P. G. (2016). The concept of urban intensity and China's townization policy: Cases from Zhejiang Province. *Cities, 55,* 22–41.

Guan, C., & Rowe, P. G. (2017). In pursuit of a well-balanced network of cities and towns: A case study of the Changjiang Delta Region. *Environment and Planning B: Urban Analytics and City Science, 45*(3).

Haggett, P., Cliff, A. D., & Frey, A. (1977). *Locational analysis in human geography.* New York, NY: Wiley.

Handy, S., Paterson, R. G., & Butler, K. (2003). Planning for street connectivity: Getting from here to there. *American Planning Association.*

Hangzhou Statistical Bureau. (2015). *Hangzhou Statistical Yearbook 2015.*

Hernández, T., & Bennison, D. (2000). The art and science of retail location decisions. *International Journal of Retail & Distribution Management, 28*(8), 357–367.

Kahr, J., & Thomsett, M. C. (2005). *Real estate market valuation and analysis.* Hoboken, NJ: Wiley.

Kang, C. (2016). Spatial access to pedestrians and retail sales in Seoul, Korea. *Habitat International, 57,* 110–120.

Kim, H., O'Connor, K., & Han, S. (2015). The spatial characteristics of global property investment in Seoul: A case study of the office market. *Progress in Planning, 97,* 1–42.

Kramer, A. (2008). *Retail development handbook.* Washington, DC: ULI-The Urban Land Institute.

Long, H., Zou, J., & Liu, Y. (2009). Differentiation of rural development driven by industrialization and urbanization in eastern coastal China. *Habitat International, 33,* 454–462.

Meyer, T. G. (1988). Site selection vs. site evaluation: Techniques for locating retail outlets. *Real Estate Issue, 13*(1), 25–28.

O'Sullivan, D., & Manson, S. M. (2015). Do physicists have 'geography envy'? And what can geographers learn from it? *Annals of the Association of American Geographers, 105*(4), 704–722.

Ozbil, A., Peponis, J., & Stone, B. (2011). Understanding the link between street connectivity, land use and pedestrian flows. *Urban Design International, 16*(2), 125–141.

Ozimec, A. M., Natter, M., & Reutterer, T. (2010). Geographical information systems based marketing decisions: Effects of alternative visualizations on decision quality. *Journal of Marketing, 74*, 94–110.

Peiser, R. B., & Hamilton, D. (Eds.). (2012). *Professional real estate development: The ULI guide to the business*. Washington, DC: Urban Land Institute.

Rabianski, J., DeLisle, J., & Carn, N. (2001). Corporate real estate site selection: A community-specific information framework. *Journal of Real Estate Research, 22*, 165–198.

Roig-Tierno, N., Baviera-Puig, A., Buitrago-Vera, J., & Mas-Verdu, F. (2013). The retail site location decision process using GIS and the analytical hierarchy process. *Applied Geography, 40*, 191–198.

Rybarczyk, G., & Wu, C. (2010). Bicycle facility planning using GIS and multi-criteria decision analysis. *Applied Geography, 30*, 282–293.

Shapin, S. (1998). Placing the view from nowhere: historical and sociology problems in the location of science. *Transactions of the Institute of British Geographers, NS 23*(1), 5–12.

Statistical Bureau of China. (2015). *China Statistical yearbook of urban-rural construction*. Beijing: China Statistical Publishing House.

Suárez-Vega, R., Santos-Peñate, D. R., & Dorta-González, P. (2012). Location models and GIS tools for retail site location. *Applied Geography, 35*, 12–22.

SURBA. (2015). *Literature review: Selected consumer services and small pilot cities of Zhejiang province*. Brooklyn, NY: Studio for Urban Analysis.

Urban Land Institute. (2016). Chinese main land real estate markets: ULI analysis of city investment prospects. *ULI Asia Pacific and ULI Center for Capital Markets and Real Estate.*

U.S. Department of Housing and Urban Development. (1992). The federal housing enterprises financial safety and soundness act of 1992. *FHEFSSA*, Pub.L. 102–550.

Wey, W. (2015). Smart growth and transit-oriented development planning in site selection for a new metro transit station in Taipei, Taiwan. *Habitat International, 47*, 158–168.

Zhang, H., Li, L., Hui, E., & Li, V. (2016). Comparisons of the relations between housing prices and the macroeconomy in China's first-, second- and third-tier cities. *Habitat International, 57*, 24–42.

Zhejiang Statistical Bureau. (2014). *Zhejiang statistical yearbook 2014*. Beijing: China Statistical Press.

10 Profiling PM2.5 pollution patterns and policy development

Jianzheng Liu, Tian Xu, Weifeng Li, and Le Yuan

China has been suffering from severe fine particulate matter (diameter < 2.5 μm, PM2.5) pollution for more than a decade. Public calls for government action to address this problem have been growing, and various measures have been proposed and implemented by Chinese government agencies. One of these measures is the well-known national action plan on the prevention and control of air pollution that specified detailed targets for air quality improvements by 2017. After the conclusion of the target year, an update about the air quality and PM2.5 pollution in major Chinese cities is necessary to help evaluate the effect of this action plan. As such, this study aims to provide an update about the PM2.5 pollution in major Chinese cities in 2017. To this end, this study provides an overview of the PM2.5 pollution in major Chinese cities in 2017, as well as the air quality attainment status against the national air standards for these cities. Further, a comparison of the air quality standards and the PM2.5 pollution in 2017 between China, India, South Korea and Japan was conducted. In addition, a brief review of some of the PM2.5 mitigation policies in China is presented. The results show that the average of daily mean PM2.5 concentrations in major Chinese cities have decreased and the attainment of air quality standards has also improved in 2017 compared with previous years. Among the cities that were evaluated, only Shijiazhuang and Ürümqi experienced bad air quality that exceeded the Chinese air quality standard grade II (75 μg/m³) on more than 30% of the days considered, while Lasa and Fuzhou had the best air quality in China in 2017. This study also found that despite these improvements, the air quality in 2017 in major Chinese cities still fell below the World Health Organization's air quality standard on most days, and the air quality in Beijing in 2017 was much worse than that in Seoul and Tokyo but better than that in New Delhi.

1 Introduction

China, the largest economy and one of the most populated countries in the world, has been suffering from severe fine particulate matter (diameter < 2.5 μm, PM2.5) pollution for more than a decade, particularly in Beijing and its surrounding cities (J. Liu, Li, Wu, & Liu, 2018; L. Liu, Silva, & Liu, 2018). Previous studies demonstrated that PM2.5 pollution in China is characterized by extremely high PM2.5

concentrations and is considered to be very severe compared with international air quality standards (Chai et al., 2014; Hu, Wang, Ying, & Zhang, 2014; J. Liu, Li, & Li, 2016; Wang, Ying, Hu, & Zhang, 2014). For example, Chai et al. (2014) calculated the PM2.5 concentrations in 26 major cities in China from August 2011 to February 2012 and determined that the mean PM2.5 concentration in these cities was approximately 57.5 $\mu g/m^3$; a value that is much higher than World Health Organization (WHO) guidelines on PM2.5 (25 $\mu g/m^3$) (World Health Organization, 2006).

PM2.5 is considered one of the most detrimental air pollutants in the world (J. Liu et al., 2016). Studies have shown that PM2.5 concentrations are associated with many cardiorespiratory-related diseases (Newell, Kartsonaki, Lam, & Kurmi, 2017), such as chronic obstructive pulmonary disease (Gu, Chu, Zeng, Bao, & Liu, 2017), cerebrovascular diseases (Leiva, Santibanez, Ibarra, Matus, & Seguel, 2013), foetal growth of newborns (Jedrychowski et al., 2009) and others. Hoek et al. (2013) found that for each 10 ug/m^3 increase in PM2.5 concentration, the risk of cardiovascular mortality increases by 11% in large geographic areas including Asia. Further, some studies have reported the potential links between PM2.5 pollution and mental illnesses such as depression and anxiety (Lim et al., 2012; Power et al., 2015). In China, it has been estimated that approximately 1.6 million deaths per year, about 17% of the annual total deaths, are attributed to PM2.5 pollution (Rohde & Muller, 2015). Public calls for government action to address this problem have been growing, and various measures for controlling the outdoor levels of PM2.5 have been proposed and implemented by Chinese government agencies.

In 2013, the Chinese State Council announced an action plan (Ministry of Environmental Protection, 2013b) to decrease the levels of particulate matter with diameter < 10 μm (PM10) levels by 10%, to reduce the PM2.5 concentration in the Beijing-Tianjin-Hebei area by up to 25% relative to the 2012 level by 2017 and to maintain the PM2.5 concentration in Beijing below 60 $\mu g/m^3$. Measures that have been taken include establishing air quality monitoring networks, publishing real-time air quality information, building regional coordination mechanisms between local governments, closing old power plants, replacing coal with natural gas and electricity, limiting vehicle purchases, forcing the retirement of outdated vehicles and enhancing the enforcement of laws and regulations (Jin, Andersson, & Zhang, 2016). Since the target year (2017) has just concluded, the public needs to know the effects of these policies and measures and whether the target goals of the national action plan on air pollution have been met. While efforts are being made to address this need, a recent study focusing on the PM2.5 pollution in Beijing showed that the pollution first intensified from 2008 to 2011 then began to alleviate in 2012 and has been decreasing significantly since 2015 (L. Liu et al., 2018). These results suggest that the measures have probably been effective in Beijing. However, how exactly the PM2.5 pollution in China developed in 2017 remains unclear. Thus, it has become necessary to provide an update about the PM2.5 pollution in major Chinese cities in 2017 and evaluate how the air quality in China is based on the air quality standards.

This study aims to provide such an update about the PM2.5 pollution in major Chinese cities in 2017. Specifically, this study has three objectives: (1) to obtain an updated overview of the PM2.5 pollution in major Chinese cities in 2017, as well as the air quality attainment status against the national air standards for these cities; (2) to compare the air quality standards and the PM2.5 pollution in China with the capital cities of China's neighbouring countries in Asia such as India, South Korea, and Japan; (3) to provide a brief review of some of the PM2.5 mitigation policies in China. It is anticipated that this study will contribute to the assessment of China's air pollution mitigation plans.

The remainder of the chapter is organized as follows. In the next section, we briefly introduce the data and method used in this study. In Section 3, we provide description statistics of the PM2.5 pollution in 2017 in China. A comparison of the PM2.5 concentrations between Beijing and the capital cities of Japan, Korea and India are also presented in this section. Then, in Section 4, we show the calculated attainment of air quality standard for 32 major Chinese cities against China's air quality standard. In Section 5, a short review of some of the PM2.5 mitigation policies in China is provided. In the concluding section, we summarize the findings of this study.

2 Data and method

We employed simple statistical analysis techniques to analyze the data. A total of 360 prefectures in China are included in this study. In particular, four directly controlled municipalities (Beijing, Shanghai, and Chongqing), the capital cities of 22 provinces and five autonomous regions (Taiwan Province was not included in this study) and the city of Shenzhen in China were selected as major Chinese cities and were examined in terms of their attainment of air quality standard. All 32 cities are characterized by large populations and rapid urban development. The total population of the 32 major cities is approximately 235.45 million, which accounts for 17.03% of the total population in China.

The ground-based air quality monitoring data were collected from each air quality monitoring station and reported daily through the official web portal of the national hourly air quality reporting platform (http://113.108.142.147:20035/emcpublish/) run by the China National Environment Protection Agency. The data contain the hourly concentrations of six pollutants: fine particulate matter with diameter < 2.5 μm (PM2.5), particulate matter with diameter < 10 μm (PM10), sulphur dioxide (SO_2), nitrogen dioxide (NO_2), ozone (O_3) and carbon monoxide (CO). At each station, automated monitoring systems consisting of a sample collection unit, sample measurement unit, data collection and transport unit and other accessory equipment were installed and used to measure the six pollutants. PM2.5 concentrations were measured using the micro-oscillating balance method and β-absorption method (Wang et al., 2014). However, the official online reporting portal does not provide access to historical data. Fortunately, third parties such as aqistudy.cn have been storing air quality data since late 2013 (www.aqistudy.cn/

historydata/). This study obtained daily mean PM2.5 concentration data from 1 January 2017 to 31 December 2017 for all 32 major cities in China.

The daily mean PM2.5 concentrations in 2017 for the capital cities of Japan, Korea and India, namely Tokyo, Seoul and New Delhi, respectively, were also collected as reference values to compare with the PM2.5 pollution in Beijing. The PM2.5 measurements in Tokyo were collected from 81 measurement stations in Tokyo and were available on the official Tokyo Environment Bureau website (www.kankyo.metro.tokyo.jp/air/air_pollution/torikumi/result_measurement. html). Unfortunately, only Tokyo PM2.5 data from January to September 2017 was accessible. The data for the remaining months in 2017 were still being finalized according to Tokyo Environment Bureau. The PM2.5 measurements in Seoul were obtained from the official Seoul Metropolitan Government website (http:// cleanair.seoul.go.kr/air_city.htm?method = measure&citySection = CITY), while the PM2.5 data from New Delhi was collected from 18 monitoring stations in New Delhi and are available from the Central Pollution Central Board India website (https://app.cpcbccr.com/ccr/#/caaqm-dashboard-all/caaqm-landing/ caaqm-data-availability).

3 Descriptive statistics of the PM2.5 concentrations in China in 2017

Air quality, by nature is volatile, as multiple known and unknown factors affect its concentrations, trends and paths. Volatile as it is, however, air quality has many interesting and highly regular patterns. Here we present the descriptive statistics of the PM2.5 measurements to provide an overview of the air quality in China in 2017.

Table 10.1 summarizes the basic statistics including the average, maximum and minimum values of the daily mean PM2.5 concentrations for 360 prefectures studied in mainland China in 2017. The results showed that in 2017 the average value of the daily mean PM2.5 concentrations was 44.5 $\mu g/m^3$, with a standard deviation of 36.9 $\mu g/m^3$, a minimum value of 1.0 $\mu g/m^3$ and a maximum value of 1292.0 $\mu g/m^3$. The maximum PM2.5 concentration of 1292.0 $\mu g/m^3$ was recorded on 19 April in Hotan Prefecture of the Xinjiang Uyghur Autonomous Region, while the minimum PM2.5 concentration of 1.0 $\mu g/m^3$ was observed at multiple sites on multiple dates.

A study that calculated the PM2.5 concentrations from August 2011 to February 2012 in 26 major cities in China concluded that the mean PM2.5 concentration

Table 10.1 Basic statistics of the daily mean PM2.5 concentrations in 2017 for 360 prefectures in China

Statistics	*PM2.5 ($\mu g/m^3$)*
Arithmetic mean	44.5
Maximum	1292.0
Minimum	1.0
Standard deviation	36.9

in these cities was approximately 57.5 µg/m³ (Chai et al., 2014). Another study reported an average PM2.5 concentration of 57 µg/m³ for the period from April 2014 to April 2015 (Y.-L. Zhang & Cao, 2015). This suggests that the PM2.5 pollution in 2017 in major Chinese cities has improved.

The results also showed that the mean value was higher than the Chinese Ambient Air Quality Standards (CAAQS; GB3095–2012) daily average Grade I level of 35 µg/m³, but lower than the Grade II level of 75 µg/m³ (Ministry of Environmental Protection, 2012a).

In order to understand how the PM2.5 pollution level in China was in 2017 compared with other countries in Asia, we selected the capital cities of Japan, Korea and India, namely Tokyo, Seoul and New Delhi, as references. As Figure 10.1 shows, the PM2.5 measurements in Tokyo were the lowest among the four capital cities of China, Japan, South Korea and India, indicating that Tokyo has the best air quality among the four capital cities. In 2017, the median daily mean PM2.5 concentration in Tokyo was 11.9 µg/m³, with an upper quantile value of 15.5 µg/m³ and a lower quantile value of 9.0 µg/m³. The maximum value of the daily

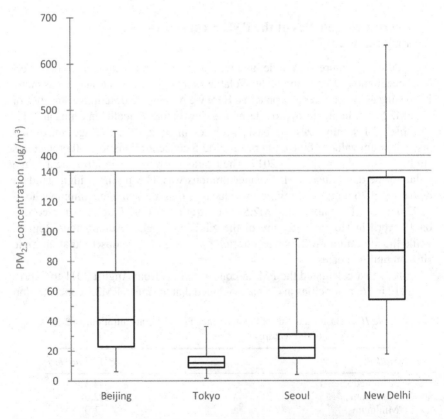

Figure 10.1 Distribution of the daily mean PM2.5 concentrations in Beijing, Tokyo, Seoul, and New Delhi in 2017

mean PM2.5 concentration in Tokyo was 36.2 μg/m³. Seoul was the second low-est with a median daily mean PM2.5 concentration of 22.0 μg/m³. The 25th and 75th percentiles of the daily mean PM2.5 concentrations in Seoul were 15.0 and 31.0 μg/m³, respectively. The median daily mean PM2.5 concentration in Beijing was 41.0 μg/m³, with an upper quantile value of 73.0 μg/m³ and a lower quantile value of 23.0 μg/m³. As seen from Figure 10.1, the lower quantile of the daily mean PM2.5 concentration in Beijing was higher than the upper quantile of the daily mean PM2.5 concentration in Tokyo, which demonstrates that the PM2.5 pollution in Beijing is more severe than in Tokyo. Figure 10.1 also shows that the capital city of India, New Delhi, had the worst PM2.5 pollution among the four capital cities in Asia. The median daily mean PM2.5 concentration in New Delhi was 87.1 μg/m³, with an upper quantile value of 135.9 μg/m³ and a lower quantile value of 54.2 μg/m³.

The data were collected from January to December in 2017 except Tokyo, because the data for the last three months of the year were unavailable. The line is the median, whereas the middle box represents the middle 50% between the upper and lower quartiles. The lower solid black line refers to the minimum and the upper line denotes the maximum.

The question regarding whether the PM2.5 concentrations meet the CAAQS Grade I or II requirements during the year was investigated. The analysis results indicated that for only a few days during the year, the PM2.5 concentrations met the WHO air quality standards. Figure 10.2 shows that for almost half of the year in 2017, the PM2.5 concentrations did not meet the United States National Ambi-ent Air Quality Standards (NAAQS), whereas most days attained China's PM2.5 standard, which is obviously less strict. It also shows that PM2.5 concentrations

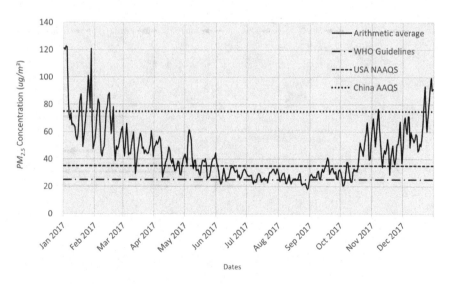

Figure 10.2 Varying daily mean PM2.5 concentrations for all 360 prefectures in China in 2017

usually reached their peak values in the winter (November, December, January and February), which is consistent with findings of previous studies (Wang et al., 2014; Y.-L. Zhang & Cao, 2015).

The blue curve refers to the arithmetic mean of the daily mean PM2.5 concentrations for all prefectures. The red line denotes China's AAQS daily Grade II, the brown line is the WHO's air quality standard guidelines published in 2005 and the violet line refers to the USA's NAAQS.

4 Attainment of air quality standards in major Chinese cities

Figure 10.2 offers insights that mainland China might set its air quality standards too lenient. What is more interesting is that after we looked at the history of evolving air quality standards and development stages in different countries, the author found that the current air quality standard in mainland China is approximate to (in fact less stringent than) the air quality standard of the United States from 1997–2006 (Figure 10.3), suggesting that the air quality control in mainland China is, in fact, a decade behind the United States.

The start of the line for each standard indicates the year in which the air quality standard was published. For example, the orange line indicates that the WHO air quality guidelines for the daily average PM2.5 concentration standard was established in 2005 and is still being used.

However, it is understandable that the environmental agencies in China set the air quality standards more leniently given that China is, to a large extent, a developing country and therefore has to compromise between economic development and environmental protection. In this regard, we examined the attainment of air

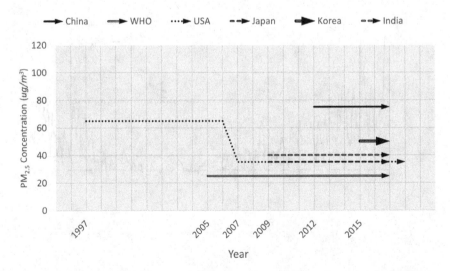

Figure 10.3 Daily (24 hours) average PM2.5 concentration standards for China, USA, Japan, Korea, India, and the WHO

quality standards in major Chinese cities in 2017. Our purpose was to see how major Chinese cities performed against China's own air quality standard.

The results show that there were obvious differences among the 32 major Chinese cities in terms of their attainment of the air quality standard (Table 10.2). Shijiazhuang and Ürümqi, capital cities of the Hebei Province and Xinjiang Uygur Autonomous Region, experienced the most serious PM2.5 pollution among the 32 cities. Both cities exceeded the CAAQS Grade II standards for 140 and 113 days, respectively, which indicates the air quality on more than 30% of the days during the study period did not attain the air quality standard. In addition, Zhengzhou, Jinan and Xi'an, the capital cities of the Henan, Shandong and Shanxi provinces, also experienced off-standard air quality on more than 100 days in 2017. Nonetheless, the air quality in China in 2017 has improved significantly compared

Table 10.2 Number of non-attainment days and population of 32 major Chinese cities

	Population (million)	# of non-attainment days 1 Jan 2017–31 Dec 2017
Beijing	13.63	85/365
Shanghai	14.50	27/365
Guangzhou	8.70	15/365
Shenzhen	3.85	3/365
Hangzhou	7.36	41/365
Tianjin	10.44	91/365
Chengdu	13.99	81/365
Nanjing	6.63	37/365
Xi'an	8.25	108/365
Wuhan	8.34	72/365
Chongqing	33.92	49/365
Harbin	9.62	77/365
Changchun	7.53	65/365
Shenyang	7.34	68/365
Shijiazhuang	10.38	140/365
Taiyuan	3.70	94/365
Jinan	6.33	100/365
Ürümqi	2.68	113/365
Lasa	0.54	1/365
Xining	2.03	35/365
Lanzhou	3.24	47/365
Yinchuan	1.84	52/365
Zhengzhou	8.27	104/365
Hefei	7.30	88/365
Fuzhou	6.87	1/365
Nanchang	5.23	35/365
Changsha	6.96	75/365
Guiyang	4.01	15/365
Kunming	5.60	4/365
Nanning	7.52	27/365
Huhehaote	2.41	56/365
Haikou	1.67	2/365

with the air quality in China during 2013–2014. According to Wang et al. (2014), 24 capital cities in China experienced severe air pollution, with 30% of the days exceeding the CAAQS Grade II standards during 2013–2014, and Shijiazhuang had the highest nonattainment rate of 86%, indicating that the air quality in Shijiazhuang on 261 out of 303 days exceeded the CAAQS Grade II standards.

In contrast to Shijiazhuang and Ürümqi, Lasa and Fuzhou, the capital cities of the Tibet Autonomous Region and Fujian Province, had the best air quality in China in 2017, and there were almost no non-attainment days in both cities. Air quality in Shenzhen, Kunming and Haikou, the latter two being the capital cities of the Yunnan and Hainan provinces, exceeded the air quality standards for fewer than 5 days.

Non-attainment days are defined as days when the PM2.5 concentration exceeds the Grade II standards. The numbers preceding the slash in the last column represent the total number of non-attainment days, and the numbers following represent the total number of days with valid data.

The attainment of air quality standards for the 32 major cities also showed great temporal variability. As shown in Figure 10.4, in spring, the non-attainment rates for most cities were about 50%, and in winter, the non-attainment rates were around 30%, while the non-attainment rates in summer and autumn varied between 0% and 20%, which are much lower than the rates in spring and winter.

5 A short review of the PM2.5 mitigation policies in China

In the wake of serious air pollution, China has been proposing and enforcing multiple policies to address PM2.5 pollution. Perhaps the most important laws and regulations that helped form the pollution mitigation policies were the Environmental Protection Law that was newly enacted on January 1, 2015 (National People's Congress of the People's Republic of China, 2014), and the National Action Plan on Prevention and Control of Air Pollution (Ministry of Environmental Protection, 2013a).

The new Environmental Protection Law was the first important amendment to China's Environmental Protection Law since it was enacted 25 years ago. Significant progress has been made since then. Under the new law, local governments are given more environmental protection responsibilities and are assessed on environmental performances in their respective jurisdictions. The new law also gives more importance to environmental information disclosure, demonstrating that the central government recognized the need for public supervision to aid environmental protection (Ker & Logan, 2014).

The National Action Plan on Prevention and Control of Air Pollution was issued by the State Council of China on September 10, 2013. Its aim was to improve China's overall air quality within five years. The targeted regions included Beijing-Tianjin-Hebei, the Yangtze River Delta and the Pearl River Delta. The Action Plan set 2017 as the achievement year for three major goals: a 10% reduction in PM10 concentrations in major cities; around 25%, 20%, and 15% decreases in PM2.5 concentrations of fine particulate matter in Beijing-Tianjin-Hebei, the Yangtze

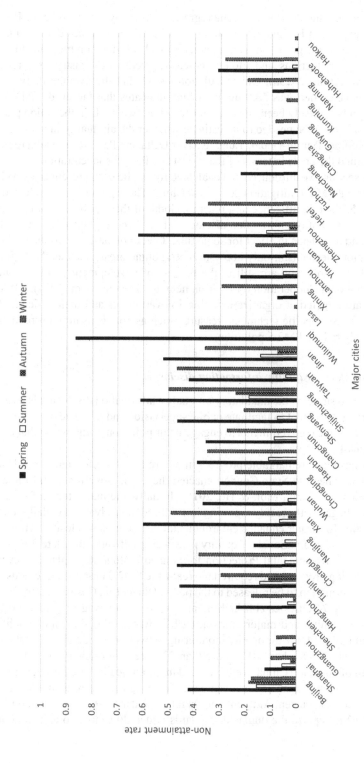

Figure 10.4 Seasonal variation of non-attainment rates in the major cities of China

River Delta and the Pearl River Delta region, respectively; and to keep the PM2.5 concentration of in Beijing below 60 $\mu g/m^3$. The action plan introduced 10 measures to address the pollution, including a regional coordination mechanism, coal consumption reductions and motor vehicle restrictions (Ministry of Environmental Protection, 2013a). Our calculation shows that the average daily mean PM2.5 concentration was 58.0 $\mu g/m^3$, which indicates that the third goal of the action plan has already been attained. For the other two goals in the action plan, a detailed study will be needed to investigate whether the air quality in major cities and the Beijing-Tianjin-Hebei, Yangtze River Delta and Pearl River Delta regions have attained the goals in terms of the PM10 and PM2.5 concentrations.

In this section, we introduced and evaluated four policies to present an overview of the current PM2.5 mitigation policies in China. These policies were selected on the basis of their significance and recency. Some of these policies, for example, mandatory air quality information disclosure, have been applied across the entire country and have been in effect for some time. Other policies, such as the regional coordination mechanism, only apply to metropolitan areas, such as the Beijing-Tianjin-Hebei area, and are still in the process of development (China Council for International Cooperation on Environment and Development, 2014). All four policies are targeted at organizations, local governments and their officials. We did not discuss specific technical measures such as coal consumption reduction that directly reduce PM2.5 pollution.

5.1 Mandatory air quality information disclosure

As a national strategy, the mandatory air quality information disclosure is used by the central government to facilitate public supervision and to create pressure from the public for local governments to engage in air pollution mitigation (Ghanem & Zhang, 2014).

China has made remarkable progress in environmental information disclosure since 2008, when the State Council enacted the Open Government Information Regulations (L. Zhang, Mol, & He, 2016). Initially, the mandatory information disclosure began with weekly reporting in 1998 and then advanced to daily reporting in 2000. To further enhance environmental information disclosure, China has been constructing a national air quality monitoring network since late 2012. The Ministry of Environmental Protection formulated a "four-step" plan to develop the monitoring program and required the real-time PM2.5 monitoring records and relevant information to be released to the public (Yuan, Liu, Castro, & Pan, 2012). In 2013, only 74 cities established the air quality monitoring program, most of which were capital and major cities in each province, plus four municipalities. By the end of 2014, the air quality monitoring network expanded to 1074 stations in 190 cities. By October 2015, more than 330 prefecture-level cities, covering almost all of mainland China, were included in the air quality monitoring network.

In the meantime, new national standards for air quality were being developed and updated. The current Ambient Air Quality Standards were published on February 2012 to replace the outdated standards issued 20 years ago and came into effect on January 1, 2016 (Ministry of Environmental Protection, 2012a). Other affiliated standards and technical regulations have been developed and implemented to facilitate the monitoring program, including the Technical Regulation on Ambient Air Quality Index (Ministry of Environmental Protection, 2012b) and the Technical Specifications for Installation and Acceptance of Ambient Air Quality Continuous Automated Monitoring System for PM10 and PM2.5 (Ministry of Environmental Protection, 2013c).

Mandatory air quality information disclosure has been proven effective. It not only urges local governments to address PM2.5 pollution but also raises public awareness that PM2.5 pollution is related to their daily motor vehicle use and other activities. This effect is demonstrated in the pollution documentary *Under the Dome*, which was produced by the well-known journalist Chai Jing (Ren, 2015). However, information disclosure and public supervision alone will not make the governments proactively mitigate PM2.5 pollution. Policies with incentives are required. This is the reason the central government set up various award schemes such as the National Environmental Protection Model City award.

5.2 National environmental protection model city

In 1997, the central government of China established the National Environmental Protection Model City award scheme to evaluate cities' environmental quality and economic performance. The purpose of this National Environmental Protection Model City award is to provide incentives for cities and to promote environmental protection. The award gives a city benefits such as a good reputation and a more competitive and livable environment that attracts more tourists and talents to boost the economy, and perhaps a potential bonus for the promotion of officials from the municipality governments.

The measures for the award cover air quality, water quality, noise, percentage of green land, consumer satisfaction with the environment, gross domestic product per capita and energy consumption, among other things (Chen, Jin, Kumar, & Shi, 2012). In 2003, to qualify for the National Environmental Protection Model City award, a city was required to have at least 80% "blue-sky" days within a calendar year. A "blue-sky" day refers to a day with an air pollution index at or below 100. However, as air pollution became more severe, people found that the "blue-sky" measures reported by the government were inconsistent with real observations. The criterion for air quality soon changed to the concentrations of air pollutants. The current air quality criterion for the National Environmental Protection Model City award focuses on SO_2, NO_2, and PM10 (Ministry of Environmental Protection, 2011).

Participation in the award evaluation is voluntary. During the application, the award committee panel organized by the central government visits the city in person, evaluates the city based on the criteria and announces the winners afterwards. The award is not permanent and is only valid for three years. After three years, each awarded city is subject to a review. If a city fails the review process, a grace period of three years will be given to the city. If the city fails again after the grace period, the National Environmental Protection Model City award will be revoked. However, none of the awards have ever been revoked, and this situation reduces the incentives for genuine improvements in air quality after the model city award has been won (Chen et al., 2012).

This award may be helpful, but it has several problems. One problem is that the criteria are outdated. For example, PM2.5, the most detrimental air pollutant, is not included in the criteria. Another problem is that the incentives provided by this award are limited, and participation in the award scheme is not compulsory. Therefore, the award scheme is not powerful enough to encourage local governments to proactively take more action. The inclusion of air quality in government performance evaluations discussed in what follows is one of the solutions to these problems.

5.3 Inclusion of air quality indicators in government performance evaluation

China has a unique political system called the regionally decentralized authoritarian system. This system means that the central government controls the personnel and the money and requires the subnational governments, including the provinces, municipalities, and counties, to provide public service, enforce laws, and initiate and coordinate reforms (Chen et al., 2012). As the central government controls the appointment, promotion, demotion and removal of the local government officials, public supervision policies such as mandatory air quality information disclosure naturally does not make a significant difference. Conversely, the inclusion of air quality indicators in governmental performance evaluations have a greater impact because it directly affects the promotions of government personnel. The system is conducted by following a top-down approach: the central government specifies a certain performance criterion for provincial governments, and the provincial leaders stipulate more precisely defined performance requirements to its sub-level governments (Chen et al., 2012).

Currently, only a few local governments have implemented this policy and include air quality indicators in the government performance evaluations. For example, on 23 January, 2015, the Zhejiang provincial government issued a regulation stipulating that the promotion of officials depends on the attainment of PM2.5 standards (H. Wu, 2015). The Zhejiang provincial government also provides economic incentives to municipal governments that attain the PM2.5 standards.

For most governments, this policy has been proposed for several years but has never been implemented. In fact, this policy is still under development and debate, and many of the interested parties are still bargaining. Some practices, for example, offering economic awards to officials who effectively mitigate air pollution, are criticized by the public (Schneider, 2013). Existing government performance evaluations did consider environmental goals but emphasized accounting indicators such as energy intensity and environmental infrastructure investment rather than environmental outcomes that have significant impacts on public health and quality of life such as PM2.5 levels (Zheng, Kahn, Sun, & Luo, 2014). There is a need to reinforce the policies regarding the inclusion of air quality indicators in government performance evaluations.

5.4 Regional coordination mechanism

Scholars have long demonstrated that addressing air pollution requires regional coordination, and pollution mitigation measures in a single city might not be helpful (J. Liu et al., 2018; Yuan et al., 2012). However, some government agencies in China appear to be unaware of this fact. In 2014, the Beijing governments initiated a campaign to relocate around 100 manufacturing factories and companies to neighbouring areas such as the Hebei Province to reduce the pollution in Beijing (Stanway & Macfie, 2015). Clearly, the governments failed to consider the regional nature of air pollution and air pollution transport (China Council for International Cooperation on Environment and Development, 2014). Air pollution does not simply go away just because the pollution sources are relocated to nearby places. Instead, the regional transport of PM2.5 pollution is significant, as indicated in the previous chapter.

Fortunately, the central government have recently recognized that the PM2.5 pollution problem is a regional issue that is not limited to a single city. Scholars have also proven that joint regional air pollution control will save the expense of air pollution control when compared with locally based pollution control strategies (Wu, Xu, & Zhang, 2015). The action plan issued by the State Council of China in 2013 proposed to establish a regional coordination mechanism and to make overall arrangements for regional environmental treatment. The action plan required the governments in the Beijing-Tianjin-Hebei area, the Yangtze River Delta area and the Pearl River Delta to establish a regional coordination mechanism for air pollution control (Ministry of Environmental Protection, 2013a).

In 2013, an initial mechanism was established to support regional decision making and consultations in the three key regions led by Beijing, Shanghai and Guangdong Provinces, respectively. The regional coordination team for air pollution control in the Beijing-Tianjin-Hebei region, for example, held its first meeting in October 2013 and determined the working principles for information sharing, mutual defence and joint control. In its second meeting in May 2014, the regional coordination team established a partnership with the National Energy Administration and signed an agreement on coal reduction.

Although the mechanism has been established, regional coordination was initially limited because it focused only on heavy pollution weather alerts and joint emergency responses. The coordination mechanism lacked unified plans, objectives, control requirements, supervision and administration (China Council for International Cooperation on Environment and Development, 2014) except during important events such as the APEC summit in Beijing in 2014 and the military parade in 2015, when a range of measures were coordinated to reduce the pollutant emissions by the central government in the Beijing-Tianjin-Hebei region. Moreover, the regional coordination mechanism in the Beijing-Tianjin-Hebei area, the

Yangtze River Delta area and the Pearl River Delta area was developed on the basis of political administrative boundaries. However, air pollution is characterized by trans-boundary transport (J. Liu, et al., 2018; J. Liu, W. Li, J. Wu, et al., 2018). The coordination teams in the three regions might need to consider which cities and areas should be included and what corresponding measures to adopt.

Recent developments show that the situation is improving, as some fundamental changes are ongoing, such as the strategic energy transition of heating from coal to gas, which is currently coordinated and implemented in the Beijing-Tianjin-Hebei region (Li, 2017)]. But still there are a lot of improvements to make.

6 Conclusion

This study provided an updated overview of the PM2.5 pollution in China in 2017, including the attainment status of the national air quality standard for 32 major Chinese cities. A comparison of the air quality standards in China, the USA, India, South Korea and Japan and WHO was presented. Furthermore, PM2.5 pollution levels in 2017 in Beijing, Tokyo, Seoul and New Delhi were compared. In addition, a short review of some of the PM2.5 mitigation policies in China was also presented. The results show that in 2017 the average value of the daily mean PM2.5 concentrations in China was 44.5 ±36.9 µg/m^3, which might suggest a decrease compared with that in previous years. The attainment of air quality standards in 32 major Chinese cities also indicated an improvement, with only Shijiazhuang and Ürümqi experiencing more than 30% of days when the air quality exceeded the Chinese air quality standard Grade II. However, despite these improvements, our results showed that for a few days in 2017, the PM2.5 concentrations in 2017 did meet the WHO's air quality standard, and for almost half of the year the PM2.5 concentrations did not meet the USA air quality standard. Although the air quality in Beijing was better than that in the capital city of India in 2017, it was much worse than that in the capital cities of South Korea and Japan.

References

Chai, F., Gao, J., Chen, Z., Wang, S., Zhang, Y., Zhang, J. . . . Ren, C. (2014). Spatial and temporal variation of particulate matter and gaseous pollutants in 26 cities in China. *Journal of Environmental Sciences, 26*(1), 75–82. https://doi.org/10.1016/S1001-0742(13)60383-6

Chen, Y., Jin, G. Z., Kumar, N., & Shi, G. (2012). Gaming in air pollution data? Lessons from china. *The BE Journal of Economic Analysis & Policy, 12*(3). https://doi.org/10.1515/1935-1682.3227

China Council for International Cooperation on Environment and Development. (2014). *Performance evaluation on the action plan of air pollution prevention and control and regional coordination mechanism.* Retrieved from http://content.lib.sfu.ca/cdm/ref/collection/cciced/id/1341

Ghanem, D., & Zhang, J. (2014). "Effortless perfection": Do Chinese cities manipulate air pollution data? *Journal of Environmental Economics and Management, 68*(2), 203–225.

Gu, X. Y., Chu, X., Zeng, X. L., Bao, H. R., & Liu, X. J. (2017). Effects of PM2.5 exposure on the notch signaling pathway and immune imbalance in chronic obstructive pulmonary disease. *Environmental Pollution, 226*, 163–173. https://doi.org/10.1016/j.envpol.2017.03.070

Hoek, G., Krishnan, R. M., Beelen, R., Peters, A., Ostro, B., Brunekreef, B., & Kaufman, J. D. (2013). Long-term air pollution exposure and cardio-respiratory mortality: A review. *Environmental Health, 12*(1), 43.

Hu, J., Wang, Y., Ying, Q., & Zhang, H. (2014). Spatial and temporal variability of PM2.5 and PM10 over the North China plain and the Yangtze River delta, China. *Atmospheric Environment, 95*, 598–609. https://doi.org/10.1016/j.atmosenv.2014.07.019

Jedrychowski, W., Perera, F., Mrozek-Budzyn, D., Mroz, E., Flak, E., Spengler, J. D. . . . Skolicki, Z. (2009). Gender differences in fetal growth of newborns exposed prenatally to airborne fine particulate matter. *Environmental Research, 109*(4), 447–456.

Jin, Y., Andersson, H., & Zhang, S. (2016). Air pollution control policies in china: A retrospective and prospects. *International Journal of Environmental Research and Public Health, 13*(12), 1219.

Ker, M., & Logan, K. (2014). *New environmental law targets China's local officials.* Retrieved from www.chinadialogue.net/article/show/single/en/6939-New-environmental-law-targets-China-s-local-officials

Leiva, G. M., Santibanez, D. A., Ibarra, E. S., Matus, C. P., & Seguel, R. (2013). A five-year study of particulate matter (PM2.5) and cerebrovascular diseases. *Environ Pollut, 181*, 1–6. https://doi.org/10.1016/j.envpol.2013.05.057

Li, X. (2017). *AIIB loans $250m for Beijing coal-to-gas conversion.* Retrieved from www.chinadaily.com.cn/a/201712/12/WS5a2f146aa3108bc8c6721954.html

Lim, Y.-H., Kim, H., Kim, J. H., Bae, S., Park, H. Y., & Hong, Y.-C. (2012). Air pollution and symptoms of depression in elderly adults. *Environmental Health Perspectives, 120*(7), 1023.

Liu, J., Li, J., & Li, W. (2016). Temporal patterns in fine particulate matter time series in Beijing: A calendar view. *Scientific Reports, 6*, 32221. https://doi.org/10.1038/srep32221

Liu, J., Li, W., & Wu, J. (2018). A framework for delineating the regional boundaries of PM2.5 pollution: A case study of China. *Environmental Pollution, 235*, 642–651. https://doi.org/10.1016/j.envpol.2017.12.064

Liu, J., Li, W., Wu, J., & Liu, Y. (2018). Visualizing the intercity correlation of PM2.5 time series in the Beijing-Tianjin-Hebei region using ground-based air quality monitoring data. *PLoS One, 13*(2), e0192614. https://doi.org/10.1371/journal.pone.0192614

Liu, L., Silva, E., & Liu, J. (2018). A decade of battle against PM2.5 in Beijing. *Environment and Planning A: Economy and Space, 50*(8), 1–4. https://doi.org/10.1177/0308518X18766633

Ministry of Environmental Protection. (2011). *Criterion and regulations for national environmental protection model city award.* Retrieved from www.mep.gov.cn/gkml/hbb/bgt/201101/W02011012532804238967.pdf

Ministry of Environmental Protection. (2012a). *Ambient air quality standards.* Retrieved from http://kjs.mep.gov.cn/hjbhbz/bzwb/dqhjbh/dqhjzlbz/201203/W020120410330232398521.pdf

Ministry of Environmental Protection. (2012b). *Technical regulation on ambient air quality index.* Retrieved from http://kjs.mep.gov.cn/hjbhbz/bzwb/dqhjbh/jcgfffbz/201203/W020120410332725219541.pdf

Ministry of Environmental Protection. (2013a). *The state council issues action plan on prevention and control of air pollution introducing ten measures to improve air quality.* Retrieved from http://english.mep.gov.cn/News_service/infocus/201309/t20130924_260707.htm

Ministry of Environmental Protection. (2013b). *The state council issues action plan on prevention and control of air pollution introducing ten measures to improve air quality.* Retrieved from http://english.mep.gov.cn/News_service/infocus/201309/t20130924_260707.htm

Ministry of Environmental Protection. (2013c). *Technical specifications for installation and acceptance of ambient air quality continuous automated monitoring system for PM10 and PM2.5.* Retrieved from http://kjs.mep.gov.cn/hjbhbz/bzwb/dqhjbh/jcgfffbz/201308/W020130802492823718666.pdf

National People's Congress of the People's Republic of China. (2014). *Environmental protection law of the People's Republic of China.* Retrieved from www.chinadialogue.net/Environmental-Protection-Law-2014-eversion.pdf

Newell, K., Kartsonaki, C., Lam, K. B. H., & Kurmi, O. P. (2017). Cardiorespiratory health effects of particulate ambient air pollution exposure in low-income and middle-income countries: A systematic review and meta-analysis. *The Lancet Planetary Health, 1*(9), e368–e380. https://doi.org/10.1016/S2542-5196(17)30166-3

Power, M. C., Kioumourtzoglou, M.-A., Hart, J. E., Okereke, O. I., Laden, F., & Weisskopf, M. G. (2015). The relation between past exposure to fine particulate air pollution and prevalent anxiety: Observational cohort study. *BMJ, 350*, h1111. https://doi.org/10.1136/bmj.h1111

Ren, Y. (2015). *Under the dome: Will this film be China's environmental awakening?* Retrieved from www.theguardian.com/commentisfree/2015/mar/05/under-the-dome-china-pollution-chai-jing

Rohde, R. A., & Muller, R. A. (2015). Air pollution in China: Mapping of concentrations and sources. *PLoS One, 10*(8), e0135749. https://doi.org/10.1371/journal.pone.0135749

Schneider, F. (2013). *The crisis of China's environmental pollution: What does it take to clean up the PRC?* Retrieved from www.politicseastasia.com/studying/chinas-environmental-pollution/

Stanway, D., & Macfie, N. (2015). *China capital to move more polluting industry to heavily polluted Hebei.* Retrieved from www.reuters.com/article/us-china-beijing-idUSKCN0QT0JE20150824

Wang, Y., Ying, Q., Hu, J., & Zhang, H. (2014). Spatial and temporal variations of six criteria air pollutants in 31 provincial capital cities in China during 2013–2014. *Environment International, 73*, 413–422. https://doi.org/10.1016/j.envint.2014.08.016

World Health Organization. (2006). *WHO air quality guidelines for particulate matter, ozone, nitrogen dioxide and sulfur dioxide: Global update 2005: Summary of risk assessment.* Retrieved from http://apps.who.int/iris/bitstream/10665/69477/1/WHO_SDE_PHE_OEH_06.02_eng.pdf

Wu, D., Xu, Y., & Zhang, S. (2015). Will joint regional air pollution control be more cost-effective? An empirical study of China's Beijing-Tianjin-Hebei region. *Journal of Environmental Management, 149*, 27–36.

Wu, H. (2015). *GDP phasing out in government evaluation.* Retrieved from www.shanghaidaily.com/hangzhou/GDP-phasing-out-in-government-evaluation/shdaily.shtml

Yuan, Y., Liu, S., Castro, R., & Pan, X. (2012). PM2.5 monitoring and mitigation in the cities of China. *Environmental Science & Technology, 46*(7), 3627–3628. https://doi.org/10.1021/es300984j

Zhang, L., Mol, A. P. J., & He, G. (2016). Transparency and information disclosure in China's environmental governance. *Current Opinion in Environmental Sustainability, 18*, 17–24. https://doi.org/10.1016/j.cosust.2015.03.009

Zhang, Y.-L., & Cao, F. (2015). Fine particulate matter (PM2.5) in China at a city level. *Scientific Reports*, *5*, 14884. https://doi.org/10.1038/srep14884

Zheng, S., Kahn, M. E., Sun, W., & Luo, D. (2014). Incentives for China's urban mayors to mitigate pollution externalities: The role of the central government and public environmentalism. *Regional Science and Urban Economics*, *47*, 61–71.

Part IV

11 Conclusion

Chapters included in this edition so far demonstrate two peculiar strengths of big data research within an urban China context. The first is inherent to the big data employed *per se* in light of Batty's (2016) '3*v*' definition, i.e., large *volume* of data which can be generated and collected in high *velocity*, often encompassing a wide *variety* of information that allows for further manipulation and integration. Big data as such have become increasingly accessible and deployable in contemporary China, thanks not only to the rapid developments in terms of information and communication technology but also to the country's large population size, hence the massive and still-expanding number of internet users (Harwit, 2004).

In the meantime, each individual study contained within this edited volume also displays a rather clear applied focus, collectively eliciting the second strength of big data research in terms of helping furnish multitudinous empirical evidence at the 'molecular' scale to serve as a 'micro-foundation' for public policy making (see Hekkila's foreword to this book). For example, Chapter 2 in the book tracks the mobility and footprint patterns of numerous social media users, revealing the underlying inequalities between core and peripheral cities in terms of urban migration. Chapters 3 and 4 identify a similar imbalance issue, albeit focussing their respective big data analyses on the aviation and motorway networks. Chapter 5 proposes a system of indices based on big data extracted from smart travel cards to monitor and evaluate the spatio-social transformation of individual cities. The authors use the municipality of Shenzhen in south China as an example, managing to illustrate the potential of big data metrics to support urban planning and management in practice.

Compared with Chapters 2, 3, 4, and 5, which all tend to concentrate on the mobility aspect of urban transformation in China, the big data research reported in the later part of the book touches upon a wider range of policy issues relating to human wellbeing and development. Notwithstanding its technical sophistication, Chapter 6 employs a set of administrative big data to examine the spatial, temporal and contextual dimensions of the residential land market in Beijing, the capital city of China, generating profound new policy insights into the local provision of affordable housing. Likewise, based upon a large sample of asking rents observed and collated from online letting websites, Chapter 7 unravels a geographical pattern of price segmentation underlying the residential rental market in Shanghai as the most populous city in China. The research work sheds some new light on how to understand the renters' housing demand and location choice in Shanghai, with policy interventions recommended accordingly on the supply side. More intriguingly, Chapter 8 presents a set of big data–based indicators to compare the degree of polycentricity between Beijing and Shanghai as the two largest cities in China. While Beijing is found to be more polycentric than Shanghai, the latter is found to have more potential in terms of the future development of subcentres. Chapter 9 marks a shift of empirical focus from large cities to small towns in China. The authors look at the location choices of retail stores in some 20 small towns across East China's Zhejiang Province, contributing practically to the retail industry's site-selection strategy supported by big data informatics. Chapter 10 is probably most unique, because it is the only study drawing on environmental policy issues within this edited book. The chapter provides an overview with regard to the concentration of PM2.5 as an air pollutant across major Chinese cities in 2017, calling for more coordinated and sustained policy endeavors to improve air quality in urban China.

Although this edited book showcases a compilation of big data research featuring both technical significance and policy relevance, coherence between the intrinsic quality and the extrinsic utility of big data is not to be taken for granted. One may argue that the innate desirability of big data in terms of volume, velocity, and variety does not necessarily warrant conscious and willing application of big data research in addressing the most pressing societal problems (see e.g., Zwitter, 2014). Indeed, despite a collection of successful examples illustrated in the current book, some scholars have warned of the emerging political economy challenge faced by big data:

> publicly available data may become private as value is added to such data, and the publicly-funded data infrastructure, due to its complexity and technical demands, are increasingly managed by private companies that in turn, potentially restricts access and use.
>
> (Thakuriah et al., 2015, p. 21)

China is not an exception in this regard. While thousands and millions of human respondents, whether voluntarily or unwarily, have been involved in the generation and collection of big data, the ownership and usufruct of big data are witnessing a worrying trend of privatisation by corporate and research organisations with privileged access to and control of the relevant hardware, software and specialised skills. The concept of big data governance is, in the meantime, still nascent in China, let alone government regulation in terms of data security, ethics, copyright etc.

While this edited volume contains a series of applied research examples in terms of deploying big data to serve public interest in mobility, development, and wellbeing, more fundamental issues which go beyond the Chinese context are yet to be discussed in depth (even though some of them are touched upon in the forewords to this book). For instance, Lane et al. (2014) suggest that, in the current information age, we should treat big data as a public good or essential infrastructure so that big data research can engage rather than exclude the general public. Arguments as such are neither supported nor refuted explicitly in the current book, due partly to its limited span and intended scope. These yet-to-be-addressed issues, however, point promisingly to the directions of our future research.

References

Batty, M. (2016). Big data and the city. *Built Environment, 42*(3), 321–337.

Harwit, E. (2004). Spreading telecommunications to developing areas in China: Telephones, the internet and the digital divide. *The China Quarterly, 180,* 1010–1030.

Lane, J., Stodden, V., Bender, S., & Nissenbaum, H. (2014). *Privacy, big data, and the public good: Frameworks for engagement.* Cambridge, MA: Cambridge University Press.

Thakuriah, P. V., Tilahun, N. Y., & Zellner, M. (2017). Big data and urban informatics: Innovations and challenges to urban planning and knowledge discovery. In *Seeing cities through big data* (pp. 11–45). Cham: Springer.

Zwitter, A. (2014). Big data ethics. *Big Data & Society, 1*(2), 1–6.

Index

Printed in the United States
by Baker & Taylor Publisher Services